5199

39.95

This book was donated
to honor
the birthday of

Anna Murdock Levin

by

*Sandra Murdock &
David Levin
1998*

DATE

THE CAMBRIDGE ILLUSTRATED HISTORY OF
Prehistoric Art

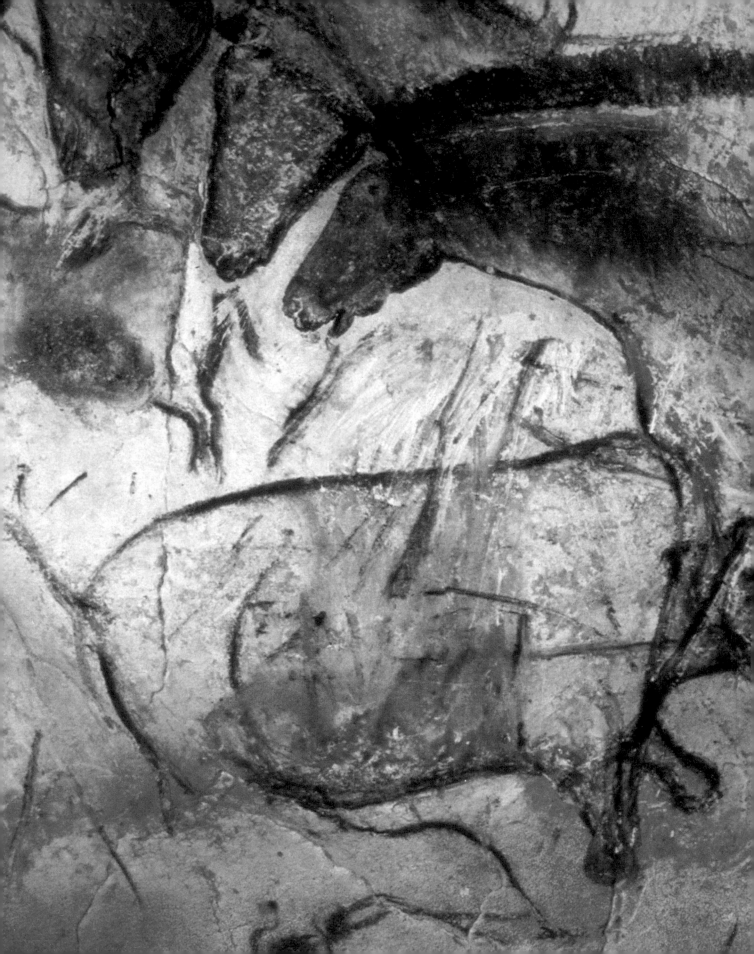

The Cambridge Illustrated History of
Prehistoric Art

PAUL G. BAHN

CAMBRIDGE
UNIVERSITY PRESS

PUBLISHED BY THE PRESS SYNDICATE OF THE UNIVERSITY OF CAMBRIDGE
The Pitt Building, Trumpington Street, Cambridge CB2 1RP, United Kingdom

CAMBRIDGE UNIVERSITY PRESS
The Edinburgh Building, Cambridge CB2 2RU, United Kingdom
40 West 20th Street, New York, NY 10011–4211, U.S.A.
10 Stamford Road, Oakleigh, Melbourne 3166, Australia

First published 1998

Printed in Italy at Rotolito Lombarda

Typeset in Berkeley 10.25/14 pt

Layout: David Seabourne, Erlestoke SN10 5TZ
Editing: Sally Carpenter, Upper Wolvercote, Oxford, OX2 8BG
Artwork: European Map Graphics Limited, Finchampstead RG11 4RF
Imagesetting by Hilo Offset, Colchester CO4 4PQ

A catalogue record for this book is available from the British Library

Library of Congress Cataloguing in Publication data
Bahn, Paul G.
The Cambridge illustrated history of prehistoric art / by Paul G. Bahn.
p.   cm. — (Cambridge illustrated histories)
ISBN 0-521- 45473-5 (hb)
1. Art, Prehistoric.
I. Title.   II. Series: Cambridge illustrated history.
N5310.B34   1998
709'.01'1—dc21   96-51099
CIP

ISBN 0 521 45473 5 hardback

Half-title: Tiny painting of a
female antelope from Hunter's
Shelter, Cederberg, South Africa
(see page 194).

Title Page: Horses and fighting
rhinoceroses, in Chauvet Cave,
France (see pages 164–5).

Contents

Author's Acknowledgements   vii

Foreword by Desmond Morris   viii

INTRODUCTION   xi

1 The 'Discovery' of Prehistoric Art   1

2 The Nineteenth and Twentieth Centuries: 30
   Prehistoric Art Comes into its Own

3 Body Art   70

4 Objets d'Art   82

5 Art on Rocks and Walls   98

6 The Appliance of Science   142

7 Matters of the Body: 170
   Literal Interpretations of Prehistoric Art

8 Matters of the Mind: 218
   Symbolic Interpretations of Prehistoric Art

9 Current Threats and Future Prospects   254

EPILOGUE   282

REFERENCE GUIDE

   Glossary   288

   Select Bibliography   289

   Map of Prehistoric Art Sites   294

PICTURE ACKNOWLEDGEMENTS   296

INDEX   298

For Lena

Yo, que soy montañés, sé lo que vale
La amistad de la piedra para el alma.
(As a man of the mountains, I know the value of
the friendship of the rock for the soul.)

Leopoldo Lugones, *A los Andes*

Author's Acknowledgements

Over the past twenty years or more I have visited a great deal of prehistoric art, and it would be an impossible task to list here all those who have helped me in various ways – through guidance, documentation, transportation and much else. I remain indebted to the numerous friends and colleagues already listed in my *Images of the Ice Age* (1988), and here would like to add some of those who have helped since then, or in other rock art areas: Mila Simões de Abreu, R.C. Agrawal, Juan-María Apellániz, Andrea Arcà, Claude, Jean and Monique Archambeau, Norbert Aujoulat, Dominique Baffier, James Baird, Rodrigo de Balbín Behrmann, Stephen Townley Bassett, Lasse Bengtsson, Magín Berenguer, Federico Bernaldo de Quiros, Margaret Berrier, Greg Bettis, Frank and A.J. Bock, Olga Boiko, John Campbell, Augusto Cardich, Edmund Carpenter, Jean-Marie Chauvet, Chen Zhao Fu, Shirley Chesney, Kathy Cleghorn, Sally Cole, John Coles, Stu Conner, Maria Soledad Corchón, Michèle Crémades, Ron Dorn, Jon Driver, C.N. (Kees) Dubelaar, Jean-Pierre Duhard, Phil Duke, Francesco d'Errico, Nick Evans, Eve Ewing, Alicia Fernández Distel, Dánae Fiore, Javier Fortea, Angelo Fossati, Céline Fournier, Natalie Franklin, Carole Fritz, Lidia Clara García, Jean-Michel Geneste, Donna and Garry Gillette, Naama Goren-Inbar, Carlos Gradin, Niède Guidon, Mariana Gvozdover, Jørg Hansen, Ken Hedges, Knut Helskog, Mauro Hernández Pérez, Bill Hyder, Anne-Sophie Hygen, Ludmila Iakovleva, Ludwig Jaffe, Vitor Oliveira Jorge, Jim Keyser, Majeed Khan, Ed Krupp, Giriraj Kumar, Joe Labadie, Jean-Loïc le Quellec, Georgia Lee, Tilman Lenssen-Erz, Larry Loendorf, the late Howard McNickle, Juana Martín, Elena Miklashevich, Elanie Moore, Breen Murray, Fred Muzzolini, Jarl Nordbladh, Laurence Ogel, George and Marvis Ogura, Marcel Otte, Shirley-Ann Pager, Nicole Pailhaugue, Anne-Marie Pessis, Jean Plassard, Maria Mercedes Podestá, Nikolai Praslov, Frans Prins, André Prous, Barbara Purdy, Roy Querejazu Lewis, Erika Rauschenbach, Sergio Ripoll, Lisa Roach, Anna Roosevelt, Marvin Rowe, Pam Russell, José Luis Sanchidrián Torti, Maria Eugenia Santa Coloma Costea, Dario Seglie, Viacheslav Shchelinsky, Jakov Sher, Vladimir Shirokov, Roberta Simonis, Jan Eric Sjöberg, Hans Christian Søborg, Kalle Sognnes, Amara Srisuchat, Jack Steinbring, Andrea Stone, Debbie Stonehouse, Matthias Strecker, Anne and Francis Thackeray, Alice Tratebas, Yvonne Vertut, Valentín Villaverde, P. Wagenaar Hummelinck, Christian and Janine Wagneur, Steve Waller, Grahame Walsh, Jesse Warner, Alan Watchman, David Welch, Margot Wellmann, Michèle Wollstonecroft, Bert Woodhouse, Hugo Yacobaccio, Daniela Zampetti, João Zilhão, and the Sir Philip Reckitt Educational Trust.

At Cambridge University Press, I would like to pay special thanks to Peter Richards for asking me to write this volume, to Pauline Graham for her help with picture research and the project in general, to Desmond Morris for his foreword, and to Sally Carpenter whose editing skills produced big improvements in structure and content.

PGB

(*Opposite*) A herd of llamas, and other figures, depicted as huge geoglyphs of piled-up dark stones (*see* pages 116-7) on a hillside at Tiliviche, northern Chile. The electricity pylons provide the scale. Late prehistoric, but precise date unknown.

Foreword

When I first visited the painted cave at Lascaux, not long after it had been discovered, I was stunned by what I saw. The skill of the prehistoric artists and the beauty of the images on the walls overwhelmed me. A companion, staring at them open-mouthed, blurted out that they must be fakes – they were clearly too good to have been produced by a Stone Age tribe. Of course, she was wrong. Much research has taken place during the half century since Lascaux was revealed to the world, and we now know that these remarkable paintings are perfectly genuine. My companion's disbelief was an impulsive reaction to the sheer quality of the portrayals. Therein lies their mystery and their greatest fascination.

It is not simply that primitive hunters, 15,000 years ago, were motivated to depict the animals that inhabited their world, but that they did so with such flair and artistry. The challenge we face when evaluating these astonishing works is not merely anthropological, it is also a matter of aesthetics.

Even if, after carefully excavating the cave floors and making delicate pigment analyses, we come to understand the chronology and technology of prehistoric art, we are still left with the most absorbing question of all – why did these prehistoric artists paint so well? Why did they create works of art that went far beyond the merely functional. If they wished to record a deer, a horse or a bull, they could easily have done so with crude little matchstick figures. But instead they laboured away in the dimly lit recesses of their caves recreating details of shape and form that would do credit to artists of any epoch in the history of painting. Indeed, when looking at animal pictures of the present century one is tempted to draw the humiliating conclusion that the best of the Stone Age painters were greater artists than many of those working of today.

This conclusion contains an important truth, namely that the aesthetic urge in *Homo sapiens* is not some recent refinement of civilization, but part of an ancient, deep-seated need of our species. The study of prehistoric art not only informs us about our Stone Age past and the way we lived then, it also tells us about what kind of species we are now and have always been. It forces us to accept that our artistic impulse sets us apart from other animals as much as our language or our technology.

One of the earlier books on the subject of prehistoric paintings used in its title the descriptive phrase *The Birth of Art*. How misleading that was. The clumsiness of the newborn is not what we see on the rock surfaces of Lascaux, Altamira or other such sites. The cave paintings that have miraculously managed to survive down the millennia are more like the adolescence of art, dextrous and talented, full of energy and vitality.

Tragically these absorbing works of art have not always been treated with due reverence. When I visited Lascaux for a second time, many years after my first visit, I was horrified to see how faded the paintings were. I assumed that my memory had been playing tricks with me and that, during the intervening decades I had, in my imagination, coloured them brighter and brighter. Sadly this was not the case. When I returned home, I found a report explaining that the paintings were rapidly deteriorating due to the huge numbers of people entering the caves. Shortly after that, Lascaux was closed to the public and, albeit too late, has remained so ever since. My memory had not played tricks with me after all. What I had seen, not long after the Second World War had ended, really had been magically vivid and bright.

Within the past few years, more painted caves have been discovered. Perhaps now, at last, these newly revealed paintings will be valued for what they are – a priceless record of human aesthetic activity. Some are twice as old as those as in Lascaux, revealing just how long the great tradition of European Stone Age art persisted.

With only a few words at my disposal, I have spoken solely of European cave art, but prehistoric art is worldwide in its distribution. New discoveries are being made all the time, especially in remote rock shelters in Africa and Australia, and at many sites in the New World. Everywhere this ancient work shows the same intensity, the same joy in imagery, colour and pattern. Some examples are more schematic and stylized, others more representational; some are heavy with myths and legends, others more concerned with the natural world. They are all, every one of them, worthy of our serious attention, and the publication of this superb volume will do much to remind us of this fact.

The author modestly points out that his brief is only to 'survey a tangible phenomenon', rather than to engage in theoretical debate. He sets out to give us the best and most up-to-date review of the data possible – and leaves it up to us to evaluate, interpret and re-interpret. But his presentation is much more than a mere catalogue. Time and again, his carefully arranged thematic treatment leads us to a reassessment of our own entrenched ideas about the true nature of prehistoric art and about its complexity when viewed on a global scale. His text is a model of scientific restraint and objectivity, but as its title indicates, this is ultimately an art book, and as such it is endlessly provocative and engaging.

Desmond Morris

Introduction

(Rock art is a) universal language of creative expression ... its intrinsic efficacy lies in its universality of appeal and its ability to endure and be sustained in a manner which can be discerned by all.

Kapila Vatsyayan

Prehistoric art is of supreme importance not because of the vast numbers of objects and images from the past that our eyes consider to be beautiful or striking, but because it is art alone that gives humankind its true dimension by showing that human activities hold meanings other than those of a purely utilitarian kind. But what *is* art?

(Opposite) **Petroglyphs of hut-like motifs on a rock at Naquane, Valcamonica, Italy. Date unknown, but probably Bronze or Iron Age.**

(Left) **Paintings of a male ancestral being with stretched ear lobes and two scrub turkeys, at Gugu-Yalanji, Laura region, Queensland, (Australia). Date unknown.**

ART?

'Art' is something which exists in every present-day human society and which also seems to have existed in every ancient one too, back to at least 40,000 years ago and probably much further. Yet it is a phenomenon which is notoriously difficult to define, not least because it encompasses such a vast array of activities and products, and because in many societies it is not perceived as a separate entity but merely as an inherent part of normal social or religious life: just as there are no clear boundaries drawn between the secular and the religious, so there are none between the aesthetic and the practical. Indeed, in some societies, such as most Australian Aboriginal cultures, there is no word for 'art' as such, and all aesthetic manifestations – paintings, carvings, woven mats and baskets, decorated musical instruments, as well as song and dance – are extensions of the cultural and natural environment, rather than divorced from it, and are related to many aspects of human experience.

Most views of art comprise some combination of two basic ideas: Plato's view of art as an individual's simple need to imitate what he or she sees; and the nineteenth-century theory which saw art as the expression of the artist's emotions. The latter idea has produced definitions of art which are elegant but of no help in the understanding of prehistoric art: for example, from the Norwegian composer Edvard Grieg – 'Art is really the surplus of longing that cannot find expression in life or in other ways'; or from the Russian novelist Leo Tolstoy – 'Art is a human activity

Art as part of the environment. Fine petroglyph panel (the Golden Disk Site) in Petrified Forest, Arizona (United States), showing a mixture of geometric and animal-like or humanoid designs. The main animal seems to be a hybrid, with horns and catlike paws. The panel is in a prominent position, visible from afar. The disk is about 60 centimetres (nearly 2 feet) in diameter. Date unknown.

consisting in this, that one man consciously, by means of certain external signs, hands on to others feelings he has lived through, and that other people are infected by these feelings, and also experience them.' The French sculptor Auguste Rodin said he was merely 'giving shape to his dreams'. Such views are of little use in the understanding of prehistoric art, since we know so little about the people and the cultures which produced it.

Another common perception of art as 'an achievement of human skill, the aim of which is to give pleasure rather than utility' is likewise of little use in archaeology, where the aim of most art – particularly in prehistoric periods – remains unknown. Some archaeologists go so far as to reject the word 'art' altogether, or at least place it between inverted commas, because it is thought to presume the aesthetic, because it lumps together such a huge variety of material into a single, monolithic category, or simply because it is impossible to provide a scientific and universally acceptable definition of the term. Conversely, one can argue that the word should be retained precisely because it is so vague, flexible and neutral and does *not* impose any particular interpretation.

The centuries-old definition of art as 'the work of people as opposed to that of nature' – that is, as being artificial and specifically human – may be more useful for a consideration of prehistoric art since it avoids any differentiation of the diversity of forms, content or intention. However, such a description would necessitate the inclusion of all kinds of artifacts which do not look like 'art' to us in any normal sense of the word. A more sharply focused version of the definition – in which a work of art is seen as a visual communication resulting from voluntary and conscious human intervention as opposed to natural phenomena – may be more appropriate. Thus art can be a deliberate communication through visual form, a message expressed in durable form, an expression of group mentality and of an artist's inner world. In short, art is art, regardless of the difference and variety of its meaning and function, regardless of qualitative or aesthetic appreciation, and whether it be prehistoric, Greek, Assyrian or anything else.

There is a feeling in some circles that the term 'rock art' is unsatisfactory – not merely in respect of debates over the meaning of 'art' itself, but also because it does not cover categories such as work in clay or chalk figures – and that some new word ending in -*ology* would be preferable. However, nobody has yet come up with a generally acceptable suggestion, let alone persuaded any of the rock art associations or journals to change their name. Nevertheless, a growing number of specialists are limiting themselves to terms such as 'rock paintings', 'rock engravings' or 'images', and avoiding the word 'art' altogether.

'An achievement of human skill', this remarkably realistic little petroglyph of a lizard is pecked into a rock at Dry Wash, Utah, United States. Date unknown.

Origins

Another basic problem for archaeology is the origins of art – not so much the why and wherefore, about which debate will probably continue for ever, but the appearance of 'proto-art'. At present, art is traditionally seen as an invention of fully

modern humans, its rise coinciding with their arrival in Europe and elsewhere over 40,000 years ago. However, since fully modern humans are now thought by some researchers to have been in Africa and the Near East since at least 100,000 years ago, one wonders why art took so long to emerge. A more realistic approach is to acknowledge the growing number and variety of apparently non-functional objects and examples of incipient decoration that are being discovered for earlier periods, produced by Neanderthals and even by *Homo erectus*, extending back some 200,000 or 300,000 years.

A related question is when tools moved beyond the strictly utilitarian into a symmetry which was perhaps more aesthetically pleasing than functionally necessary: many researchers would point to the sophisticated forms, proportions and high degree of symmetry of the handaxes of the Lower Palaeolithic period, several hundreds of thousand years ago, as the first visible example of this trend. Not only did such toolworking exceed functional requirements, but often particularly attractive or otherwise special rocks were carefully selected, such as fossiliferous flint or rock crystal, the procurement and transport of which presumably involved some effort. Non-functional fossils were also transported long distances.

Of course it is possible that these early tools as well as many later artefacts were primarily conceived in terms of practical use, and that any aesthetic effect they may have on ourselves was unintended or at best incidental. For example, much of the simplest 'decoration' of tools and weapons, such as incisions near the base, was probably intended to strengthen the adherence to the shaft and to improve the

(Opposite) **Petroglyphs of humans pecked into granite at Site 19 of the Spear Hill Complex, Pilbara, north-west Australia. The large figure is over 2 metres (7 feet) long, and has eyes, a rayed head and a wavy line down the length of his body, while the smaller figure below is clearly female. Date unknown.**

(Below) **Hunting scene painted in a low cleft at Main Caves, Giant's Castle, in South Africa's Drakensberg. A running man with a penis attachment and a stick appears to be driving an eland towards a third figure in the scene, a crouching archer to the right of the picture, which is barely visible today. Date unknown.**

user's grip: this has been called 'technical aesthetics'. Apparently non-figurative art – motifs which convey nothing to our eyes other than patterning – has existed from the beginning: indeed, it often dominates the art of the Palaeolithic period and its study is one of the long-neglected challenges of archaeology.

Trying to understand prehistoric art

The art of the past speaks to us, even though no longer in the language of its creators. But since our own ideas about what art is are continually changing, how can we possibly understand the art of thousands of years ago and other parts of the world? We need to be wary of using too aesthetic an approach, and to look beyond any beauty or formal qualities we may perceive in the art of the past, in order to try and recreate the perception and use of images of ancient peoples. It is important to remember that in remote periods (as in certain traditional societies today) some images were probably considered as the work of the supernatural, not merely as products of the human mind. They were seen as more or less direct manifestations of the divine and sometimes even as spontaneous miracles (like the image on the Turin Shroud): for example, many Australian rock engravings and paintings were

Possible supernatural images, painted at Head of Sinbad, Utah, United States. The central bug-eyed humanoid has a tapering body, short limbs and long fingers, as well as vertical stripes. Above its head is a wavy line, perhaps a snake, while on either side are very elongated, thin, striped figures. The panel, on a sandstone cliff, is about 1.5 metres (4–5 feet) wide and 6 metres (20 feet) above the ground. Date unknown.

(and in some areas still are) interpreted by the Aborigines as imprints left on the rock by the Dreamtime heroes. In other cases, ancient artists were anonymous go-betweens, conveying the decisions of the spirits and interceding between them and the people, whereas today artists in many cultures have lost their social and religious function.

Figurative images are more easily recognized as 'artistic' than non-figurative, though they too may well be utilitarian rather than simply decorative: 'art for art's sake' may theoretically have occurred in any culture, but in most cases individual artistic inspiration was related to some more widespread system of thought and had messages to convey – signatures, ownership, warnings, exhortations, demarcations, commemorations, narratives, myths and metaphors. The function of most prehistoric art was probably to affect the knowledge or behaviour of the people who could read those messages. We cannot read it in the same way as its intended public (and it is worth remembering that much cave art, for example, was intensely private,

Australian petroglyphs. This startling panel of female figures with clear (and sometimes apparently flowing) vulvas is at Lukis Granites in the Pilbara. Date unknown.

This accumulation of superimposed paintings was carefully placed within a niche in the great rock shelter of Pedra Furada in the Piauí region of Brazil. There are both animals (deer, lizards, etc) and humans, as well as a long string of enigmatic figures resembling paper dolls. Date unknown.

Petroglyphs of an emu, two eggs and a crab, at Skew Valley on the Burrup Peninsula, in Western Australia. Note how the emu has been drawn to fit the top of the rock. Date unknown.

meant to be seen only by the artist and perhaps by some deity – it was the act of producing the image, and its location, which seem to have been important) and the way in which vision, sound, movement, etc. may have been combined into a single experience has gone for ever. Without informants, we can use art only as a source of hypotheses; without the artists or (in later cultures) the presence of some explanatory label or writing, our chances of correctly interpreting the content and meaning of ancient art are small. Meaning can only be conjured up from our imaginations or – more reliably – from comparisons with images from historic cultures.

Taphonomy

Another fundamental problem in the study of ancient art is that of taphonomy – the question of what has or has not survived and what has or has not been discovered. Prehistoric art has reached us in a highly distorted and incomplete sample: except in sites with special conditions of preservation – the frozen, the arid or the water-logged – where objects made of fragile organic materials can survive, the art of the past is mostly made of more durable materials such as stone, pottery and metal. This is only the tip of the iceberg and may be completely unrepresentative of what existed originally.

A huge amount of artistic creation involving perishable materials has of course gone for ever – work in wood, bark, fibres, feathers or hides; objects made of mud, sand or snow; and, of course, body-painting and tattooing which probably have very distant origins. In addition, dance and song leave no traces at all and most musical instruments will have disintegrated.

Even those durable objects which have reached us are often no more than a pale shadow and indeed false image of their former selves. For example, it is known from residual traces of colour that many Ice Age portable art objects and most Ice Age bas-relief sculpture on rock-shelter walls, were originally painted, often in gaudy colours – as were Greek and Roman statuary, Aztec temples and the Medieval cathedrals of Europe. To our modern eyes, colouring would probably ruin these things; whereas the original artists and their contemporaries might well be horrified at the present lack of colour.

Where rock art is concerned, vast amounts have already disappeared thanks to weathering, farming, dams, etc. and much is threatened by pollution, vandalism, etc. There are many other causes of deterioration – properties of the rock itself (some kinds flake and weather rapidly, others remain virtually unchanged), action by animals and insects, algae and other organisms, human occupation, damage by fire or deposits of soot, and even geomorphological processes or tectonic activity. Some art has survived purely by chance, some because succeeding generations reused it or renewed it out of respect or piety. Untold quantities of art still remain undiscovered. Even in well-documented areas, new images and whole new sites are constantly being found: for example, the carvings of a dagger and axes on the stones at Stonehenge were not spotted until July 1953!

Petroglyph panel at Cottonwood Creek in Nine Mile Canyon, Utah (United States), containing thirty-two sheep of different sizes, several hunters and several other stylized human-like figures. Date unknown.

In caves too, many images may have been destroyed by water-flows or masked by stalagmite; others are still being discovered even in the best-frequented sites. So all studies of the content and distribution of motifs, techniques or sites are inevitably tentative, since they rely on an incomplete or distorted set of data.

PREHISTORIC?

As for 'prehistoric', this is simply a convenient category denoting the arrival of written records in a place: so, in the Near East, it ends about 3100 BC, whereas in Australia, Polynesia and elsewhere, it ended only a couple of centuries ago. In recent years, as a reaction against what is considered 'Eurocentric' or 'neocolonialist'

archaeology, some Third World scholars have rejected the term 'prehistoric', when applied to their regions, as somehow patronizing – implying that their oral traditions and histories were less valid or reliable, less worthy of regard, than written documents of the Western tradition. Such is not the case, however: 'prehistory' is simply a convenient chronological division, not a value judgement. (One could just as easily choose the arrival of the wheel, and 'pre-wheel' cultures such as those of the pre-conquest New World were clearly perfectly mobile and in no way inferior.)

However, to focus on the term 'prehistoric' where art is concerned is particularly ironic since prehistoric art, and particularly rock art, was clearly a means of recording and transmitting information. It constitutes the earliest and most universal

The Climbing Man panel near Dampier on the Burrup Peninsula, Western Australia, features a unique and bizarre set of petroglyphs. The face-like motif is 26 centimetres (10 inches) high. At either end of the panel are what look like humans climbing up both sides of trees or poles. Date unknown.

form, therefore, of 'proto-writing' and documentation. Of course, it was not true writing, which must have a grammar, a word order and a direct relationship to spoken language; but writing is basically a standardized form of recording, narrating, counting – all of which, it seems clear, prehistoric art could do.

ABOUT THIS BOOK

Prehistoric art comprises many millions of images from hundreds of thousands of sites – for example, according to a recent estimate, Sweden alone has about a quarter of a million images and marks in its rock art; and yet this is little when compared with countries such as the United States or Australia. The Australian Kakadu National Park alone has 5,000–6,000 sites, and Queensland has an estimated 50,000; the Burrup Peninsula of Western Australia is thought to have half a million petroglyphs. One researcher has hazarded a guess that there are well in excess of 100 million motifs in world rock art, and – since a single Thai grave contained more than 120,000 beads (see Chapter 4) – prehistoric portable art objects are certainly to be counted in their hundreds of millions, if not their billions!

Writing a book on such a huge, varied and complex phenomenon presents an enormous challenge: it is hard enough to write a meaningful volume on a single artist or period or culture. To attempt to encompass prehistoric art in all its forms (portable and parietal) and all its periods (from the earliest traces of 'art' up to a couple of centuries ago in some regions) is to tackle most of the world's art history, and it is impossible for a single book to do the subject justice. Previous efforts have focused, understandably, on specific areas such as Europe (N.K. Sandars, *Prehistoric Art in Europe*, 1968; W. Torbrügge, *Prehistoric European Art*, 1968). Others, despite more general titles, have in reality done the same (E.A. Parkyn, *An Introduction to the Study of Prehistoric Art*, 1915; R. Myron, *Prehistoric Art*, 1964; T.G.E. Powell, *Prehistoric Art*, 1966); or, worse, focused almost entirely on European Palaeolithic art, thus fuelling the 'Eurocentric' accusations (H. Delporte, *L'Image des Animaux dans l'Art Préhistorique*, 1990; D. Vialou, *La Préhistoire*, 1991).

In putting together this volume, therefore, and intending it to have a more global coverage, it was decided to avoid a simple chronological or a regional approach, neither of which could have been dealt with adequately in the space available. Instead a thematic approach seemed useful, focusing on just a few of the many varied topics involved in the content, context and conservation of this fragile and precious universal heritage. The very title of this series of books encouraged the inclusion of the early history of the discovery of prehistoric art by the world of scholarship. Unfortunately, lack of space has precluded a more exhaustive coverage of themes. Emphasis has been placed on the earlier periods, which in any case constitute the bulk of prehistory, and on parietal (cave and rock) art rather than portable objects, which are so diverse as to require several volumes. Some entire categories – such as architecture, standing stones, vessels, weapons and textiles – have had to be omitted. Similarly, the endless purely theoretical and largely pointless debates about how and why 'art' arose, and about the psychological, sociological or cultural factors at work, have no place here; our brief is to survey a tangible phenomenon.

We cannot know how prehistoric people regarded art, or if they had any concept of 'art' as such. Hence this book will include such images as stencils of hands, feet and tools, even though some scholars consider them to be mere impressions, mechanically reproduced, which do not 'represent' anything.

Petroglyph panel in Petrified Forest, Arizona, United States. Note particularly the intricate geometric design, 65 centimetres (over 2 feet) wide, comprising twenty-seven squares each featuring one of three motifs. Date unknown.

It cannot be guaranteed that all of the art mentioned or depicted in this book is truly prehistoric. For while it is fairly straightforward to date portable art, either from its stratigraphic position or through direct dating of its organic materials, comparatively little cave or rock art has been directly dated as yet. And while some is certainly of prehistoric age – as shown, for example, by caves which have been blocked since the Ice Age or rock panels masked by prehistoric occupation deposits – the vast majority is merely assumed to be prehistoric, based on evidence of varying degrees of validity and reliability such as patination, style, depicted objects, dress or vehicles and species of animal. But since it is known that much rock art was produced in the historical period, and even earlier this century in some areas such as parts of Australia, one cannot be absolutely sure that no 'historic art' has crept in here and there.

Hand stencil on a particularly coarse rock surface in the Laura region of Queensland, Australia. Date unknown.

THE GROWING POPULARITY OF ROCK ART

Rock art exists in all but a couple of countries of the world (Holland, for example, has almost no rocks, and although Poland does have rocks no rock art has yet been found) and it is a subject which has seen a huge upsurge of interest during the last few decades – witness the abundance of publications and conferences, as well as the proliferation of calendars, T-shirts, mugs and jewellery which it spawns in some places. In Scandinavia one can even find prehistoric art images on fabric designs, socks, ties, tea towels and oven gloves! Some researchers have rather grumpily

Large and extremely toothy 'mask' petroglyph in the Helan Mountains of the Ningxia region of northern China. Date unknown.

Petroglyph panel in Nine Mile Canyon, Utah (United States), depicting humanoids and a variety of animals, including two bighorn sheep facing an archer and what may be a scorpion. Date unknown.

Painted panel at the site of Ngarradj Warde Djobkeng, Arnhem Land (Australia), which includes a large X-ray style fish and, at top left, a hunter spearing a bird. The bird is about 25 centimetres (10 inches) high. Date unknown, but probably less than 1,000 years old.

objected to such 'frivolous' uses, either because they believe the motifs were origi-nally of deep religious significance (though we have no idea whether this is so) or because it deflects attention from the sometimes sad fate of the indigenous people who originally made the art (but of course we know nothing of the prehistoric artists, only the fate of their recent supposed descendants). Criticism of those rock art researchers who find amusement and relaxation in the subject is equally patron-izing and misplaced. Since prehistoric art images probably meant different things to different people when they were made, and still do so, there can be no objection to their popularization or to their being a source of fun and enjoyment. The images are used on T-shirts and mugs because they are seen to be beautiful or striking or funny – all positive attributes – or as a means of celebrating and promoting indi-genous art. Surely art, whatever its original motivation, exists for our enjoyment at some level. Would Michelangelo object to atheists deriving pleasure from the

Sistine Chapel? And would he expect all its visitors to curb their enjoyment by recalling the hardship and suffering he endured during the project?

Many people who are famous for other things have worked on or published rock art – for example, scholars such as Mary Leakey or authors like Joy Adamson and Erle Stanley Gardner. Rock art studies have always been the domain of the amateur as well as the professional. Amateurs remain of huge importance in this field and indeed many of the principal rock art organizations, such as ARARA (the American Rock Art Research Association), AURA (The Australian Rock Art Research Association), SARARA (The Southern African Rock Art Research Association) or SIARB (Sociedad de Investigación del Arte Rupestre de Bolivia), along with their important journals, were created by, are run by, and consist largely of amateur enthusiasts who include some of the world's foremost specialists. These associations are dedicated to the discovery, recording and conservation of rock art. The growing popularity of the art brings an ever-increasing risk of pollution, damage and vandalism, as well as outright thefts of objects and even of wall or cave images. The rock art associations are playing a major role in striving to teach schoolchildren and adults alike about the incalculable importance of this irreplaceable, universal heritage and about the need to respect and protect it.

In closing, I must stress that not only is it impossible to guarantee that all the art presented in this book is truly prehistoric, but it is equally impossible to be sure what it represents. In the absence of the original artists, and without readable labels or a written history, we simply do not know for sure what is depicted. (In the same way, without classical literature and without the names which are sometimes painted on the vessels, we would understand virtually nothing of the mythology depicted on Ancient Greek 'vases'.) In many cases, it seems fairly clear that humans or animals are represented in prehistoric art and we can even try and identify objects, but nothing is certain. So throughout this book, any labels or descriptions applied to prehistoric markings spring inevitably from the eye and mind of a twentieth-century European archaeologist, and they refer to form, not to meaning. The reader should assume that every statement is followed, in invisible parentheses, by the words – 'at least that's what this looks like to me, but what do I know?'

(Following page) **Etching by Debrie of paintings in the rock shelter of Cachão da Rapa (Portugal), published in 1734 in Contador de Argote's** *Memórias para a História Eclesiástica do Arcebispado de Braga.* **These prehistoric paintings (date unknown) were first mentioned in a manuscript by Father João Pinto de Morais in 1721. Debrie's etching is the earliest published picture of European rock art.**

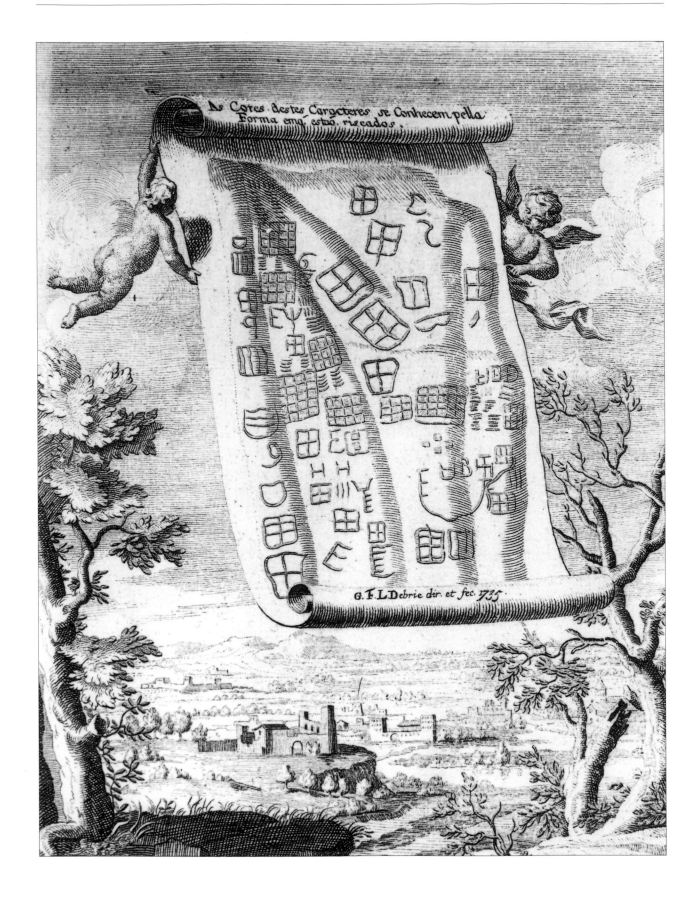

The 'Discovery' of Prehistoric Art CHAPTER 1

With the obvious exception of caves blocked since the Ice Age, sites and objects buried by deposits (which had to be excavated), and areas no longer frequented by humans (deep jungle, remote desert), prehistoric art was never really 'discovered' at all. Local inhabitants always knew it was there – often seeing it as the work of devils, evil spirits, sorcerers or fairies – and would sometimes point it out to visiting explorers or scholars. So this chapter might more accurately be called 'The Discovery of Prehistoric Art *by the World of Written Scholarship*', and it will concern primarily rock art (parietal art), since most portable art became known through excavation, as archaeology got under way around the world.

EARLY 'DISCOVERIES'

Most early 'discoveries' came about accidentally, as missionaries, scholars or explorers travelled around, reporting on anything of interest which they encountered. It was only in recent times (especially in the late nineteenth and twentieth centuries) that systematic searches began. Naturally, the early reports had no conception of the age of the art (even today, most rock art remains undated), since archaeology had not yet become established and there was as yet no inkling of the antiquity of humankind or of the very concept of prehistory.

The Far East
It seems to have been the Chinese who – in this domain as in so many others – were the pioneers. The earliest known written reports of rock art are to be found in *Han Fei Zi*, written about 2,300 years ago by the philosopher Han Fei (280–233 BC).

Petroglyphs of archers, deer and goats in the Inner Mongolia area. Date unknown. Describing part of the Yinshan Mountains of Inner Mongolia in the fifth century AD, the geographer Li Daoyuan wrote: 'The (Yellow River) passes to the west of a rock cliff. The cliff has pictures on it and is thus called Picture Rock Mountain ... The cliff has pictures of deer and horses on it.' He believed the images to have been 'made by nature'. It is largely thanks to this book that archaeologists have recently found much rock art in Inner Mongolia. In the Yinshan Mountains, guided by a shepherd, they rediscovered over 10,000 figures between 1976 and 1979, followed, between 1980 and 1983, by another 10,000 in the Ulanqab grasslands to the north. However, despite all these finds, it has been estimated that 90 per cent of Inner Mongolia's petroglyphs remain to be discovered. Much of the rock art of the Yinshan Mountains is in remote and windy locations. Wild animals and hunting are a dominant theme, while in the grasslands to the north there are many scenes of people with domestic animals.

In the fifth century AD, Li Daoyuan, a geographer of the northern Wei dynasty (386–534 AD), wrote a famous geography book called *Shui Jing Zhu* (Notes on the Systems of Rivers). The book consists mostly of Li Daoyuan's personal experiences, and describes places he has seen. He mentions numerous rock art sites in about half of China's provinces, and states that he has also heard of rock art in what are now India and Pakistan. The book also describes techniques (painting and engraving) and subjects (such as tigers, horses, goats and chickens, as well as divinities, masks and foot and hoof prints).

The rock art in other regions of China has probably long since disappeared, through agricultural activity and repeated human occupation. There are further Chinese texts on rock art from the tenth, fifteenth and seventeenth centuries, with local chronicles citing paintings and engravings in vague, magical and poetic references. For example, the spectacular pictographs (paintings) of Huashan (long considered prehistoric, but recently dated to about 2,000 years ago) in south-west China were mentioned in the fifteenth century; chronicles in the following three centuries state that they were discovered by shepherds who thought them to be magical. They were only rediscovered by modern scholars in 1950!

Eurasia
The earliest known reference to rock art in Europe occurred 1,000 years after Li Daoyuan's book, when, in 1458, Calixtus III, one of the Borgia popes, from Valencia in Spain, forbade cult ceremonies in a cave with horse pictures (presumably a decorated cave of Ice Age date) – showing the persistence of beliefs attached to

(*Opposite*) Pictographs, Huashan (Mountain of Flowers), China. The great cliff face of Huashan, one of about eighty rock art sites along the Zuojiang (or Ming) River, is the world's biggest rock art panel, over 200 metres (600 feet) wide and 40 metres (130 feet) high, and comprising 1,819 figures. The figures are from about 30 centimetres (12 inches) to 3 metres (10 feet) high, and form distinct groupings: large full-frontal figures, arms raised and knees bent, usually wearing a sword and often with a dog-like animal at their feet and a bird above their heads, are surrounded by smaller humans, both in full-frontal view and in profile. The artists must have used ladders, scaffolds or poles.

The Sorcerer petroglyph of Monte Bego (Vallée des Merveilles), located at an altitude of over 2,000 metres (6,000 feet) in the southern Alps. This schematized figure is located on a vertical surface facing the mountain peak. It looks like a human face, possibly with moustache and teeth and beard, and has two raised five-fingered hands and two daggers. In 1460, a traveller, Pierre de Montfort, mentioned the valley in a letter as an infernal place. This epitomizes the traditional view of prehistoric art as something diabolical which alarmed Christians. Date unknown, but probably Bronze Age.

prehistoric images. Only two years later, in 1460, a traveller, Pierre de Montfort, wrote a letter to his wife which described the Vallée des Merveilles in the Alps as follows: 'C'estait lieu infernal avecques figures de diables et mille démones partout taillez en rochiers.' (It was an infernal place with figures of devils and a thousand demons carved everywhere on rocks.) In the sixteenth century, Onorato Lorenzo, a priest from the region, wrote a large unpublished manuscript called *Accademio dei Giordani di Belvedere*, including information obtained from shepherds: he mentions the 'Meraviglie' and provides a long list of motifs and subjects in the rock art.

Further references to rock art can be found in southern Europe in the sixteenth century. In 1598, the Spanish dramatist Lope de Vega, in his comedy *Las Batuecas del Duque de Alba* (The Backwoods of the Duke of Alba), refers to the schematic (that

The Cobbler panel of petroglyphs at Backa, Bohuslän (Sweden) is about 8 metres (26 feet) long and 3 metres (10 feet) wide. At the top are small animals (deer?) and boats. In the middle are humans, including the Cobbler, a 1.5-metre (5-foot) male with exaggerated penis, large head with a necklet (or perhaps a small head surmounted by a disc?) and raised arms brandishing a battle-axe. At his feet is a chariot and to the left is a 'boat' carrying six humans. Lower down there are some long-legged birds and a 'boat' with hands at either end. Probably Bronze Age (*c.* 1000 BC).

is, highly simplified or stylized) paintings of Las Batuecas (Cáceres), the woods in which demons were said to live. (Ponz, in his *Viaje de España*, 1778, also speaks of the frieze of 'painted goats' at this place, but they were only rediscovered in 1910.) A certain Señor del Coto de Racemil de Parga, who was hunting for treasure at the beginning of the seventeenth century, noted that in the Iberian dolmen-tumulus of Anafreita, Fial, there were 'shields and letters engraved'.

In Sweden, the earliest known documentation of petroglyphs are some seventeenth-century drawings of rock carvings at Backa Brastad near Tanum, Bohuslän (at that time part of Norway, itself linked to Denmark), which were made by Peder Alfssön, a schoolmaster from Kristiania (Oslo) and sent to Professor Ole Worm, doctor to the King of Denmark. Worm, a renowned polymath and founder of museums, had sent questionnaires to educated people in the provinces, mainly priests, asking them to make a note of the location, setting and dimensions of ancient monuments and, if possible, to make drawings, investigate how the monuments were constructed and ascertain what the local population said or believed about them. Alfssön, who provided information on south-east Norway for Worm, produced freehand wash drawings and accompanying text which, amazingly, still survive in Copenhagen, having escaped several wars and great fires. (They remained forgotten until reproduced as small copperplate engravings by P.F. Suhm in 1784, in his *Samlinger til den Danske Historie*, Collections from Danish History.) It is not known exactly when the drawings were made, but they entered the

Copperplate engravings of petroglyphs at Bohuslän, Sweden, made from the wash drawings of Peder Alfssön and published by Suhm in 1784.

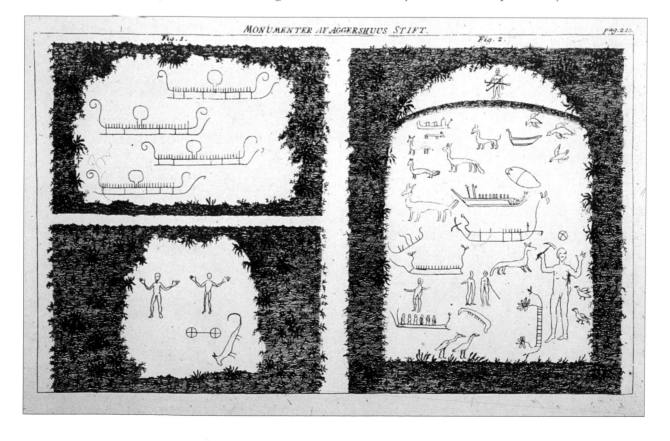

Drawing of the main Cobbler panel by the schoolmaster Peder Alfssön. For his depiction – 33 x 40 centimetres (13 x 16 inches) – Alfssön clearly drew its figures separately and then placed them together in a way that is somewhat different from reality. He showed the rock surface as grey and marked its limits with vegetation. The human figures were left unsexed, except for the largest which, astonishingly, he drew as a woman, omitting its prominent penis. The Cobbler panel was the first European rock art to be recorded by drawing as far as is known.

(*Opposite*) The oldest known depiction of megalithic art, at Newgrange (Ireland), dates to 1699. We owe this account of a decorated passage grave (a form of megalithic chambered tomb) to Edward Lhwyd (1660–1708), the famous Welsh antiquary and Keeper of Oxford's Ashmolean Museum, who visited Newgrange in 1699, shortly after it was first opened up. In a letter to the Royal Society in December of that year, he mentions that at the door there is a 'broad, flat stone, rudely carved' and inside the chamber '(the stones) about the Basons, and some elsewhere, had such Barbarous sculpture (*viz.* spiral like a Snake, but without distinction of Head and Tail), as the fore-mentioned stone at the entry of the Cave'.

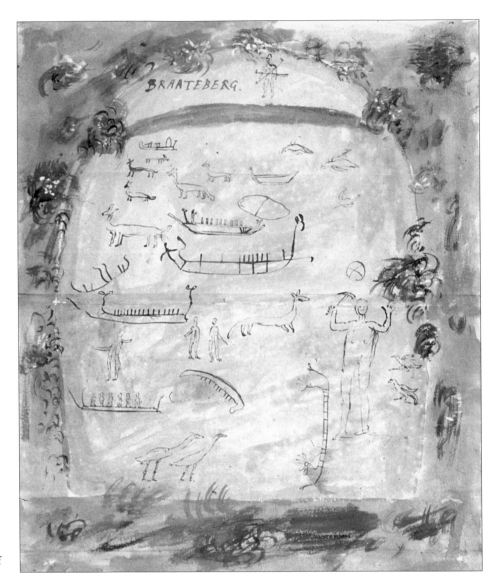

Copenhagen Archives in 1627, which makes them the oldest known drawings of rock art panels in the world.

Alas, Worm made no mention of rock art in his 1643 book on ancient Denmark. Alfssön, of course, had no inkling of the panel's antiquity, and believed that the carvings – including the large human figure subsequently nicknamed Skomakeren (The Shoemaker) – had been made as graffiti in Medieval times by apprentice stonemasons working on the construction of a church in the vicinity. It was only in the eighteenth century that scholars came to realize that such carvings were very old, though at first it was believed that they depicted historical events, such as battles between Viking ships.

In the Alps, the Nice historian Abbé Pietro Gioffredo, in his *Storia delle Alpi Marittime* (*c.*1650), basing his somewhat fanciful description of the Vallée des Merveilles

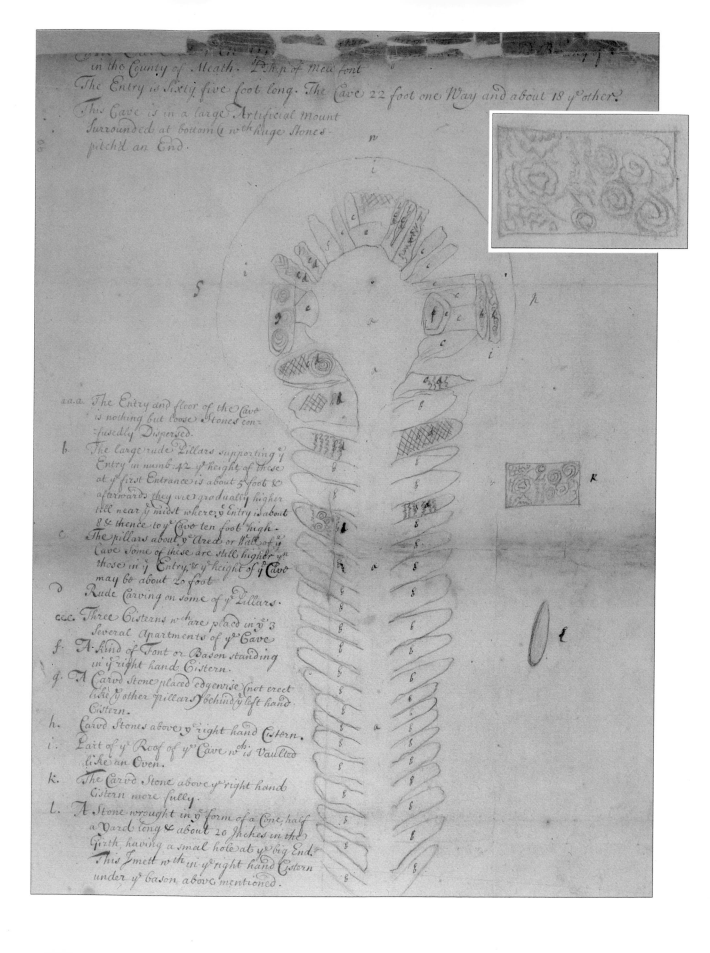

... in the County of Meath. Dioph. of New font

The Entry is Sixty five foot long. The Cave 22 foot one Way and about 18 y other.

This Cave is in a large Artificial Mount
Surrounded at bottom (with huge Stones
pitch'd an End.

aa.a. The Entry and floor of the Cave
    is nothing but loose Stones con=
    fusedly Dispersed.

b.   The large rude Pillars supporting y
    Entry in numb: 42 y height of these
    at y first Entrance is about 5 foot &
    afterwards they are gradually higher
    till near y midst where y Entry is about
    8 & thence to y Cave ten foot high.

c.   The pillars about y Area or Wall of y
    Cave Some of these are still higher yn
    those in y Entry, & y height of y Cave
    may be about 20 foot

d   Rude Carving on some of y Pillars.

ccc. Three Cisterns wch are placd in y 3
    Several Apartments of y Cave

f.   A kind of Font or Bason standing
    in y right hand Cistern.

g.   A Carvd Stone placed edgewise (not erect
    like y other pillars) behind y left hand
    Cistern.

h.   Carvd Stones above y right hand Cistern.

i.   Part of y Roof of y Cave wch is Vaulted
    like an Oven.

k.   The Carvd Stone above y right hand
    Cistern more fully.

l.   A Stone wrought in y form of a Cone, half
    a Yard long & about 20 Inches in the
    Girth, having a smal hole at y big End.
    This I mett wth in y right hand Cistern
    under y bason above mentioned.

on Onorato Lorenzo's account, mentioned 'various stones of all colours, flat and smooth, decorated with engravings of a thousand imaginary subjects, representing quadrupeds, birds, fish, agricultural or military mechanical instruments ... This leads one to think of a work dating from several centuries, and that the authors of such merry jokes were shepherds trying to avoid boredom.'

In Russia, petroglyphs (originally known as *pissanye kamni*, or inscribed stones) were mentioned in the notes made by travellers, ambassadors and merchants during the seventeenth and eighteenth centuries. For example, the Moldavian prince Nikolai Milesku Spafarii, ambassador for Tsar Alexei Romanov, mentioned petroglyphs in the Yenisei Valley in his travel notes of his journey through Siberia to China in 1675. The site of Tomskaya Pisanitsa was described in a Russian chronicle of the seventeenth century as a 'big stone with the images of animals, birds and people'. In 1692, the Dutch traveller and scientist Nicolaas Witsen, a friend of Peter the Great, published *Nord und Ost Tartaray* (2nd edition 1705): this book – in effect the first Siberian encyclopedia – contained descriptions of 'ancient paintings', including rock pictures on the River Irbit in the Urals.

Drawings of petroglyphs by Ambrósio Brandão. These drawings – the earliest known reproductions of rock art motifs in the world – appeared in Brandão's chronicle of an expedition through part of Brazil.

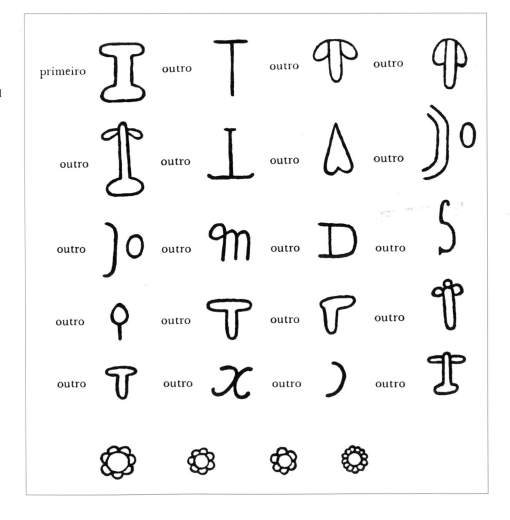

The New World

It was in the New World that the major development of the sixteenth century occurred, as 'inscriptions' of various kinds were spotted, and sometimes described and illustrated, by conquering Europeans – such as the Bandeirantes (carriers of the royal Portuguese banner) – exploring the interior of Brazil. During the first centuries of the conquest, members of various religious orders also penetrated the interior of Amazonia. The earliest known information on rock art here is attributed to Ambrósio Fernandes Brandão, who in 1598 recorded the existence of rock engravings in the present state of Paraíba, on the River Araçai. In 1618, Brandão included drawings of motifs in Brazilian petroglyphs in his *Diálogos das Grandezas do Brasil*, probably the world's earliest-known reproduction of rock art. In this account, he records that on 29 December 1598 a group of soldiers found a cavern on the western bank of a river called 'Arasogipe'. The cavern was

> …formed of three boulders touching each other, capable of sheltering fifteen men … All over the curved surface of the rocks were markings which from their shapes showed they had been made artificially. Firstly, on the west side of the cave, on the upper part were fifty depressions or 'pits' close together, running in a line from bottom to top, looking like Our Lady's rosary on an altar piece, and at the end of the row of 'pits' was shaped a rose …
>
> There were more characters in the cave on the west side … Above these was another rose painted, like the first, and below it, another similar rose near which was a sign like the skull of a dead man. Near this, on the left, were twelve more pits like the others, and above them, near the first group of fifty pits were some signs like skulls. On the right side was a cross and nearby, on the left side of the rock face, were fifty pits divided into six groups. In one of the groups was a rose badly eroded by time, and near that another nine pits like the others. All over the bulges of the rock were painted another six roses … It should be noted that all the roses were the same except for one which had twelve petals with the one in the middle.

Later, in 1641, the poet and adventurer Elias Herckmans noted stones worked by humans in the Serra da Cupaóba in Brazil. In 1656, while on a trip to catechize Indians in the state of Pará, Father João de Sotto Mayor noted demonic figures across the River Pacajá (a tributary of the Pará): 'I found on the boulder, worked with iron tools, some faces, so ugly and

Drawing showing a Christian cross superimposed on a prehistoric petroglyph (of unknown date) at Peña Escrita (Bolivia), showing a human or animal. This example of Christianized rock art epitomizes the attitude of sixteenth-century clerics in Latin America, who felt the need to combat native respect or veneration for such images by attempts to exorcize, neutralize or convert them. (After Bednarik.)

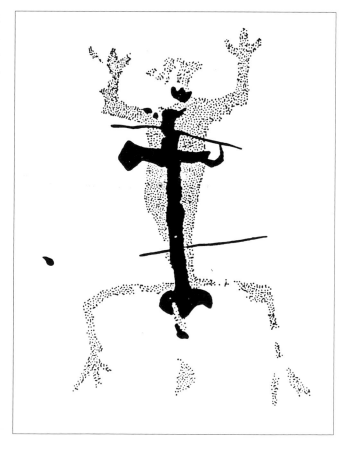

deformed that one might be led to think they had been made by the Devil. This I realized from the observation of their shape and from the figure of a crocodile depicted on another side of the boulder.'

The earliest mention of rock art in Mexico is in the sixteenth-century book *Monarquía Indiana* by Fray Juan de Torquemada, who linked it with Quetzalcoatl (the feathered serpent god): 'Quetzalcoatl arrived at another place, a hill near the village of Tlalnepantla, two leagues from this city of México, where he sat down on a stone, and placed his hands on it, and left their imprint there, of which traces can still be seen today ... and at present it is called Temacpalco, which means, in the palm of the hand.'

Quetzalcoatl was also linked to engravings at Coatepec-Chalco in Mexico. *La Relación de Coatepec y su Partido*, by Comendador Christobal de Salazar, 1579, mentions that the feathered serpent also came to this sierra – 'where he climbed up there can be seen – and it seems as if they had been made today – the prints and signs which he made with his feet, and the hollow where he lay down'. A bit later, in 1592, Fray Diego de Azevedo said he saw in the Cerro de Cempoaltepec, Oaxaca: 'two big stones, marked with two human footprints, one opposite the other'.

During the sixteenth century, some Spanish missionaries in Latin America realized that certain rock art sites which were of a religious nature remained sacred to the native population. For example, a late sixteenth- or early seventeenth-century document from Mexico, written by Padre Andrés Pérez de Ribas, mentions that a cleric, trying to catechize the Guazaves in the north of Sinaloa, saw a native stop in front of a sculptured stone decorated with some crude images and make some demonstrations of reverence. Such attitudes so concerned the clerics that they either destroyed the images or they engraved crosses in high or prominent places at the sites to demonstrate the superiority of Christianity.

The first investigations of Bolivian rock art began early in the colonial period. A Spanish priest, Padre Alonso Ramos Gavilán, in his book *Historia de Nuestra Señora de Copacabana* (1621), mentions four rock art sites. In three of these, the Spanish found engraved 'footprints' in the rock, but here, instead of attributing them to Quetzalcoatl, as in Mexico, they assumed them to be the traces of a Christian saint – this fitted their theory that there had been a Christian missionary in the Andes in prehistoric times. Some believed this to have been St Thomas himself, who was said to have preached in this continent and left his footprints when he moved on. The fourth site had 'letters written on a rock'. Early explorers often saw rock art as ancient writing. For instance, in a document of 1615 addressed to the Padre General, Padre Rodrigo de Cabredo wrote about a legend which circulated in the area of the bay of Banderas in the south-west of the state of Nayarit, Mexico: on a crag of a sierra here 'there is sculpted a most devout Christ, and below it some lines of ancient characters; and the letters ... contained many little dots, and must be Hebrew ... in these mountains can be seen a little crag on which, in the manner of a ladder, there are imprinted the tracks of this saintly man (a preacher called Matias or Mateo).'

In Colombia, in about 1620, Padre Simón saw signs of the cross – so deeply engraved into the rocks that 'neither age nor the waters have been able to wipe them out' – near Bosa and Soacha, south-west of Bogotá. De Zamora, in 1635, also mentioned engraved figures in Colombia which he associated with St Thomas. Breton, in 1635, was the first to observe the deeply engraved rocks in the Lesser Antilles. The missionary Antonio de Calancha, in his *Crónica Moralizada de la Orden de San Agustín en el Perú*, 1638, reproduced a drawing of petroglyphs on a rock at Calango, near Lima, including a footprint which he believed was that of the saint, and other motifs which he saw as keys, an anchor and letters.

Drawing of the decorated petroglyph rock of Calango, near Lima (Peru), as published in 1638 in a book by Antonio de Calancha – probably the earliest known published reproduction of a rock art panel. The rock stood just by the old church and was 'of bright white and blue marble'. De Calancha described it as being about 2 metres/7 feet high at one side, about 6 metres/20 feet long, and 4 metres/13 feet wide.

> There is depicted and imprinted a left foot print ... above it there are signs or letters like XX ... below there are some circles and other figures like keys ... (The) stone's name (is) Coyllor Sayana, which means 'stone where the star stopped', and in the local dialect it was called ... Yumisca Lantacaura, which means 'clothing or skin of the star'; it has this name because a male and a female Indian got up on the stone to perform the venereal act, and while they were looking at the sky a star fell down and merged them ... and this is why no Indian dared to offend the stone or to look at the stars during such acts ... The two sensual people who, without respect, offended God over the print of the Saint called it 'stone where the star stopped' ... The two keys, one bigger than the other, were unknown to the Indians and not used in their houses, nor did they see anchors or characters or letters until the Spaniards arrived ... Maybe this was meant to signify that they must wait because in the future the keys of St Peter's church would enter these lands, where he left his print but could not introduce his faith.

De Calancha reported that, because the stone was still the object of superstitious worship on the part of the Indians, Hispanic visitors had had the images ground down, and a cross placed at the head of the rock. He felt that this was enough to eliminate any superstition, and that the perpetrators were wrong to 'erase a footprint that was so worthy of veneration, but perhaps it was an impulse from heaven'.

In 1671, missionaries living at the confluence of the Sinaruco and Orinoco Rivers, Venezuela, found petroglyphs along the Orinoco. In Mexico in 1694, Padre Francisco de Florencia said that in some part of the valley of Chacala, Jalisco, 'on a small crag St Thomas left his tracks imprinted'. This stone was removed to the Franciscan convento of Guadalajara.

In 1695, a remarkable book, *Amerikaansche Voyagien, Behelzende een Reis na Rio de Berbice* (English translation 1925), appeared in Amsterdam. The author, a traveller called Adriaan van Berkel, refers to an Indian tribe in Guyana called the Acquewyen (Akawai): near their trading place, he says, are 'many cliffs upon which can still be seen the marks of the Spaniards who first discovered the coast and penetrated the river through'. Once again, therefore, petroglyphs were explained away as marks by Europeans.

Drawings of the pictograph known as the Piasa Bird, at Alton (United States). The missionary and explorer Jacques Marquette described the image as winged monsters. The pictograph became a well-known landmark, remarked on by many river travellers, until 1856 when it was destroyed to provide stone for a rock quarry. 'Piasa' is an Indian term meaning 'the bird which devours men'. (*Top right*) The drawing made by William Dennis on 3 April 1825 was marked 'flying dragon'. (*Top left*) The simpler drawing is from an old German publication entitled *The Valley of the Mississippi Illustrated* by H. Lewis, published around 1839 in Düsseldorf.

In the mid-seventeenth century, the first reports of rock art in North America also emerged. In 1673 a Jesuit missionary and explorer, Jacques Marquette, while exploring the upper Mississippi River, noted in his journal hideous, painted, winged monsters high on a cliff near Alton in modern Illinois. Marquette described the image as follows:

> On the flat face of a high rock were painted, in red, black and green, a pair of monsters, each as large as a calf, with horns like a deer, red eyes, a beard like a tiger, and a frightful expression of countenance. The face is something like that of a man, the body covered with scales; and the tail so long that it passes entirely round the body, over the head, and between the legs, ending like that of a fish.

Unfortunately, Marquette's original drawing of the main monster was lost when his canoe capsized on the St Lawrence River on the return voyage from Illinois.

Other North American discoveries soon followed, such as the markings on Dighton Rock – a large rock covered with deeply incised abstract designs and highly stylized human figures on the east bank of the Taunton River in Massachusetts. These have been attributed by the lunatic fringe of archaeology, even today, to

Dighton Rock, Massachusetts (United States). This boulder of bluish grey rock by the Assonet or Taunton River was noticed by New England colonists as early as 1680, when Dr Danforth made a drawing of it. At least five other drawings of it are known from the eighteenth century and three from the early nineteenth – all of them different and imperfect. These petroglyphs (date unknown) were pecked into the rock, not cut or chiselled. By 1886 its surface (about 3.5 x 1.5 metres/11 x 5 feet) was already rapidly deteriorating owing to frequent scrubbings with brooms and water to remove the sand and dirt deposited by every tide.

Norsemen, Phoenicians, Scythians and Portuguese explorers. In fact, these are native American petroglyphs and the first drawings of them were made by colonists in 1680. The pictograph site of La Roche-à-l'Oiseau on the Outaouais River, Quebec, was mentioned in 1686, in connection with Indians throwing down offerings of tobacco when they passed close to the rock.

THE AGE OF ENLIGHTENMENT

In the eighteenth century, a time when so many fields of enquiry began to be transformed into serious topics of study, a more profound and sustained interest began to be taken in rock art and sites were reported in two more continents.

Eurasia

In Portugal, the first documentation of rock art was by Padre António Carvalho da Costa in 1706, when he published some notes on paintings in the rock shelter of Cachão da Rapa at Montecorvo, on the River Douro. An etching by Debrie (see page xxxii) of some schematic art from this shelter was included by Jerónymo Contador de Argote in his *Memórias para a História Eclesiástica do Arcebispado de Braga*, 1734;

Sketches of schematic rock art motifs at Fuencaliente, Ciudad Real (Spain), made by López de Cárdenas in 1793. Date unknown.

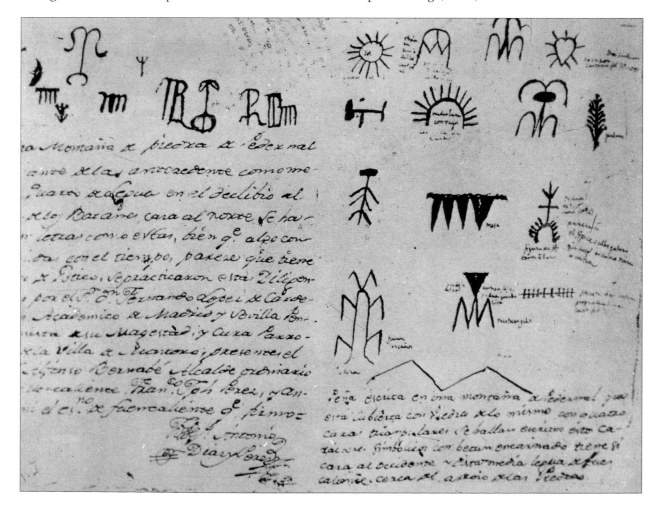

(*Above*) Sketch of petroglyph, Balsfjord (Norway). In 1799 Martin Vahl from Bergen, Professor of Botany at Copenhagen, visited northern Norway for his botanical fieldwork. In 1913 this sketch was found among his papers (part of his travel diary) in Copenhagen's Botanical Museum. Under the drawing he had written: 'At a farm in Balsfjord a buck is pecked on the rock.' This image is said to be the first record of the 'hunters' art' in these northern lands. In the mid-twentieth century Gustav Hallström, the Swedish archaeologist, went to Tennes in Balsfjord to find the unnamed farm. On showing the drawing to the locals he was directed to the oldest man in the place, who exclaimed 'the buck at Bukkhammar!' Although the images there were now overgrown, the figure had actually given its name to the hill (Buck Hill). Date unknown.

in this same work, reference was also made to, and a sketch given of, a monument near Esposende which comprised four upright stones 'all decorated with diverse characters and figures' and covered by another stone. In Spain, sketches of the schematic rock art of Fuencaliente (Ciudad Real) were drawn in a notebook by López de Cárdenas in 1793. In Ireland, Newgrange and the other decorated Boyne tombs were frequently described and illustrated in the eighteenth and nineteenth centuries, while 'rude carvings' at Killin, Co. Louth, were reported by the antiquarian Thomas Wright in 1758.

There were also further reports of rock art in Scandinavia. In 1751, a letter from a superintendent of the Swedish–Norwegian border mentions carvings in Bohuslän: 'In the parish of Tanum, not far from the sea, I have also visited a sloping rock, where a man with spear in his hand is cut, and about whom is said that a Scottish commander had been killed in his flight during a military campaign and that the position of his dead body was reproduced in the rock.' The letter included a plea for an inventory to be started in the county but this fell on deaf ears. Also in the mid-eighteenth century, the great cairn of Kivik in Skåne, southern Sweden, was discovered, and the carved images on the stone slabs of its central cist (chamber) were drawn in very professional fashion by Carl Gustaf Hilfeling, an antiquarian

who specialized in depiction and description. The much-travelled Hilfeling also visited Bohuslän, and his travel books, published after 1792, include several drawings of monuments and rock carvings in that region. He produced measured drawings done to scale, not freehand sketches, and his pictures are full of comments on size, distances and locations. Unfortunately, he had a tendency to see non-existent runic inscriptions on some rocks. Rock art was also mentioned by Suhm in 1784, and in 1760 in Carl Fredrik Broocmans's *History of East Götland* – he said the places with pictures were sacrificial altars.

(Left and opposite bottom) **Drawings of rock art in the area of Gordovaja Stena (Siberia) made by the young doctor and naturalist Daniil-Gotlieb Messerschmidt in 1722.**

In 1719, Tsar Peter the Great sent a young doctor and naturalist, Daniil-Gotlieb Messerschmidt, to lead a scientific expedition to study the nature and population of Siberia. In Tobolsk, Messerschmidt met Philip Johann Tabbert von Strahlenberg, a Swedish officer who was a prisoner in Siberian exile, and together they carried out the first scientific excavations in the region. In 1722 Messerschmidt made a drawing of a rock with symbols, images of animals and a man. He also discovered runic inscriptions on rocks: in 1893 these were found to be old Turkish but at first they conjured up, for Messerschmidt, romantic ideas about Vikings and Germans. The discovery of these inscriptions encouraged him to investigate ancient rock images more closely and to make copies of them. In his diary entry for 23 February 1722, he reports that by the Yenisei River, not far from the village of Birjusa, near Krasnoyarsk, 'there are all kinds of "characters" and figures, written in red, to which the locals ascribe all kinds of meanings, because the motifs are quite high above the river on smooth, steep rocks, so the locals could not understand how people could make them there. They call them "Pisannyj kamen".' On 18 August of the same year, Messerschmidt saw numerous Scythian graves bearing stones covered with images, some of which he reproduced as drawings. His diary entry for

(Below and opposite)
Drawings by Johann Tabbert von Strahlenberg of motifs in Siberian rock art (date unknown).

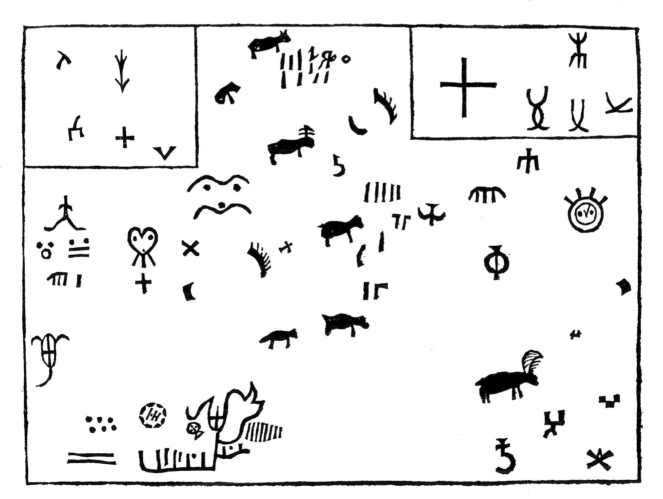

26 September mentions that at Gordovaja Stena he once again saw characters and images about 8 metres (26 feet) above the river level, and made with a crimson and indelible colour 'in time immemorial'.

In 1730, liberated and back home in Sweden, von Strahlenberg published a book (*Das Nord- und Östliche Theil von Europa und Asia*) which constituted the first

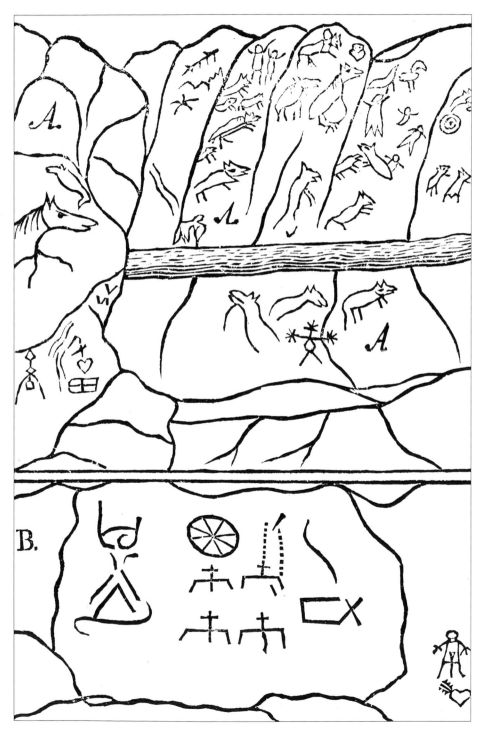

scientific publication on the archaeological monuments of the Yenisei region, including petroglyphs. Of the 'characters' in this rock art, von Strahlenberg wrote:

> ... many are to be found in Siberia and Tartary, upon Rocks and Stones, either carved, or painted, in the same Manner almost, as the Lapplanders are wont to paint their Drums; ... those which are in Great-Permia, near the city of Tzerdyn, which either are burnt in, or written by some other Means, upon Rocks there, with a red indelible Colour ... The same Sort of Figures cut or carved in Rocks, are also to be seen on the Banks of the River Tomm, between the cities of Tomskoi and Kusnetskoi ... But the Figures [on page 17, B], which are likewise painted or stained with a red colour ... were found in the farther Part of Siberia, between the Cities of Crasnoyahr and Abakan, upon the Rocks which are on the Banks of the River Jenisei ... And considering that the said River Jenisei runs close under the Rocks, which in some Places are very smooth and steep, like a Wall, and as high as a Steeple, it is hard to conceive how these Painters, or other Artificers, could come at them, to make these Figures, which are mostly on the middle of the flat Surface of these Rocks. They could not do it in Summer, by Means of Ladders, because the River is, in those Places, deeper than the Rocks are high; And in Winter, the Snow which lies there above Man's deep, and the terrible Frost would, by no Means, allow them to climb up, and paint them at all. There is, therefore, Room to conjecture, that they either found Ways to let themselves down from above, or climb'd up from below, by the Help of Stone-Wedges drove into the Rock.

Other expeditions to Siberia followed, which also examined the archaeology and rock art of the region. For example, in 1750 the historian Gerhard-Friedrich Mueller produced a book in Russian (*Opisanie Sibirskogo Carstva*, later also published in German) in which he reproduced sketches of some images and refuted the supposition that these ancient rock drawings could be taken as a special form of writing.

Drawings of Siberian rock art in its landscape, by the historian Gerhard-Friedrich Mueller, published in 1750.

The New World

Discoveries continued in the Americas. In 1711 Father Eusebio Kino described and mapped the Painted Rocks – actually engravings – near Gila Bend, Arizona. In Quebec, the Nisula site on Lac de la Cassette was mentioned on Father Pierre-Michel Laure's maps, drawn between 1731 and 1733, during the French regime in Canada and showing the so-called Domaine du Roy in Nouvelle France, with 'Pepéchapissinagan' (the stone thing on which there are paintings) where 'naturally painted figures can be seen on the rock'.

Pierre-Joseph Céleron de Blainville, part of a French expedition of 1749 which had come from Canada to the area around the northern Ohio River to bolster French claims to the region, mentioned the Indian God Rock petroglyphs in Pennsylvania as being clearly visible on the rock surface. In 1776 Father Silvestre de Escalante, who was trying to find a land route from Mexico to Monterey, saw carved rock images in western Colorado, while a pictograph on a tree in Kentucky

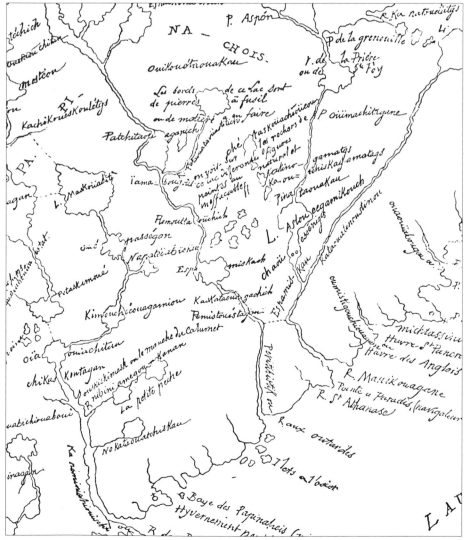

On this map of Canada, drawn in 1731 by Father Pierre-Michel Laure, one can see the words 'Chétaskouachioueou, on voit sur les rochers de ce lac diferentes figures peintes au naturel et ineffaçables.' (On the rocks of this lake one can see different figures painted true to life and indelible.)

was noted by explorer Christopher Gist in his journal in 3 April 1751: 'a small Creek on which was a large Warriors Camp, that would contain 70 or 80 warriors, their Captain's Name or Title was the Crane, as I knew by his picture or Arms painted on a tree'.

Heads or faces carved at the foot of the Great Falls on the Connecticut River in the village of Bellows, Vermont, have been commented on by travellers and researchers since 1789, the petroglyphs being described variously as Indian chiefs, families, symbols of male authority, memorials of noteworthy events, idle artwork, and the work of shamans recording vision experiences.

In the eighteenth century, a Jesuit missionary called Schabel visited Pedrazza, Venezuela, and thought the petroglyphs there had been 'engraved by angelic hands'. In 1740, Nikolas Horstman, a surgeon from Germany, was the first explorer to report seeing petroglyphs in Guyana with his own eyes – he found drawings along a tributary of the Rupununi River. These were thought to be Indian by the Prussian nobleman and explorer Alexander von Humboldt, who quoted Horstman's journal: 'Rocks with figures, or, as they say in Portuguese, covered in various letters'. Humboldt himself saw many petroglyphs during his travels through South America at the end of the century. He put forward some interpretations of petroglyphs in the Orinoco region, and mentioned that he had met Ramón Bueno, a missionary who 'hoped to return to Madrid and make known the result of his investigations of the paintings and rock drawings of Uruana'. In 1740, Pieter Tollenaer mentioned engraved signs in the Upper Rupununi area. Father Pedor Lozano, in about 1730–60, interpreted the abundant engravings and paintings of Colombia, Brazil, Paraguay and Peru as tracing the itinerary of St Thomas, with all footprints, as usual, being attributed to the saint! (Conversely, red handprints were often attributed to the Devil in Latin America.) But Filippo Salvadore Gilii, another Jesuit missionary in Venezuela, reported in 1781 that, according to the Tamanaco Indians, rock inscriptions there were made by the creator-god Amalivaca.

There was a great deal of exploration in Mexico. In 1763, the capuchin Francisco de Ajofrin, who was collecting alms on behalf of Spain's papal nuncio, wrote about a hill of modest height, two leagues from Mexico City 'and in the rocks of the edge that faces Texcuco there are many ancient characters engraved, and some of them finely worked and beautiful'.

A 1792 compilation commissioned by the Spanish Viceroy of New Spain, Conde Revilla Gigedo, contained a natural history of Baja California attributed tentatively to the Jesuit Juan Bautista Mugazábal who died in 1761. If correct, this would be the oldest known reference to rock art on this peninsula:

> In all of civilized California, from south to north, and particularly in the caves and smooth cliffs, rustic paintings can be seen. Notwithstanding their disproportion and lack of art, there can be easily distinguished the likenesses of men, fish, bows and arrows, and diversely assembled lines in the fashion of written characters.

The colours of these paintings are four: yellow, red, green and black. The majority of the images are painted in very high places, and from this, some infer that there is truth in the constant tradition of giants among the ancient Californians. Be that as it may, at the Mission of Santiago, which is located in the south, there is exposed to view on a very high, smooth cliff a series of stamped red hands. In the tall boulders near the beach, fish of different shapes and sizes, bows and arrows, and some obscure characters can be seen. In other places, there are Indians armed with bows and arrows, and at their feet various species of insects, snakes and mice, with lines and characters of a different form. It has been impossible to ascertain what these figures, lines and characters mean, despite extensive questioning of the California Indians. The only thing which has been determined from what they say, is that they are from their ancestors, and that they have absolutely no knowledge of their significance.

In his *Historia Natural y Crónica de la Antigua California* (1972), the Mexican historian Miguel Leon-Portilla includes an extended reference to the great murals of Baja California, and quotes Joseph Mariano Rothea (a missionary at San Ignacio from 1759 until 1768):

> ... the propositions that probably argue that there were giants in California can be reduced to three. First, the bones that are encountered in various places. Second, the painted caves, and third, the general belief of the elders ... I happened to investigate several painted caves ... one would be (about 9–10 metres/30–35 feet long, and about 5 metres/16 feet wide) ... From top to bottom it was all painted with various figures of men, women, and animals. The men had loose shirts with sleeves; beyond this a greatcoat and breeches but no shoes. They had their hands open and somewhat raised with extended arms. Among the women was one with loose hair arranged on the head and a dress of a native Mexican type called *huipil*. The paintings of the animals represented all those now known in the land, like deer, jack rabbits, etc., and others now unknown like the wolf and pig. The colours were the same that are found in the volcanoes of the Tres Virgenes: green, black, yellow and flesh-coloured.

Leon-Portilla also quotes the missionary Padre Francisco Escalante concerning another cave, over 10 metres (35 feet) long, about 5 metres (16 feet) or more wide and about 5 metres high. According to this account it appears that the Cochimí, the local people, had legends dissociating them and their ancestors from the painters, and that the missionaries thought the paintings impressively old. '(Its) flat ceiling is painted and full of figures now of animals and now of men armed with bows and arrows representing the hunts of the Indians ... he says that it is untutored painting, that it is very far from the niceties of this art. Nevertheless, he gives us to understand that its authors had more application, more talent and more understanding than the (present) natives of that country.'

A few of the huge, splendid rock paintings of animals and humans at Cueva Pintada, Baja California (Mexico). Date unknown. The eighteenth-century missionary Joseph Mariano Rothea described the paintings in this region as follows:

The durability of these colours seemed notable to me; being there on the exposed rock in the inclemencies of sun and water where they are no doubt struck by rain, strong wind or water that filters through these same rocks from the hill above, with all this, after much time, they remain highly visible ... Without scaffolds or other implements suitable for the purpose, only giant men would have been able to paint at so much height.

This and other nearby painted rock shelters were first 'rediscovered' by the wealthy crime writer Erle Stanley Gardner in the early 1960s – he went into the area by helicopter, and later brought in American rock art specialist Clement Meighan to do a proper study.

An eighteenth-century Jesuit missionary, the Spaniard Miguel del Barco, wrote hundreds of pages about California, which were not published until they appeared in Leon-Portilla's book. Commenting on the size of the paintings, del Barco says that:

> ... the people of this land say that the giants were so large that, when they painted the ceiling of a cave, they lay on their backs on the ground and that even thus they were able to paint the highest part. An enormous fable that, for its verification, would necessitate those men to have a height of at least (9 metres/30 feet), unless we imagine extremely long paint brushes in their hands! ... It is simpler to persuade oneself that, for this work, they found and conveyed to the cave, or caves, some wood with which to form a scaffold.

Africa

The eighteenth century also saw the first discoveries of rock art in Africa. The earliest reference is from 1721, when, in a report to the Royal Academy of History in Lisbon, an ecclesiastic in the Portuguese colony of Mozambique mentioned paintings of animals on rocks. In 1752, Domingo van de Walle de Cervellón reported engravings in the cave of Belmaco on Las Palmas (Canary Islands). He considered these meandering motifs as mere 'doodles' produced by 'chance or the imagination

One of the drawings of pictographs (date unknown) made by Colonel Robert Jacob Gordon in South Africa in 1777, now housed in Amsterdam's Rijksmuseum. This one features an elephant, an ostrich and four men with prominent penises; its inscription mentions that these drawings by 'the so-called Chinese Bushmen' were done with coloured clay, ochre and charcoal on the rocks. The Bushman rock paintings left Gordon unimpressed.

of the ancient barbarians'. That same year, explorers led by Ensign August Frederick Beutler, when more than 320 kilometres (200 miles) out from their Cape Town base, noticed rock paintings in the valley of the Great Fish River in the eastern Cape, which they recognized as the work of the 'Little Chinese' (Bushmen/San). The first known copies of rock art in Africa were made in 1777–78 on an expedition to the Sneeuwbergen (Snowy Mountains) of the eastern Cape led by Governor Joachim van Plettenberg. They were made by Colonel Robert Jacob Gordon and his draughtsman servant Johannes Schumacher – the latter had already copied probable petroglyphs or rock paintings (he called them *teekeningen* – drawings) in 1777 on an expedition to the south or west area of the Cape led by the Governor's son, H. Swellenberg. According to Gordon's account:

> Here for the first time I saw their drawings on the rocks. Some of them were fair but as a whole they were poor and exaggerated. They had drawn different animals, mostly in black or red and yellow; some people too. I can easily understand why it is said that they have drawn unknown animals because one had to make many guesses as to what they were. Made a drawing of the best, where the cave lay deep in baboon droppings and left for our wagons.

The earliest mention of a northern Cape rock art site seems to be a hearsay account of a flat rock said to bear 'the spoor of animals', noted by H.J. Wikar, a Swede, as he travelled along the Orange River in 1778; while in 1790–91, on an expedition, Jacob van Reenen noted in his diary that 'on a rocky cliff the Bushmen had made a great many paintings or representations of wildebeeste, very natural, and also of a soldier with a grenadier's cap'.

The French traveller Le Vaillant published a book on South Africa at this time in which he dismissed the Bushman paintings as 'caricatures', and said of pictures in a cave in the eastern Cape: 'The Dutchmen believe them to be a century or two old and allege that the Bushmen worship them, but though it is quite possible, there is no evidence to show it.'

One of the first people who made an attempt to understand the rock art of Southern Africa was Sir John Barrow, secretary to the Governor of Cape Colony. Journeying through the colony and beyond in 1797 and 1798, Barrow was excited to see rock paintings and amazed that they could have been produced by people described by one writer in 1731 as 'Troops of abandon'd Wretches' lacking laws, fixed abodes and religion. Barrow comments:

> In the course of travelling, I had frequently heard the peasantry mention the drawings in the mountains behind the Sneuwberg made by the Boujesmans; but I took it for granted they were caricatures only, similar to those on the doors and walls of uninhabited buildings, the works of idle boys; and it was no disagreeable disappointment to

A book by Sir John Barrow, published in 1801, contained this copy of a pictograph (probably by a Bushman) of an animal head (date unknown). This was the first copy of African rock art to be published, but not a very accurate one – Barrow thought the animal was a unicorn:
We came at length to a very high and concealed kloof, at the head of which was a deep cave covered in front by thick shrubbery. One of the party ... gave us notice that the sides of the cavern were covered with drawings. After clearing away the bushes to let in the light, and examining the numerous drawings, some of which were tolerably well executed, and others caricatures, part of a figure was discovered that was certainly intended as the representation of beast with a single horn projecting from the forehead ... The body and legs had been erased to give place to the figure of an elephant that stood directly before it.

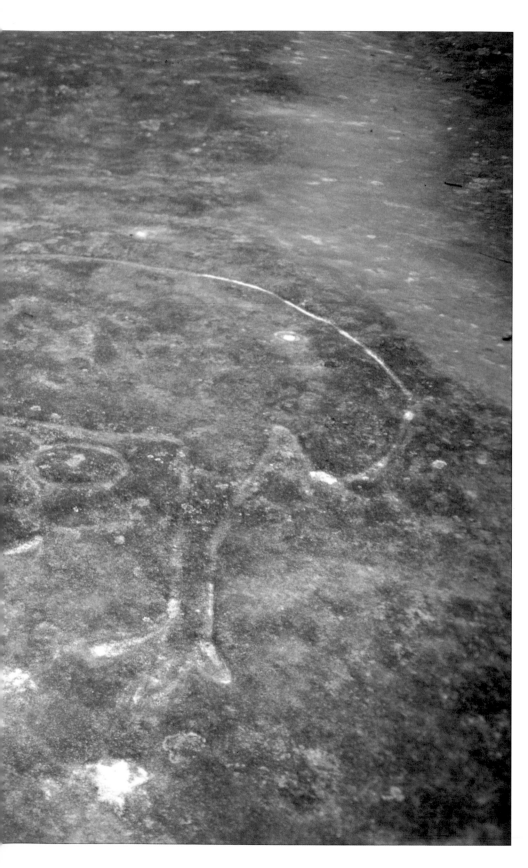

Rock engraving of an emu with eggs at Devil's Rock, Maroota, near Sydney (Australia) – over 2 metres (*c*. 6 feet) from beak to tail. Date unknown. The only known account of a Sydney Aborigine's comments on the region's engravings is by 'Queen Gooseberry', widow of the chief of the tribe in the area settled by the First Fleet. Some time before 1847, she was asked to show and explain local rock engravings to a group of Europeans at some sites on the north head of Sydney Harbour. She said her father told her that 'black fellow made them long ago' and that the tribespeople kept away from the area except for special occasions, in which dances or ceremonies took place, because 'too much debble walk about there'.

find them very much the reverse ... In one place was a very large and curious cavern formed by a waterfall ... a little on one side of the cavern, and under a long projecting ridge, of smooth white sand-stone, were several sketches of animals, and satirical attempts to represent the colonists in ridiculous situations and attitudes, characterizing them by some of their most common and striking habits ... The long-necked cameloparadalis was easily distinguished among the rest; as was also the rhinoceros and the elephant ... Among the several thousand figures of animals that, in the course of the journey, we had met with, none had the appearance of being monstrous, none that could be considered as works of the imagination, 'creatures of the brain'; on the contrary, they were generally as faithful representations of nature as the talents of the artist would allow.

(*An Account of Travels into the Interior of Southern Africa in the Years 1797 and 1798*, Vol. 1)

The beauty of this rock art made Barrow think that the Bushmen had been rendered more 'savage ... by the conduct of the European settlers'. He was especially interested in the aesthetic aspects of the art, which he assumed was indeed 'art' in the European sense. On enquiring about their age, he was told that some paintings were known to be new while others 'had been remembered from the first settlement of this part of the colony':

On the smooth sides of the cavern were drawings of several animals that had been made from time to time by these savages. Many of them were caricatures; but others were too well executed not to arrest attention. The different antelopes that were there delineated had each their character so well discriminated, that the originals, from whence the representations had been taken, could, without any difficulty, be ascertained. Among the numerous animals that were drawn, was the figure of a zebra remarkably well done; all the marks and characters of this animal were accurately represented, and the proportions were seemingly correct. The force and spirit of drawings, given to them by bold touches judiciously applied, and by the effect of light and shadow, could not be expected from savages; but for accuracy of outline and correctness of the different parts, worse drawings than that of the zebra have passed through the engraver's hands. The materials with which they had been executed were ... charcoal, pipe-clay, and the different ochres. The animals represented were zebras, qua-chas, gemsboks, springboks, reeboks, elands, baboons and ostriches ... Several crosses, circles, points, and lines, were placed in a long rank as if intended to express some meaning; but no other attempt appeared at the representation of inanimate objects.

Australia

The other continent whose rock art was 'discovered' in this period was Australia. In fact, there had been a report in 1678 by J. Keyts, a Dutch trader, of rock paintings on a cliff face in Speelmans Bay, western New Guinea (Irian Jaya), but it was ignored at the time. European discoveries in Australia began during the first months of colonization, and continued sporadically over the next century as explorers and pioneers pushed further into the country. But at first, very few rock art sites were discovered or documented, and the colonizers made little effort to enquire about the meaning of motifs and designs. The art was seen as childish attempts by primitive people to produce paintings and as radically inferior to the European art of the period.

The first known European discovery of Australian rock art was made in Bantry Bay, near Sydney, by Governor Arthur Phillip, commander of the First Fleet and of the first settlement at Port Jackson in 1788, when he led short expeditions into the surrounding area. In his journal, John White, surgeon to the First Fleet, describes how, on 16 April 1788, 'We saw ... some proofs of their ingenuity in various figures cut on the smooth surfaces of some large stones. They consisted chiefly of representations of themselves in different attitudes, of their canoes, of several sorts of fish and animals; and considering the rudeness of the instruments with which the figures must have been executed, they seemed to exhibit tolerably strong likenesses.'

In his first despatch of 15 May 1788 to Lord Sydney, Phillip mentions:

In Botany Bay, Port Jackson and Broken Bay we frequently saw the figures of men, shields, and fish roughly cut on the rocks; and on the top of a mountain I saw the figure of a man in the attitude they put themselves in when they are going to dance, which was much better done than I had seen before, and the figure of a large lizard was sufficiently well executed to satisfy every one what animal was meant.

By the end of the eighteenth century, therefore, prehistoric rock art was being noticed and even copied with increasing frequency, though no great accuracy. In the next century a turning point would be reached – not only in numbers of discoveries, but also in the realization that some of the art was of great antiquity.

The Nineteenth and Twentieth Centuries: Prehistoric Art Comes into its Own

Just as archaeology became established by the mid-nineteenth century, when the great antiquity of humankind and the concept of prehistory were accepted, so the study of prehistoric art gradually began to grow more widespread, more systematic and better documented.

THE NINETEENTH CENTURY

Australia and Oceania

In Australia, discoveries multiplied in different areas. It was Matthew Flinders, a British navigator and explorer, who, while exploring and mapping the coastline during the first circumnavigation of the continent, made the first discovery of rock shelters with pictographs (paintings) and stencils – on Chasm Island (Northern Territory) near north-east Arnhem Land, on 14 January 1803. His account describes the location, identifies some images, considers the materials used, and even attempts an ethnographic interpretation:

> In the deep sides of the chasms were deep holes or caverns undermining the cliffs; upon the walls of which I found rude drawings, made with charcoal and something like red paint upon the white ground of the rock. These drawings represented porpoises, turtle, kanguroos [*sic*], and a human hand; and Mr Westall, who went afterwards to see them, found the representation of a kanguroo,

(*Opposite*) There are very few early photographs of people posing next to rock art. This 100-year-old, hand-tinted photograph of apparently non-figurative pictographs was an advertisement for the Murrieta Hot Springs Resort in Riverside County, southern California (United States). Owing to development and flooding, only a trace of this impressive painted boulder now remains above ground level. Date unknown.

Watercolour of a pictograph panel, painted in 1803 by William Westall, the artist on Matthew Flinders's voyage round the coastline of Australia. The image was included in Flinders's published account of 1814 – the first Australian rock art to be reproduced. Westall's painting is quite accurate except that, in reality, there are thirty-four people and they appear to be aboard a high-prowed canoe, with the tall person in the bow, holding a spearthrower in one hand, and, in the other, ten harpoon lines leading towards a dugong. Date unknown.

Lithographs from George Grey's 1841 book, *Journals of Two Expeditions in Northwest and Western Australia*, showing a rock shelter *(opposite)* and its pictographs *(right)*. Grey was a young British army officer when he explored the north-west. It was while he was attempting to get through some broken sandstone ranges of the Glenelg headwaters that he came upon the rock art. 'I was certainly rather surprised at the moment that I first saw this gigantic head and upper part of a body bending over and grimly staring at me ... It would be impossible to convey in words an adequate idea of this uncouth and savage figure ... Its head was encircled by bright red rays.' The rayed-head figure is about 100 x 78 centimetres (*c.* 40 x 30 inches). Date unknown.

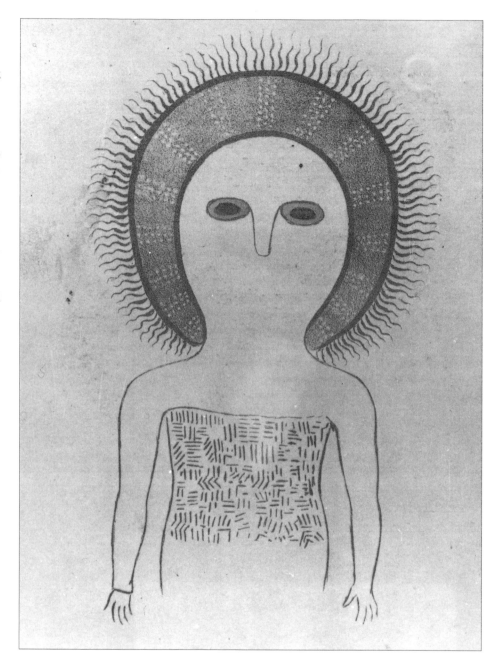

with a file of thirty-two persons following after it. The third person of the band was twice the height of the others, and held in his hand something resembling the whaddie, or wooden sword of the natives of Port Jackson; and was probably intended to represent a chief. They could not, as with us, indicate superiority by clothing or ornament, since they wore none of any kind; and therefore, with the addition of a weapon, similar to the ancients, they seem to have made superiority of person the principal emblem of superior power, of which, indeed, power is usually a consequence in the very early stages of society.

Some eighteen years later, the explorer and botanist Allan Cunningham made further discoveries on Clack Island, off Queensland, which he compared to those of Flinders. On 22 June 1821, he found a major collection of rock paintings, the first in Queensland: the images discovered by Flinders had been produced with a burnt stick 'but this performance, exceeding a hundred and fifty figures ... appears at least to be one step nearer refinement than those simply executed with a piece of charred wood'.

Tasmania was next. On 4 September 1830, George Augustus Robinson, Protector of the Aborigines in Tasmania and Victoria, found an engraved circle surrounded with dots on the island's north-west coast; three years later, in the same region, he 'saw large circles cut on the face of rocks done by natives. Some of them were a foot and eighteen inches in diameter.'

The first galleries of the Kimberley region containing paintings of wandjinas (ancestral spirits) were seen by the British explorer George Grey on 26 March 1838: 'on looking over some bushes, at the sandstone rocks which were above us, I suddenly saw from one of them a most extraordinary large figure peering down upon me. Upon examination this proved to be a drawing at the entrance to a cave, which, on entering, I found to contain besides, many remarkable paintings.'

Although he interpreted the patterns on the figure's 'halo' as an oriental script in his *Journals of Two Expeditions of Discovery in Northwest and Western Australia* (1841), Grey was a true pioneer in that he made a great effort to produce detailed descriptions, measurements and coloured sketches of some panels at the site over the next few days. He later became Sir George, and Governor of Cape Colony

(Following page) Identified by some local Aborigines as Kuion, a bad news messenger, this finely painted round-headed figure belonging to the Tassel Bradshaw Group in Australia's Kimberley is about 79 centimetres (*c.* 31 inches) long. Note the arm raised above the head, with a broad-meshed appendage dangling from the armpit and tassels hanging at its elbow. Date unknown.

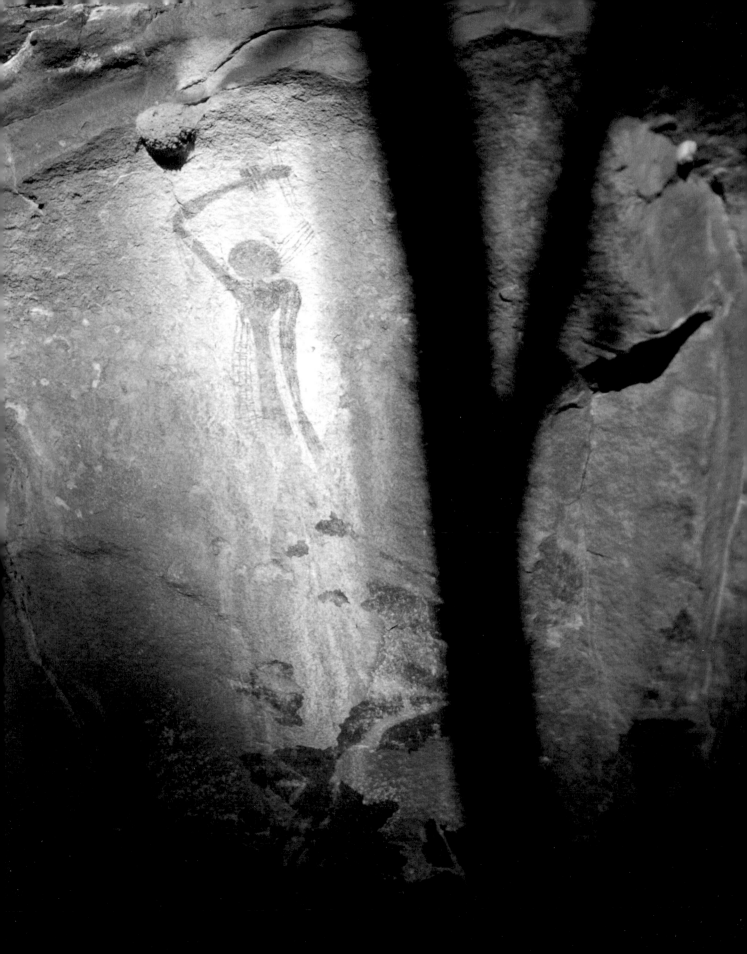

(South Africa), where he was again a pioneer, this time in encouraging the recording of the Bushman (San) language and mythology.

In 1891, the explorer Joseph Bradshaw found an entirely different kind of rock art in the Kimberley – the delicate painted human figures which were to become known as 'Bradshaws'. He published sketches of these, which he described as 'numerous aboriginal paintings which appeared to be of great antiquity, and I do not attribute them to the presentations of the Black race'.

The earliest report of the rock paintings of Arnhem Land was made by the German explorer and geologist Dr Ludwig Leichhardt in 1845: his first discovery was a rock shelter containing an image of a long-necked turtle. However, it was only with the incursion of European buffalo shooters into Kakadu in the early 1880s that its paintings became better known. In the 1870s, on a voyage in the McCluer Gulf (Teluk Berau), a Dutch trader T.B. Leon came across some rock paintings in New Guinea, which he took to be Hindu symbols. Photographs were taken of New Guinea rock art in 1887.

Discoveries soon occurred in Polynesia too. In New Zealand, a surveyor, Walter Mantell, made the first record of rock paintings at the rock shelter of Takiroa (North Otago) in 1852 – elaborate, apparently non-figurative designs in red and black. In Hawaii, William Ellis observed petroglyphs (rock carvings) in 1824. Mantell made a note of the meaning of some motifs – and this is one of the few existing first-hand accounts recorded anywhere in the world during a period when petroglyphs were still being made.

Duché de Vancy, the artist on the French expedition to Easter Island of 1786, produced this drawing which presents the islanders and their statues as somewhat European in appearance. It also depicts the islanders' predilection for, and skill at, stealing any of the visitors' possessions which took their fancy, often using the island women as bait or as distractions. The expedition's leader, the Comte de La Pérouse, is shown measuring a *moai* (giant statue), with its *pukao* (stone head-dress) still in place.

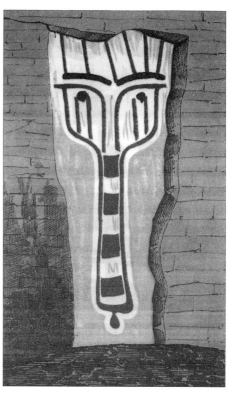

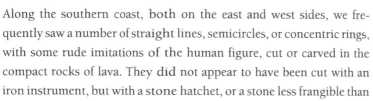

Along the southern coast, both on the east and west sides, we frequently saw a number of straight lines, semicircles, or concentric rings, with some rude imitations of the human figure, cut or carved in the compact rocks of lava. They did not appear to have been cut with an iron instrument, but with a stone hatchet, or a stone less frangible than the rock on which they were portrayed. On inquiry, we found that they had been made by former travellers, from a motive similar to that which induces a person to carve his initials on a stone or tree, or a traveller to record his name in an album, to inform his successors that he had been there.

As for Easter Island, its hundreds of giant *moai* (statues) were obviously seen and mentioned by the first known European discoverers – the Dutch in 1722 – and by all subsequent visitors. However, its rock engravings and paintings were not noticed, or at least mentioned, until the four-day visit by a German vessel under the command of Lieutenant-Captain Wilhelm Geiseler in 1882: Geiseler's report of this visit included a study of the painted slabs inside some houses, and the bas-relief petroglyphs of 'the god of the seabird eggs' and carvings of 'the feminine sex' which festoon the rocks around the ceremonial clifftop village of Orongo.

Africa and the Near East

In various parts of Africa, rock art was, understandably enough, the first evidence of the past to attract the attention of explorers: for example, in 1816, at the mouth of the River Congo (Zaïre), J. Tuckey, a British captain, observed a rock with engravings in what is now Angola; he named it Pedra do Feitiço (Fetish Rock) and published a detailed description of its human figures and animals, as well as various objects such as boats, rifles and palanquins.

Lithographs produced by the German expedition to Easter Island in 1882, commanded by Captain Geiseler, and printed in its report *Die Osterinsel, eine Stätte prähistorischer Kultur in der Südsee*. These are the first known reproductions of the island's petroglyphs and pictographs. Date unknown. *(Top left)* Painting of two birdmen on a slab, 0.95 metres (3 feet) high, inside a house at Orongo. *(Top right)* A painting of a god (?) on a slab, 0.94 metres (3 feet) high, inside a house at Orongo.

South African pictographs, probably by Bushmen (date unknown), drawn by Major C.C. Mitchell and reproduced in Sir James Alexander's *A Narrative of a Voyage of Observation Among the Colonies of Western Africa*, 1837.

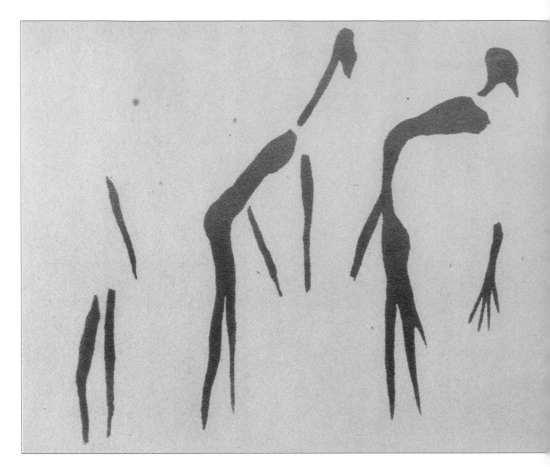

(Right) Alexander described this as follows:

The group ..., appears on the face of a rock near the waterfall on the northern extremity of the estate of Misgund, in the Lang Kloof ... It seems to represent an embassy of females suing for peace; or what my also be a dance of females, for it is thus that they range themselves in either case. No one can deny that their reception is a gracious one, to judge by the polite attitudes of the male figures, perhaps chiefs.

(*Bottom*) **Alexander wrote:**

The subjects ... are found in a ravine on the mountain side to the northward of the Cromme River ... The use of the bow, as here shown, may afford speculation to South African antiquaries: as Kaffirs are never known to employ that arm.

(*Opposite bottom*) **The subject ... was found in the defile through which the Braek River runs from the Lang Kloof into the Kamnassie country ... We are unable to assist the reader, even by a conjecture, in elucidating the meaning of that which he here sees represented: but it may, perhaps, have allusion to the amphibious nature attributed to the whites by some natives in the olden day.**

This image from the Langkloof near modern Oudtshoorn is now known as the Ezeljagdspoort rock painting. Descendants of the southern Bushmen, who still go to rock shelters for rituals and festivities, have a belief system containing extensive reference to 'watermeide' (water maidens), with accounts identical to a legend recorded in 1875 from an old Bushman. These beings are linked to puberty ceremonies, and diviners still make offerings to water ancestors.

Plate 1.

Drawings of the Aborigines of Southern Africa

Sir James Alexander, another Briton, travelling in 1835 near modern Oudtshoorn in South Africa, was taken to overhanging rocks with paintings. In his 1837 book, *A Narrative of a Voyage of Observation Among the Colonies of Western Africa*, he included three copies of these paintings, which had been made by his guide, Major C.C. Mitchell, a civil engineer and Surveyor General of Cape Colony. Like Barrow (see Chapter 1), Alexander was surprised to find

> ... that these rude attempts of uncivilized artists are not utterly devoid of merit; and that although defective in proportions, there is more resemblance in them to the human figure than is ever seen imparted by persons, however educated, who have a total negation of graphic talent. This, indeed, is rendered most evident on the spot, by sundry miserable attempts at figures, made beside them by some civilized bungler.

Alexander realized that some of the art must be ancient, stating that Mitchell 'made faithful copies of all of these drawings such as still remain uninjured by time and the weather, by which great numbers have been almost entirely effaced'. He also noted that the colour of the paintings 'seems to have been produced by a preparation in which the rust of iron forms a principal ingredient'. He saw the images as narratives and tried to 'read' them (see Chapter 7).

In 1857, David Livingstone, the famous missionary-explorer, mentioned the existence of engraved footprints on rocks at Pungo A Ndongo, Angola, which, according to local oral tradition, were those of Queen Ginga.

A geologist, George Stow, made copies of rock art in the Orange Free State and eastern Cape (South Africa) from 1867, and in 1870 he said in a letter:

> I have been making pilgrimages to the various old Bushman caves among the mountains in this part of the Colony and Kaffraria; and as their paintings are becoming obliterated very fast, it struck me that it would be as well to make copies of them before these interesting relics of an almost extinct race are entirely destroyed ... I have fortunately been able to procure many facsimile copies of hunting scenes, dances, fightings, etc, showing the modes of warfare, the chase, weapons, disguises, etc.

However, most of Stow's copies, including watercolours and pencil tracings, were not published until 1930. He was very selective, often ignoring hundreds of figures of animals and humans doing ordinary things, and only copying some small part which he imagined to represent a ceremony. He also displayed typical Victorian prudishness, omitting apparent ejaculations or infibulations, presumably because they were unsuitable for publication. His method was to make a preliminary copy on rough paper, then trace this onto art paper. (Sometimes lack of paper seems to have led him to group together images from different parts of a site or even from different shelters.) He then coloured the tracings, using the original Bushman pigments which he picked up from the shelter floors. By the end of his life he had made

(Opposite) Drawings of rock engravings in Algeria -'a family out hunting' *(bottom)* and 'a warrior's lesson to his son' *(top)* by François Félix Jacquot. These were the only two of Jacquot's drawings to appear in his book of 1847: others, he said, were so indecent that they should never emerge from his files. 'One can see, in full view and with no secrecy, the unnatural intercourse that brought the storm of fire down on the cities whose names you know well; a hideous coupling ... the strange perversion of desire which, according to Theocritus, brought together the shepherds of Sicily and their goats, also has its analogues at Thyout, only here that peaceful animal is replaced by the lion.'

seventy-four illustrations. He tried to interpret them by asking Bushman acquaintances what they meant.

   Another pioneer copier was Joseph Orpen, a magistrate in the Cape in the 1870s, who published a book including some of his drawings in colour and who listened to Bushmen talking about the art – notably a San called Qing. Orpen's work, in turn, acted as a great stimulus to Wilhelm Bleek, the German philologist who, in the 1870s, together with his sister-in-law Lucy Lloyd, spent years investigating the

languages and culture of the South African Bushmen, recording verbatim 12,000 pages of testimony about Bushman life, rituals and beliefs. Bleek also appealed for faithful copies of rock art to be made, backed up by photography, so that the art could be understood in terms of their folklore. Unlike earlier writers who had adopted a somewhat patronizing or simplistic view of African rock art, Bleek urged that the paintings should be considered 'not as the mere daubing of figures for idle pastime, but as an attempt, however imperfect, at a truly artistic conception of the ideas which most deeply moved the Bushman mind, and filled it with religious feelings'. Copies of paintings were made by enthusiasts in the Cape and shown to Bushmen for explanation and comment. It was also Lucy Lloyd who bought Stow's drawings after his death, later willing them to Bleek's daughter Dorothea who finally managed to get them published in 1930, almost fifty years after Stow's death.

Rock images were also observed by Europeans in North Africa, the Sahara and the Nile Valley by the mid-nineteenth century. Their weathered appearance, alien style and exotic subjects suggested that they must be of some antiquity and had possible associations with vanished peoples. The first discoveries of rock art in these regions were made in 1847 by two soldiers (Dr François Félix Jacquot and Captain Kook of the Foreign Legion), part of General Cavaignac's expedition against the Ksour tribes. They reported large engravings of animals (elephants, lions, antelopes, ostriches, gazelles) and of humans with bows at Thyout and Moghar-et-Tathani in the Ksour Mountains (southern Oran, Algeria). On the evidence of the costumes and scenes depicted, they believed that these were ancient works, dating from an era before the Arab invasion but after the time of Carthage (in 1847 the concept of prehistory had not yet become established). They thought that the artists were Tuareg and assumed that they were idolaters, believing in fetishes, who had been brought to the oases of southern Oran in caravan expeditions from the south of Africa.

In 1848, in his *Voyage et Recherches en Egypte et en Nubie*, the French scholar and traveller Jean-Jacques Ampère mentioned engravings of Nubia on the banks of the Nile, as did the 1842–45 expedition of the German Egyptologist Karl Lepsius. Ampère focused on the engraved rocks on the west bank near Philae: 'These signs are not hieroglyphs and bear no resemblance to the letters of any known alphabet.' Among the figures he noticed the 'symbol of life' and various animals 'grotesquely drawn' – lions, giraffes, elephants and ostriches. He also mentioned some not very artistic depictions of humans, often indecent.

In 1849, the German explorer Heinrich Barth set out from Tripoli for a four-year trip during which he discovered a large number of rock engravings, including the now-famous site of Wadi Telisaghé (Telizzharen) and the first engravings in Fezzan, Libya. He included some reproductions in a series of five volumes published in Gotha in 1857 and 1858 (*Reisen und Entdeckungen in Nord und Central Afrika in den Jahren 1849 bis 1855*), commenting that some parts of the pictures seemed unfinished, especially the lower extremities of animals' limbs. He interpreted some scenes as allegories and noted differences in quality and technique between engravings, which he saw as representing different periods. The animals represented in the engravings, especially the herds of cattle, led him to the conclusion that the climate of these desert regions had once been very different.

Scarcely had we pitched our tents, when we became aware that the (Wadi Telísaghé) valley contained some remarkable sculptures deserving our particular attention ... the sandstone blocks which studded it were covered with drawings

Sketch by the German explorer Heinrich Barth, reproduced in his book of 1857–58, showing a rock art panel of engravings and petroglyphs in its landscape at the Wadi Telisaghé, Libya. Date unknown.

representing various subjects, more or less in a state of preservation. With no pretensions to be regarded as finished sculptures, they are made with a firm and steady hand, well accustomed to such work, and, being cut to a great depth, bore a totally different character from what is generally met with in these tracts. The most interesting sculpture ... represents a group of three individuals ... To the left is seen a tall human figure, with the head of a peculiar kind of bull, with long horns turned forward and broken at the point; instead of the right arm he has a peculiar organ terminating like an oar, while in the left hand he carries and arrow and a bow – at least such is the appearance, though it might be mistaken for a

(Right) Engravings at Wadi Télisaghé described by Barth as two half-human figures and a bullock.

(Below) 'On the cliff itself there is another sculpture on a large block which, now that the western end is broken off, is about (3.5 metres/12 feet long and 1.5 metres/5 feet high) ... It represents a dense group of oxen in a great variety of positions, but all moving towards the right ... Some of these bulls are admirably executed, and with a fidelity which can scarcely be accounted for, unless we suppose that the artist had before his eyes the animals which he chiselled ... The only defect ... is in the feet, which ... have been negligently treated.'

shield: between his legs a long tail is seen hanging down from his slender body. The posture of this figure is bent forward, and all its movements are well represented. Opposite to this curious individual is another one of not less remarkable character, but of smaller proportions, entirely human as far up as the shoulders, while the head is that of an animal which reminds us of the Egyptian ibis, without being identical with it. The small pointed head is furnished with three ears, or with a pair of ears and some other excrescence, and beyond with a sort of hood ... This figure likewise has a bow in its right hand, but, as it would seem, no arrow, while the left hand is turned away from the body. Between these two half-human figures, which are in a hostile attitude, is a bullock, small in proportion to the adjacent lineaments of the human figure, but chiselled with the same care and the same skilful hand, with the only exception that the feet are omitted, the legs terminating in points ... There is another peculiarity about this figure, the upper part of the bull, by some accident, having been hollowed out, while in general all the inner part between the deeply-chiselled outlines of these sculptures is left in high relief. The animal is turned with its back towards the figure on the right (*sic*), whose bow it seems about to break. The block on which it was sculptured was about four feet in breadth and three in height. It was lying loose on the top of the cliff. No barbarian could have graven the lines with such astonishing firmness, and given to all the figures the light, natural shape which they exhibit ... the sculptures have nothing in them of a Roman character, Some few particulars call to mind the Egyptian sculptures. But on the whole it seems to be a representation of a subject taken from the native mythology ... two divinities disputing over a sacrifice.

A Frenchman, Henri Duveyrier, set out in 1859 on a journey which took him to western Tripolitania and the eastern Algerian Sahara; in 1865, he reproduced copies of rock engravings in Tassili in his *Les Touaregs du Nord*, and concurred with Barth about allegorical interpretations and about the existence in earlier times of abundant pastures and water resources. Farther east, in 1869, among the Tuareg of Tibesti (in modern Chad), the German military doctor G. Nachtigal noted the presence of rock engravings of cattle, camels and humans (described in his *Sahara und Sudan*, 1879). To the west, in Algeria, Captain Charles de Vigneral included a drawing of an engraved rock in his *Ruines Romaines de l'Algérie* of 1867. His somewhat incorrect drawing included humans, cattle, dogs and an ostrich.

On a journey of exploration in south-west Morocco in 1875, Rabbi Mardokhai-Abi-Sourour discovered numerous rocks bearing animal figures and inscriptions. He was the first explorer, in this part of the world at least, to make a stamped copy by pressing a thin layer of clay, contained between two sheets of paper, onto the reliefs and depressions of the rock surface (by coincidence, in 1874–78 the famous Finnish linguist and ethnographer Matias-Alexander Castren was working in the Yenisei Valley, Siberia, and likewise developed a mechanical stamping method for

copying petroglyphs and inscriptions). Some sixty-eight stamps, including forty-six of engravings, were sent by the Rabbi to the Société de Géographie de Paris, where they were studied by Duveyrier. The stamps featured elephants and rhinoceroses, as well as horses, giraffes, foxes, birds, etc, and also objects such as harnesses and shields. Duveyrier noted a difference between lines drawn deeply and clearly, made with a metal point, and lines that were broad and blurred, made by percussion or rubbing with a hard stone. However, he attributed everything to a single period – inevitably, working from a uniform stamped impression, he could not see differences in patinas and weathering. Rejecting an attribution to modern people, Portuguese merchants, Romans and Phoenicians, he eventually ascribed the pictures to an indigenous black race, the 'Ethiopians-Daratites' mentioned by the Romans. It was not until 1882 that Dr V. Reboud suggested that the North African engravings might be prehistoric.

In 1889 Dr Bonnet of the Paris Natural History Museum, on a botanical expedition in Algeria, was the first to note the presence of worked flint tools by some of the rock art sites. He also produced some exceptionally accurate copies of the engravings of Moghar-et-Tathani, and was less shocked than Jacquot by what he saw: 'it is true that a few hunters brazenly display monstrous phalluses, but in most cases it is easy to recognize, from the form and colour of the line, that these organs are later additions to the rest of the figure'. Bonnet is especially important for his archaeological observations: he noticed prehistoric weapons and tools on the ground around the engraved rocks – worked flints, arrowheads, knives, scrapers, etc. – and came to the conclusion that it was probably with a fragment of worked flint that 'the primitive artists engraved this gigantic page of their history'. He was thus able to concur with Reboud that the images were prehistoric, particularly those depicting pachyderms or ruminants which had already left this region for Central Africa by Roman times.

During this century, the deserts of the Near East were being thoroughly explored by archaeologists, theologians and historians, looking for holy sites relating to the origins of Judaism and Christianity. Some of them noticed rock art: for example, a French theologian, Caignart de Saulcy, in his book *Voyage autour de la Mer Morte* (1856), described what he thought were 'astrological signs' engraved on rocks in the desert of Judea (these are now known to be territorial markers or tribal emblems in pasture areas). In 1871, an English explorer E.H. Palmer discovered rock engravings in a cave at Wadi Muwilikh, in northern Sinai. In fact, inscriptions (sometimes mingled with figures of humans and animals) carved into the rocks had been noticed long before and many had been reproduced in books of the seventeenth and eighteenth centuries – for example, *Voyages* by Balt. de Monconys (1665), *Description de l'Orient et de Quelques Autres Contrées* by Richard Pococke (1743–45), *Voyage en Arabie et d'Autres Pays Circumvoisins* by the famous Carsten Niebuhr (1776) and books by many other subsequent travellers.

India

It was in the second half of the nineteenth century that India was placed on the rock art map, in particular by one astonishing and farsighted pioneer, Archibald Carlyle (or Carlleyle), first assistant to the Archaeological Survey of India. In the 1860s, Carlyle discovered rock paintings in shelters at Morhana Pahar, above the Ganga Valley – for example, in 1867–68 at Sohagighat in the Mirzapur district (south of Benares) of Uttar Pradesh. He wrote in his notebooks:

> Lying along with the small implements in the undisturbed soil of the cave floors, pieces of a heavy red mineral colouring matter called *geru* were frequently found, rubbed down on one or more facets, as if for making paint – this *geru* being evidently a partially decomposed haematite ... On the uneven sides or walls and roofs of many of the caves or rock shelters there were rock paintings apparently of various ages, though all evidently of great age, done in the red colour called *geru*. Some of these rude paintings appeared to illustrate in a very stiff and archaic manner scenes in the life of the ancient stone chippers; others represent animals or hunts of animals by men with bows and arrows, spears and hatchets ... With regard to the probable age of these stone implements I may mention that I never found even a single ground or polished implement, not a single ground ring-stone or hammer-stone in the soil of the floors of any of the many caves or rock shelters I examined.

Since Carlyle only found stone tools and bits of pottery in the vicinity, he attributed the paintings to various periods, including that of the makers of thousands of microliths. His recognition that some of the paintings must be prehistoric had no precedent in Europe and was probably the first in the world. But alas he published nothing on them; he merely placed some notes with a friend and these were published in 1883 by A. Smith. It is known from the index-books of his microlith collections that he prepared copies and tracings of rock pictures, but unfortunately these have never been found.

The first scientific article on Indian rock art – *A Short Account of the Petrographs (drawings) in the Caves and Rock-shelters of the Kaimur Range in the Mirzapur District* – was published in 1883 by John Cockburn, a government 'opium agent'. Cockburn had found paintings of rhinoceroses and boars. The 'exceedingly numerous' rock shelters contained drawings in red pigment of 'men, women and animals, weapons, utensils, symbols of religion, etc'. In the Sorhow ghat cave he found pieces of haematite and a pointed pencil of chalk: on grinding these up with oil – in what may be the first piece of experimental archaeology related to rock art – Cockburn was able to produce colours exactly like those used in the cave paintings. He did not consider them to be more than six or seven centuries old. In 1899 he published an account of all his finds and compared the paintings with those found in Australia, South Africa, and North and South America. He made tracings of several pictures, using paper made transparent by petroleum.

Panel of small red pictographs of cattle and other animals, an archer and a rider, in a rock shelter at Bhimbetka, northern India. Date unknown.

(*Opposite bottom*) Some of the elaborate, apparently non-figurative Chumash paintings on the ceiling of the rock shelter of San Emigdiano (Pleito Creek) in southern California, United States. Date unknown.

The New World

In Central and South America, there were comparatively few discoveries during the nineteenth century. In Mexico, for example, nobody during this century seems to have taken much notice of the great murals of Baja California until 1882. Shortly afterwards, in 1888–90, the German explorer Teobert Maler visited the cave of Loltun, in Yucatán, and made drawings and photographs of its rock engravings and paintings.

Down in South America, the French naturalist Alcide d'Orbigny published detailed descriptions and plans of a number of Bolivian rock art sites, such as Samaipata in the department of Santa Cruz (*Voyage dans l'Amérique Méridionale*, 1826–33, Paris). In Guyana in the 1830s and 1840s, petroglyphs were seen by travellers, some of whom later published sketches of them. Other observations were made in Brazil in the early part of the century, while Argentina was added to the rock art map in the 1870s when Francisco P. Moreno found the first rock paintings on the shores of Lake Argentino in Patagonia in 1877. In 1854, the explorer Sir Robert Schomburgk published an account of the Borbon or del Pommier Caves in the Dominican Republic, where he had discovered rock paintings five years earlier.

In North America, however, there were major developments in prehistoric art – as the West was won and frontiers pushed back. As early as 1804, in west Virginia, Bishop James Madison published an account of a rock near Burning Springs, which bore images of humans and animals. He made some interesting observations on the technique used:

> We see the outlines of several figures, cut without relief ... and somewhat larger than the life. The depth of the outline may be half an inch; its width three-quarters, nearly, in some places ... The labour and the perseverance requisite to cut those rude figures in a rock so hard that steel appeared to make but little impression upon it, must have been great.

Historic accounts from 1816 describe 'human footprints' found in limestone at the edge of the Mississippi at St Louis. Three years later these were removed to Indiana by the Rappites, a German religious group. In an intriguing echo of the early missionaries' interpretation of such prints, they were associated with the Angel Gabriel. Some early visitors, including Henry Rowe Schoolcraft, the famous American explorer and ethnologist, discussed whether these were actual footprints in solidified mud or petroglyphs, but a geologist eventually proved that they were definitely the work of human hands.

A military expedition into New Mexico in 1846 led to a government report, by Lieutenant W.H. Emory, which included copies of petroglyphs along the Gila River.

(Above) These illustrations by Edward Thompson, the American consul in Yucatán (Mexico), of two Loltun paintings in 1897, as well as of some rock carvings, were included in what was the first published account of Maya cave painting. However, Thompson accorded them scant importance, merely observing:

Upon the walls of a tunnel-like passage with a general trend toward the northwest, we found curious symbols outlined in black pigment, showing remarkably clear and distinct against the yellow-white surface of the stone wall. One distant chamber ... had death's heads carved upon the wall surface and the many projecting knobs of stone were so carved that grinning skulls confronted one at every turn ... In another chamber the projections were fashioned in the shape of tigers' heads instead of death's heads.

Date unknown.

Petroglyphs in the distinctive style of America's north-west coast are still being discovered, masked by moss or vegetation. For example, in recent years, a number have been found on Gabriola Island, near Vancouver (Canada), including these 'seawolves', mythical beings which are part killer whale, part wolf. Date unknown.

In California, strange abstract designs cut into basalt rock were copied into J. Goldsborough Bruff's diary in 1850. The first written record of rock art in Utah dates from 1852, in Lieutenant J.W. Gunnison's *Mormons or Latter-Day Saints*: he had been sent to survey the region, and included sketches of a rock art panel near Manti. In 1853, Schoolcraft published a drawing of pictures from two rock art sites, one on the south shore and the other on the north shore (which he called Inscription Rock): the drawing had been given to him by Chingwauk, his informant in the Agawa Bay area (Lake Superior), whom he had hired in 1822 to teach him the meaning of pictures on birch-bark scrolls and stone; Chingwauk had supplied a reading of the images and this was included with the drawing.

The earliest investigator of the paintings of the Chumash Indians in California was the Reverend Stephen Bowers, who sketched two sites near the San Marcos Pass in 1877. Further north up the coast, petroglyph carving continued on the British Columbia coast until the nineteenth century – Newcombe learned this from Indian informants near Beecher Bay in the 1860s and 1870s, while the anthropologist Franz Boas (1895) recorded an historical account of a petroglyph-carving ceremony by the Kwakiutl at Fort Rupert before 1882.

The major American pioneer of this period was Lieutenant-Colonel Garrick Mallery, a US army colonel in command of Fort Rice on the Upper Missouri, who retired in 1879 and collected and interpreted a vast amount of material. His first account, *Pictographs of the North American Indians* (1886), contained only twenty-one pages on rock art, but he followed this with his definitive work *Picture-Writing of the American Indians* (1893), containing no less than 150 pages on the subject. In it he noted that 'one of the curious facts in connection with petroglyphs is the meager notice taken of them by explorers and even by residents other than the Indians, who are generally reticent concerning them'.

Eurasia
It was in Europe that the most momentous developments in the study of prehistoric art were to occur during this century, when the existence of Palaeolithic (Ice Age) portable and cave art was discovered, authenticated and eventually accepted.

This type of petroglyph, found at Monte Bego in the Alps, is thought to represent a pair of oxen (schematized as 'corniforms') yoked to a plough. In the petroglyphs of the neighbouring region of Fontanalba (but, curiously, never in Monte Bego), the plough is sometimes guided by a human figure. Date unknown.

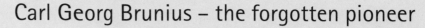

Carl Georg Brunius – the forgotten pioneer

Brunius (1792–1869) was one of the greatest pioneers of rock art recording, though his name remains largely unknown outside Scandinavia. Born in the parsonage of Tanum, west Sweden, to a clergyman father with an interest in antiquities, he was surrounded throughout his childhood by the wealth of ancient monuments and rock art in this region. From an early age, Brunius showed talent as a draughtsman. Later he became Professor of Greek at the University of Lund, a stimulating institution for the budding field of archaeology. Lectures on prehistoric monuments and objects were given there, mainly by natural scientists, and the university had its own archaeological museum from 1806, with the finest prehistoric collections in Sweden.

Brunius was inspired to undertake some field work, which he carried out in Bohuslän in the three summers from 1815 to 1817, and which led him to write a book, *Hällristningslära* (A Doctrine of Rock Art) in 1818. This was translated into French (*Rapport Succinct sur les Hiéroglyphes Trouvés sur les Rochers de la Province de Bohus*), but for financial reasons it was never printed – the many illustrations made it far too expensive. Nonetheless, it comprised the first professional record of sixty-five rock art sites in this part of the world.

Eventually, various publications appeared, written by other people, some of whom had been Brunius' pupils or, like Holmberg, had been influenced by him. But it was not until fifty years later, in the year before he died, that Brunius himself produced his only publication on rock art, *Försök till Förklaringar över Hällristningar* (Attempts at Explanations of Rock Carvings), which examined what others had written during the previous half century and included lithographs of a few of his drawings. His original drawings are preserved in Stockholm's Topographical Archives.

Brunius saw petroglyphs as hieroglyphics, a remnant of a writing method based on images, although he could perceive no connection with runes. He referred to runes and to the Lapp magic drums as evidence that symbols could have been created in the Nordic countries as in the great civilizations. He could see that the petroglyphs were older than the alphabet, and so assumed them to be older than runes – especially as they are not mentioned in the Icelandic sagas. Although they were located far from the present Scandinavian coast, he thought they might be several thousand years old and have originally been cut next to the shore: presumably the dominance of ship motifs suggested this, as well as his observation of several ancient beaches and inland shell-middens. Brunius argued like a natural scientist and even used weathering processes as indicators of antiquity. However, he had no comparable studies from which to work: for his somewhat simple narrative interpretations (seeing the images as memorials, a kind of picture writing, depicting fighting, embarkation, etc.) he used classical sources such as Tacitus and Pytheas, as well as the emerging ethnography of the Eskimo – for example, by drawing on knowledge of Greenland canoes and some Siberian carvings on rocks published earlier by von Strahlenberg (see Chapter 1).

Brunius left a detailed account of his working methods which reveal what a true pioneer he was. He maintained that careful and true observations create the best conditions for interpretation:

> The earth on the carvings was taken away, the mosses were scratched off by an iron scraper, the water was led another way and the bedrock was cleaned and washed somewhere. If the figures were small and unclear, I had to – in order to be sure – visit the place at that hour of the day when the sun was shining so that a separation of the figures was possible by light and shadow. It is possible to have the same effect after the sun set by the help of a lantern. If the observation was difficult I had to revisit the place. On these occasions chalk was brought to make contours. It was also rewarding to use the finger tips to know if a line was natural or artificial.

To produce his drawings, Brunius laid a grid system over the rock surface, and copied the images onto a corresponding grid paper, all within a controlled scale. Images that were hard to identify were visited several times in different conditions – in oblique sunlight, by night lantern, or after rainfall. The images were marked on the rock with chalk and then drawn onto paper with pencil in such a way that a darker line denoted a deeper carving.

He also made notes about the location and possible age and significance of the images, noted differences in their condition (from intact to almost totally disappeared), and looked at the sites' environs, their setting in the landscape, and the presence of monuments nearby. Since Brunius was such a pioneer, he had very little comparative material to help him with interpretation. He also had a moral problem in his

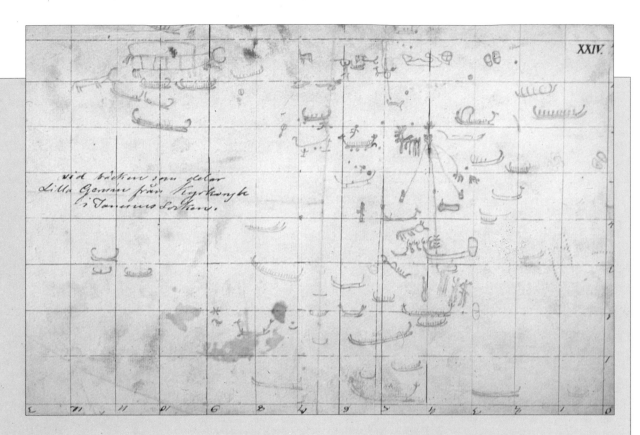

documentation – should the impressive sexual organs of the male figures be depicted or not? He consulted his colleagues, but some were for and some against. Brunius therefore referred to other tribes such as the Lapps or Huns as the creators of the rude customs shown on the rocks, but claimed the original Nordic people were above this cultural level.

(Above and below) **Drawings of petroglyphs by Brunius.**

In parallel with those events, however, more recent rock art continued to be found or studied. For example, in 1821 the French doctor François-Emmanuel Fodéré mentioned the petroglyphs of the Vallée des Merveilles (Monte Bego) in the Alps, when referring to Hannibal's passing through the region – he saw them as blocks prepared for the construction of a monument which the makers never had the time to erect. There were several studies of these petroglyphs in the 1860s and 1870s, before two major figures entered the scene: the French prehistorian Emile Rivière, in 1877, was the first to recognize that they were prehistoric, and the English amateur botanist Clarence Bicknell carried out the first systematic studies of Monte Bego from 1881 onwards.

In Spain, schematic paintings, erroneously described as engravings, were reported in a rock shelter called Portell de Les Lletres at Rojals, Catalonia, by Félix Torres Amat in 1830, in a memoir to the Real Academia de la Historia. (The site was then forgotten until 1893 when a copy of the rock art was published.) The first references to Andalucian schematic art, well illustrated and approximately dated, appeared in 1868 in a book by Manuel de Góngora y Martínez, *Antigüedades Prehistóricas de Andalucia*. The first description of decoration in a stone monument in Spain was that of Santa Cruz, Cangas de Onis, in 1871. Other descriptions followed in the 1870s. The earliest mention of Spain's famous Levantine rock paintings came in 1892, in a book called *Los Toros de la Losilla* by J.E. Marconell: the author described the white rock paintings of the Sierra de Albarracín, although he did not realize they were prehistoric.

In Brittany, the earliest known drawings of decorated stones (Les Pierres Plates and La Table des Marchands) were done in 1814 by Maudet de Penhoët. Many such sites were reported in Ireland in the nineteenth century, including Loughcrew in the 1860s.

In Britain, the decorated sandstone blocks known as the Calderstones, from a chambered tomb in Liverpool, were noted in 1825. They were in fact already well known and had been referred to in a boundary dispute as early as 1568, although there is no indication that the spirals, cup marks and feet pecked into the slabs were above ground at that time. The decorated stones of Orkney were discovered by

This drawing of the Chaffaud reindeer bone, with its engraving of two hinds, is the first known reproduction of Ice Age art. The drawing was made by the writer Prosper Mérimée, France's Inspector General of Historical Monuments and sent with a letter in April 1853 to the eminent Danish archaeologist Jens Worsaae. The bone (total length 13.5 centimetres/ 5½ inches, height 3.7 centimetres/1½ inches) was discovered in Vienne (France) in 1852 and was donated to the Musée de Cluny, Paris, where it was mistakenly catalogued as part of a series of Celtic objects.

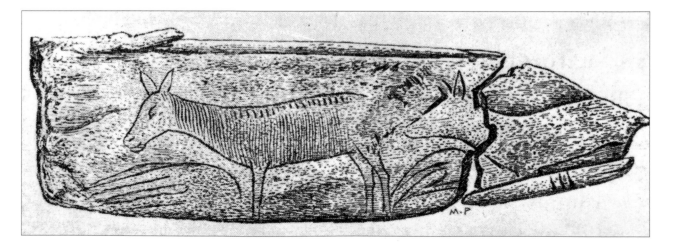

excavation in the nineteenth century. The first person to describe English rock art was George Tate in 1864 – he mentioned fifty-five sites, including Roughting Linn. Sir James Simpson, Queen Victoria's physician in Scotland and the discoverer of chloroform as an anaesthetic, wrote a book called *Archaic Sculpturings* in 1867, about some Scottish cup and ring marks.

The Lake Onega engravings in Russia were discovered in 1848, and fanciful copies of them were published by P. Schwed in 1850. Other discoveries were made in the Urals and Siberia in the nineteenth century.

In Scandinavia, some copies of rock carvings were made by Carl Georg Brunius in the early nineteenth century, though it was only after the clergyman Axel Emanuel Holmberg began his work in 1843 that really useful catalogues of the art were put together. Holmberg's *Skandinaviens Hällristningar* (Rock Carvings of Scandinavia), 1848, was illustrated with 165 drawings, only a small part of his collection. The most remarkable work is considered to be that of a Danish art teacher Lauritz Baltzer who, in the period 1881–1908, published an outstanding volume of prints, *Hällristningar fran Bohuslän I 1881–1890 och II 1891–1908*, containing 248 drawings and descriptions, all of great accuracy. Plaster casts of rock engravings were made as early as the mid-nineteenth century by the great Danish prehistorian Jens Worsaae.

Art of the Ice Age

Until the mid-nineteenth century, there was no real conception of prehistory or of how old prehistoric art might be – in Europe, for example, it was simply 'pre-Roman'. The bombshell of Palaeolithic (Ice Age) art came after decades of sporadic and misunderstood finds. The first pieces of the Palaeolithic portable art known to have been discovered were found in about 1833 in the cave of Veyrier (Haute Savoie), near France's border with Switzerland – an engraved antler pseudo-harpoon and a perforated antler baton decorated with an engraving. A horse head, engraved on a reindeer antler, was found in 1842 at Neschers (Puy-de-Dôme), and a reindeer foot-bone, bearing a fine engraving of two hinds, was discovered in the French cave of Chaffaud (Vienne) in 1852. The latter piece was believed to be Celtic in date, since there was as yet no concept of an Old Stone Age, and was only properly identified some years later through comparison with examples excavated from Palaeolithic occupation layers.

It was not until the 1860s that the existence of Palaeolithic art was first established and accepted through the discovery of engraved and carved bones and stones in a number of caves and rock shelters in south-west France, particularly by the French palaeontologist Edouard Lartet and his English associate, the businessman and ethnologist Henry Christy. These objects were found with Palaeolithic stone and bone tools and the bones of Ice Age animals, which proved their great age – for example, the famous engraving from La Madeleine depicts a mammoth engraved on a piece of mammoth tusk. There followed a kind of 'gold rush', with people plundering likely sites for ancient art treasures.

According to the French palaeontologist Edouard Lartet, a piece of antler with chevrons engraved on it was found in 1827–8 by Paul Tournal in the Grande Grotte de Bize (Aude, France) but it was never published and is now lost. The first definite finds of decorated objects from the Ice Age were made in Veyrier by Dr François Mayor of Geneva in about 1833. The antler harpoon, about 11 centimetres (*c.* 4 inches) long, is engraved so as to resemble a budding plant. The perforated antler baton bears a simple engraving which may perhaps be a bird. (Drawings after Pittard.)

Don Marcelino Sanz de Sautuola (1831–88) (above) and
his daughter Maria (opposite
bottom), who first spotted the
bison painted on the ceiling of
the cave of Altamira (Spain).
At the time of the discovery, in
November 1879, Maria was
around five to nine years old.
She said that while her father
was excavating in the cave
floor she was 'running about in
the cavern and playing about
here and there ... Suddenly I
made out forms and figures
on the roof.' She exclaimed,
'Mira, Papa, bueyes!' (Look,
Papa, oxen!)

(Right) One of the cluster of
great polychrome bison on
the ceiling of Altamira which
had lain concealed in total
darkness for 14,000 years,
awaiting the gaze of a little girl.

(*Above*) The first published drawing of cave art, these apparently abstract black motifs from the back of the cave were included in Sanz de Sautuola's little pamphlet on Altamira in 1880. He had noticed these motifs in 1875, but paid them little attention until the revelation of the decorated ceiling in 1879.

(Top left) **Sketch of the animals painted on the Altamira ceiling by Dr José de Argumosa, a friend of Sanz de Sautuola, which was published in** *La Ilustración Española y Americana* **in October 1880.**
(Top right) **Drawing of the Altamira ceiling published by Sanz de Sautuola in his own pamphlet of 1880.**

However, the identification of Palaeolithic portable art did not lead immediately to an awareness of the age and significance of cave art. The pioneer who made the crucial mental leap was a Spanish landowner, Marcelino Sanz de Sautuola, who noticed in 1879 that the bison figures painted on the ceiling of the cave of Altamira, near the north coast of Cantabria, were very similar in style to the images in Palaeolithic portable art. Unfortunately, most of the archaeological establishment refused to take his published views seriously, dismissing him as naive or a fraud. One prehistorian who did accept Altamira, however, was Edouard Piette, who, in the late 1880s, was to find the famous painted pebbles in the eponymous cave of Le Mas d'Azil in the French Pyrenees, a discovery which the establishment found equally hard to swallow. One of the doubts raised about Altamira had been that the cave was too humid and the rock too friable to have preserved painting for so long, but the stratigraphic position of the Azilian pebbles finally brought the proof that ochre could adhere to rock for millennia.

It was in south-west France, once again, that the final breakthrough occurred when engravings were found, in 1895, in a gallery of the cave of La Mouthe (Dordogne). Since the gallery was blocked by Palaeolithic deposits, it was obvious that the engravings must be of the same age. Further discoveries soon followed in other caves in southern France, culminating in those of Les Combarelles and Font de Gaume in 1901, which at last established the authenticity of Palaeolithic cave art.

THE TWENTIETH CENTURY

The study of prehistoric art in the twentieth century is a vast subject which can be given only the briefest overview here. Discoveries have involved not just individual sites, but whole classes of art, and have brought entire countries onto the map of prehistoric art.

It was in 1903 that there occurred the first scientific discovery of a site of Levantine art in Spain – red paintings of three deer and an aurochs (wild ox) at Roca dels

Moros at Calapatá, Teruel – by Juan Cabré y Aguiló, a photographer. Mindful of the ridicule and furore caused by Altamira in 1880, he did not dare publish his findings until 1907, but eventually his find aroused national interest. The same year, the Roca dels Moros at Cogul (Lérida) was reported by the local parish priest, Ramón Huguet, and an account of it published in 1908, although the locals had always known about its images and attributed them, like all ancient things, to the Moors. Elsewhere in Europe, the rock art of Valcamonica in the Italian Alps was first pointed out by a shepherd in 1914.

One might think that the rock art map of Europe is well established nowadays: in fact, not only do new decorated caves come to light every year in France and Spain, and new petroglyph sites in the Alps and elsewhere, but thousands of petroglyphs have been discovered in the far north of Norway (especially around Alta) since 1973, while major collections of hundreds of open-air, Palaeolithic-style engravings and petroglyphs have been found in Spain and Portugal since 1980 and especially in the 1990s!

This painting of a red deer stag, a few centimetres long, is in the rock shelter of Arpan in the valley of the River Vero, Aragón (Spain). It is of classic Levantine art style yet its inland and northerly location in the central Pyrenean foothills shows that the term 'Levantine' was poorly chosen for this category of rock paintings, which are found predominantly but by no means exclusively in Spain's eastern coastal zone.
Date unknown.

Henri Breuil – the 'pope of prehistory'

Henri Edouard Prosper Breuil (1877–1961), one of the towering figures in Old World prehistory during the first half of the twentieth century, trained as a priest in his youth. However, although he remained a priest till his death, it was only a title since he was allowed to devote his whole existence to prehistory, undertook virtually no religious duties, and made almost no contribution to the reconciliation of prehistory's findings with religious teachings.

The son of a lawyer, his childhood in northern France infused him with an intense love of nature – not only of animals and plants, but especially of insects which remained a lifelong interest. Breuil's determination to be both priest and scientist was aided by the fact that one teacher at the seminary, the Abbé Guibert, not only encouraged his bent towards natural history but even expounded the theory of evolution and lent him the works of Gabriel de Mortillet, the anticlerical prehistorian.

As a young man with a talent for drawing animals, he had the supreme good fortune to make the acquaintance of Edouard Piette and Emile Cartailhac, two of France's greatest prehistorians at the turn of the century, when they needed help with the study and illustration of Palaeolithic portable

Breuil's tracing of an engraved panel in the cave of Bernifal, Dordogne (France), *c.* 15,000 years old. The panel is about 2 metres (7 feet) long and 1.5 metres (5 feet) high. The tracing shows a series of mammoths, with a bison, deer and horse below. On top of the mammoths there are several shapes described as 'tectiform' by early researchers, who thought they looked like huts. Some interpret these as pit-traps or gravity-traps, but this motif is so localized in space and time that others see it as some kind of tribal emblem.

and cave art respectively. This led to Breuil's becoming the world's leading authority on Palaeolithic art until his death. He discovered many decorated caves or galleries himself, and copied their art – by his own reckoning he spent about 700 days of his life underground. Although now seen as excessively subjective and incomplete, his tracings are nevertheless recognized as remarkable for their time. In some caves they constitute our only record of images that have since faded or disappeared.

Palaeolithic art, Breuil believed, had developed in two consecutive cycles, each from crude to good – that is, from simple to complex forms. This concept was inconsistent and unsatisfactory, and was eventually replaced by André Leroi-Gourhan's four 'styles' (the whole sequence developing from crude to good): this, too, is now being abandoned.

Breuil saw Palaeolithic art primarily in terms of hunting magic, thanks to a simplistic use of selected ethnographic analogies, and he generally considered decorated caves to be accumulations of single images, unlike Leroi-Gourhan who saw them as as carefully planned compositions.

Although he carried out a few small excavations at the start of his career (for example, at Le Mas d'Azil and Abri Dufaure in the Pyrenees), Breuil went on to concentrate on other aspects of prehistory – not only Palaeolithic art, but also the megalithic art of France and (during the First World War) the Iberian peninsula. In the Second World War he began a long campaign of copying rock art in parts of Southern Africa, an episode which led to the spectacular blunder of 'the priest and the white lady'.

A panel of human and animal figures had been discovered in a small shelter by Reinhardt Maack, while he was surveying the Brandberg massif in South West Africa (Namibia) in 1917. On a visit to South Africa in 1929 Breuil saw Maack's sketch of the panel and for eighteen years was haunted by a figure on it, which he saw as a 'white lady'. When he managed to reach the remote site himself in 1947, he declared that the White Lady and her companions were Caucasian visitors – Cretans or Minoans – from the Mediterranean area. This idea that Southern African art could be attributed to 'foreigners' fitted the common misconception at that time that the Bushmen were too 'primitive' to have produced the huge quantities of sensitive rock art to be seen in Southern Africa. A certain Colonel Imker Hoogenhout, Smuts's administrator of the territory, declared on seeing Breuil's copy, 'This is no Bushman painting: this is Great Art.'

An irascible and egotistical man, Breuil nevertheless had a lasting influence on numerous devoted friends and pupils. So ingrained was his image as the 'pope of prehistory' that he was often thought virtually infallible. It is only in recent years that it has become possible in France to criticize and re-examine his work openly. His huge legacy of publications and tracings has been found to contain many errors and misjudgements, but equally an abundance of profound insights which are only now being supported by new finds: for example, the new direct dates and pigment analyses in European caves often tend to support Breuil's views rather than Leroi-Gourhan's.

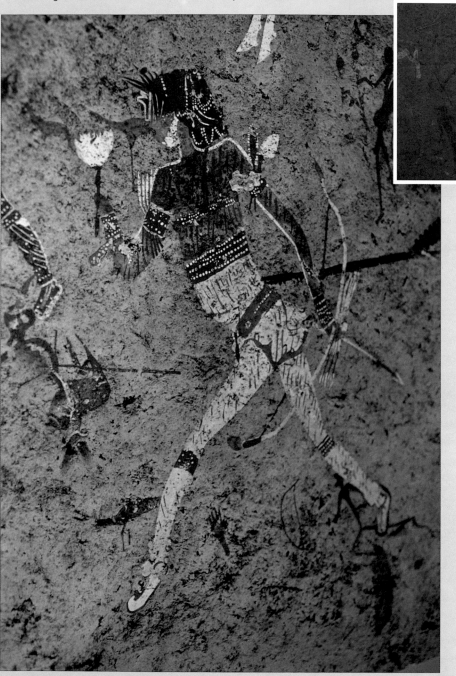

(*Above*) The famous White Lady in Namibia, painted by Bushmen. Date unknown. Breuil's interpretation of the 'White Lady of the Brandberg', immortalized in his book of the same name, was influential for a long time, until it was established by less subjective researchers that this painting is in fact a male figure (it has a penis), carrying male equipment (a bow and arrow). But Breuil never doubted it was female, even after seeing and copying it in person: he described it as 'rosy white from her waist to her feet ... the face is very delicately painted and has nothing native about it', and even speculated that it might be Isis herself. (*Left*) Harald Pager's meticulous copy of the figure. Being somewhat more accurate than Breuil's, it shows clearly that this is a male. Date unknown.

The rock art in the Valcamonica area (Italian Alps) – probably the biggest concentration
in Europe – comprises approximately 300,000 petroglyphs,
though hundreds of decorated
rocks doubtless remain buried.
This panel, at Naquane, shows
a warrior, thought to date to
the Iron Age, a few centuries
BC, and some enigmatic grids.

In Asia, Thailand entered the lists thanks to a French military surveyor L.L. Lunet
de Lajonquière, who was there in 1903–09; his descriptive records, published in
1912, include references to painted rock art sites, notably Khao Kian (Mountain of
Paintings), a shallow cave containing geometric designs and naturalistic animals.
More sites were found in the 1920s and later. In China, a Hong Kong engraving had
been mentioned in newspapers in 1819, but the first real research took place in 1915,
on the engravings in Fujian Province, after Professor Hua Zhongjin had been
informed of them by villagers. In 1927, the Swedish archaeologist Folke Bergman

found engravings in Inner Mongolia, and filled them with white powder to take photographs. Amazingly, however, it was not until the 1980s that rock art research really got under way in earnest in China and the outside world learned of that country's enormous wealth in prehistoric rock art. Major discoveries continue in China even today – for example, scores of rock art sites with thousands of pictures were discovered in Tibet during the 1990s. Meanwhile, in India, research flourished throughout the century, with the result that we now know of more than 1,000 rock shelters with paintings, in over 150 sites – there is rock art in almost all the states of India.

In Australia, the first clues that rock art might be really ancient came in 1929, with the excavations of the Devon Downs Shelter on the Murray River, which exposed engraved art on the rock face, the earliest of which was associated with debris four metres below the surface. In the last few decades dates have been pushed back – 13,000 years for engravings at Early Man Shelter in Queensland, more than 40,000 years for organic material trapped in varnish on top of simple petroglyphs at Wharton Hill and Panaramittee North in South Australia (see Chapter 6), and perhaps up to 75,000 years or more for thousands of cup marks at Jinmium in north-west Australia. In some areas, such as the Kimberley, more than 100 new sites per year have been found in the 1990s; and a large number of previously unsuspected decorated caves have also been discovered.

In North America, there was relatively little interest in rock art until Julian Steward wrote a doctoral thesis on the subject, which was published by the University of California at Berkeley in 1929: he was the first person to use the terms 'petroglyph' (rock carving) and 'pictograph' (rock painting), and he shunned the use of ethnographic data as speculative, preferring to focus on defining a series of rock art

Bears and reindeer, part of the huge abundance of petroglyphs found at Alta, far above the Arctic Circle in northern Norway, since 1973. Many more still lie undetected beneath soil or vegetation in the area. The date of the petroglyphs is unknown, but, from their position in relation to the shore line, they are thought to be between 4200 and 500 BC.

'areas'. In recent years the New World has emerged as housing one of the world's richest and most diverse bodies of prehistoric art, with whole new areas still being put on the rock art map, especially in vast territories like Brazil, where, for example, the hundreds of painted rock shelters of the Piauí region have only become known since the 1970s.

The continent where knowledge of prehistoric art was perhaps most transformed in the course of the twentieth century is Africa. In East Africa, the first discovery of rock art occurred in 1908, when some missionaries on the western shore of Lake Nyanza (Tanzania) found red figures in rock shelters. The first decorated cave in the République Centrafricaine was found in 1912, and engravings were discovered in Cameroon in 1933. In North Africa, rock paintings (as opposed to engravings) were not documented till 1933 when a camel-corps officer, Lieutenant Brenans, ventured into a deep canyon of the Tassili n'Ajjer (Algeria) during a police operation; as he rode slowly on his camel, he saw strange figures on the cliffs of the wadi – the animal and human engravings of Oued Djerat. He also saw very delicate paintings, the very first to be seen by Europeans. New discoveries continue to be made in Africa – for example, the first rock art (engravings) was found in Gabon only in 1987!

A splintering of approaches

The twentieth century has seen a huge number of discoveries of Palaeolithic art – not only of caves (an average of one per year, even today, including such major sites as Niaux, Les Trois Frères, Pech Merle, Lascaux and Chauvet) but also of thousands of pieces of portable art – and in recent decades it has become apparent that art of the same age also exists outside Europe, in every other continent. The subject was dominated by the Abbé Henri Breuil until his death in 1961; renowned for his tracings of cave and portable art (primarily in Europe, but also in Southern Africa), he

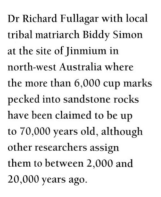

Dr Richard Fullagar with local tribal matriarch Biddy Simon at the site of Jinmium in north-west Australia where the more than 6,000 cup marks pecked into sandstone rocks have been claimed to be up to 70,000 years old, although other researchers assign them to between 2,000 and 20,000 years ago.

was less noteworthy for his interpretations, which remained firmly entrenched in simplistic notions of hunting and fertility magic based on selected ethnographic analogies. In the 1960s and 1970s this field was dominated by André Leroi-Gourhan who undertook no tracing but revolutionized interpretation by rejecting ethnography and conducting a structuralist analysis of cave art's contents. He found a basic male–female dualism: the art was dominated by horses and bison, which he interpreted as male and female symbols respectively, and he likewise saw the non-figurative 'signs' in sexual terms, dividing them into phallic and vulvar groups. He also believed that caves were not simple collections of individual images (as Breuil had thought) but carefully planned homogeneous compositions, laid out according to a preconceived blueprint. Since Leroi-Gourhan's death in 1986, approaches to Palaeolithic art have splintered; it has become apparent that no single great all-embracing theory can hope to account for such a widespread, long-lasting and varied phenomenon.

Paintings of human figures at Sefar, Tassili, Algeria. Date unknown.

Different approaches to prehistoric art in the twentieth century

During the early decades of the century, attention was focused on discovering and copying prehistoric art, interpreting it in fairly simple and literal terms – often distorting or selecting the facts to fit a preselected pet theory derived from ethnographic accounts – and great effort was devoted to building up local chronological schemes for each region. This was the period when searches became systematic, although accidental discoveries continued to be made and indeed still do. In these early days, the study of rock art was akin to that of stone tools or any other artifacts – being based on stratigraphy (superimposition of images) and typology (styles), with the primary aim being the development of a classificatory framework. The regional stylistic sequences that were built up were equivalent to the geological and artifactual sequences of other fields. Interpretations were simplistic, drawn largely from the history of religion, and uncritically incorporating elements from a wide array of places, periods and cultures.

It was during the second half of the century that attention was devoted to developing more complex (and more accurate) interpretations. Some of these were based on structuralism, most notably the interpretations of Leroi-Gourhan, while researchers such as Frederick McCarthy in Australia or Patricia Vinnicombe and Tim Maggs in Southern Africa placed great emphasis on qualtification and urged that the rock art corpus should be recorded as objectively and comprehensively as possible.

However, counting and listing require enormous amounts of time and labour, and at the end of the day do not reveal anything much about meaning – they merely provide the raw material on which hypotheses can be based (although they can lead to fascinating insights, as shown by current wide-ranging studies based on the thousands of images traced accurately by the graphic artist Harald Pager in Namibia's Brandberg). More recently, therefore, there has been a move towards environmental and spatial studies – examining the art in its landscape – and greater efforts have been made to integrate rock art with contemporary archaeological data and cultural contexts (where its date can be at least estimated). Some researchers have attempted a semiotic approach, treating rock art as complex, symbolic messages. There has also been renewed interest in ethnographic information (see Chapter 8), with an avowed intention (not always successful, it must be said) to avoid the simplistic and all-embracing explanations for which ethnography was misused in the past and with a renewed ability to tell new kinds of stories about the individual images and scenes in the art.

As in archaeology itself since the 1960s, there has also been a desperate desire to find some new approach, some fresh fashion to adopt, with every other discipline imaginable being trawled for any useful titbits of theory or insight. So in rapid succession we have passed through structuralism, processualism, post-structuralism, structural-marxism and contextualism. Overall, there has been a splintering of approaches, which can only be healthy; and a new emphasis on the non-material, the ideological and the social aspects of prehistoric art. Once again, this is reflected in the Scandinavian ship images, which are now seen by some researchers as ambiguous symbols of social interaction and unity, with rock art sites marking social boundaries or ownership of places and resources.

More serious, and far more important, has been the growing realization that indigenous people have rights which need to be respected. Just as it came as a profound shock to

There are more than a thousand petroglyphs of 'boats' on the rocks of Bohuslän (Sweden), thought to date largely to the Bronze Age, about 3,000 years ago. The ubiquitous 'ships' in the rock art of southern Scandinavia, originally interpreted as Viking battleships, were, during the early part of the twentieth century, seen as cult ships linked with a fertility god, myths and rituals – a magico-religious interpretation based on northern folklore as well as on the religions of the Mediterranean!

Tally marks and other motifs can be seen in this early photo of Painted Rocks, Montana, around 1890. In the foreground are Charles A. Stillinger (centre), William Wade (right), and a companion. The site is on Flathead Lake. Date unknown.

archaeologists and anthropologists in the late 1970s and 1980s to find that some indigenous people objected vociferously to having their ancestors or sacred objects excavated and stored in museums without their knowledge or permission, so rock art researchers in several parts of the world (especially Australia) have had to modify their procedures and outlook, as the Aboriginal groups campaign for control of their own culture, and provide input into – and demand feedback from – research into their art. It is safe to say that, today, nobody in Australia would dream of beginning a study of rock art without consulting the Aboriginal custodians of the region in question. This is a welcome move for many reasons, not least for its role in taking such studies out of the ivory towers and making them more relevant to the Aboriginal people and the world at large.

On the technical side, photography was adopted quite early – for example, the first photograph of an African rock painting was taken by von Bonde in 1885, and by a decade later it had become commonplace. Much later, colour photography began to be used, at first by pioneers such as the rock art specialist Alex Willcox in South Africa from 1951, and new technology such as video and computer enhancement are now coming into their own. In the last few years, the new techniques of direct dating (see Chapter 6) have begun to revolutionize (in some cases) or at least fine-tune (in others) the traditional chronologies built up over decades, and newly dated rock art has at last joined the already well-dated portable art in being embraced by mainstream archaeology as data worthy of attention.

Harald Pager (1923–85), a South African immigrant born in Czechoslovakia and brought up in Austria, devoted his skills as a graphic designer to the painstaking recording of Bushman rock paintings in the South African Drakensberg and Namibian Brandberg, and is widely recognized as the world's greatest recorder of rock art. Here he is working at Sebaaieni Cave in Ndedema Gorge, in the Drakensberg, South Africa's richest rock art area. Living here in the late 1960s, Pagar documented almost 4,000 paintings in its seventeen rock shelters. He is shown duplicating the images of three hartebeest, visible on the rock face, using oils on a same-size photographic black-and-white print.

CHAPTER 3   *Body Art*

Virtually all peoples around the world paint their bodies on certain occasions, and we have no reason to doubt that the same was true in prehistoric times – indeed, this was probably one of the very first forms of aesthetic expression. Unfortunately, owing to the decomposition of bodies there is no direct proof of the practice in prehistory and we therefore have to infer it from other evidence.

COLOURING MATERIALS

Lumps of natural pigments are known from archaeological sites of very remote periods – in fact pieces of haematite or ochre appear to have been carried into sites in South Africa up to 800,000–900,000 years ago. A small ochre pebble, faceted and with oblique striations (scratches), was found in an Acheulian layer at Hunsgi, southern India, dating to 200,000–300,000 years ago, and seems to have been used as a crayon on rock. Another piece of red mineral, with vertical striations resulting from use, was found in the Acheulian (*c.* 250,000 BC) rock shelter of Becov (Czech Republic) which had been occupied by *Homo erectus*, the early human ancestor. The even earlier site of Terra Amata (*c.* 300,000 BC) at Nice (France) produced seventy-five bits of pigment ranging in colour from yellow to brown, red and purple: most of them have traces of artificial abrasion and were clearly introduced to the site by the occupants, since they do not occur naturally in the vicinity.

During the period of the Neanderthals (*c.* 200,000–30,000 BC) such pigments become increasingly frequent, not only in occupation deposits but also in burials which now occurred for the first time. In France, for example, the cave of Le Pech de l'Azé yielded 103 blocks of manganese dioxide (black/blue), plus three of iron oxide (red), sixty-seven of which were rounded or polished into a crayon shape, as if they had been used on some soft surface. A Neanderthal skeleton at Le Moustier was sprinkled with red powder, and red pigment was also found around the head of the famous skeleton of La Chapelle aux Saints, near two skeletons at Qafzeh (Israel) and many others. In addition, there is evidence for actual mining of haematite (iron oxide) in Southern Africa from around 45,000–50,000 BC onwards – indeed it is esti-mated that 100 tonnes were mined at the site of Ngwenya alone, dating to about 43,200 years ago – and in Hungary from 30,000 BC. Much later, in the New Stone Age, pigment was also mined in areas such as France and Portugal. In Australia's North-ern Territory, used blocks of red and yellow ochre and ground haematite have been found in occupation layers at the shelters of Malakunanja II and Nauwalabila I, dating to around 60,000 years ago. Most notable, in the latter site, is a piece of high-quality haematite weighing a kilo, which was brought in from some distance and whose facets and striations are clear signs of use.

However, it was in the Upper Palaeolithic period (30,000–10,000 BC) that pig-ments became really abundant and ubiquitous, being transported in tens of kilos. For example, in some French sites it is not rare to find habitation floors impregnated with red to a depth of about 20 centimetres (8 inches). Well over 100 sites with pig-ment are known, as well as at least twenty-five burials. Since the decoration of cave walls seems to have begun in this period, some of the finds can plausibly be linked directly to that practice – for example, the colouring materials found in the caves of Lascaux (France) or Tito Bustillo (Spain) in close proximity to the paintings. But what about open-air sites or unpainted caves? Can we assume that the presence of pigments here necessarily indicates body-painting, let alone the decoration of arti-facts or walls?

(*Opposite*) This magnificent engraved panel at Niola Doa, on the Ennedi Plateau (Chad), was reported for the first time in 1993, but resembles one found in the same area in the 1950s. The name 'Niola Doa' means 'Dancing Maidens', but these large, apparently round-buttocked figures are unsexed. Note the intricate labyrinthine patterns engraved on the bodies, and the batons which they seem to be carrying. The height of the panel is over 2 metres (*c.* 7 feet). Date unknown. Drawing by R. Simonis.

BODY-PAINTING

Unfortunately, things are not so straightforward, for the simple reason that mineral pigments of this type have a number of properties. It is known from ethnographic studies around the world that ochre is often used in the treatment of animal skins, because it preserves organic tissues, protecting them from putrefaction and from vermin such as maggots. Ochre is also widely used for the decoration of animal skins. It is probably these kinds of function which explain the impregnated soil in some habitation sites, and the traces of red mineral on many stone tools such as scrapers. Similarly, red pigment may have been applied to corpses not so much out of pious beliefs about life-blood, as is commonly believed, or in order to restore an illusion of health and life to dead cheeks, but rather to neutralize odours and help preserve the body.

Even if, as most prehistorians assume, the people of the Stone Age did indeed paint their bodies, the practice may in some cases have been purely functional – rather than symbolic (as in female puberty rites) or aesthetic. For example, ochre is very effective in cauterizing and cleaning injuries, and is still used by the Barougas of South Africa to dry bleeding wounds. In fact, until the end of the nineteenth century, ochre was still used by country doctors in parts of Europe as an antiseptic in the treatment of purulent wounds. Another function which must have been important during the last Ice Age is that of protection against the elements and insects. Peoples such as Tasmanians, Polynesians, Melanesians and Hottentots (Khoikhoi) used red pigments to maintain bodily warmth and ward off the effects of cold and rain; among the Navaho, Walapai, Pima and other North American tribes, a mixture of red ochre and fat was often applied to the cheeks of women and children as a hygienic measure to protect their skin against the sun and dry winds.

Similarly, certain South American tribes, such as the Karaja of Brazil or the Warran Indians of the Orinoco, generally used red paint as a protection against mosquitoes, while the Tasmanians put a mixture of fat and ochre on their hair as an effective protection against vermin. The Walbiri of Australia still smear their upper torso with fat and powdered red pigment (which they explicitly associate with blood, health and strength) as an insulation against both heat and cold, and as protection against flies. (Among many such peoples, fleas were sometimes virtually unknown until white people arrived!) In Arnhem Land, men used to daub themselves with white pigment before setting out on a hunt, in order to suppress their body odour.

The more aesthetic uses of pigment on the body may well have arisen from practices such as these. For instance, the medicinal properties of ochre may have led to the painting of the dead or dying: if members of Australia's Arunta tribe felt ill, their bodies were rubbed with red ochre, while the Sioux Dakota used to paint women and children red before they died. For burials of the Stone Age and later periods it is often difficult to tell whether a body had its flesh painted or merely its bones. Some Neolithic bodies, such as a skull at Sgurgola, near Rome, seem to have been

Living designs

In the 1850s, festivals in different parts of Australia were witnessed and described by travellers. The 'incredible transformation of men into living designs' was done with ochre and white pipe clay, and the intricate patterns of stripes and dots were faithfully reproduced in lithographs. Study of these, as well as of the accounts of more recent explorers, can help us to understand how and why the painting may have been done in prehistoric times.

The technique employed varies. The motif is first sketched with either the juicy end of an orchid stem, or with blood from the arm. The paint is then applied with twig-brushes, or the motif is enhanced with down or charcoal. As the work is done, the man lies quite still, eyes closed, impassive – almost in a trance. The painting is done with extreme care, every detail being supervised by the older members of the cult lodge, and being memorized by the younger members, who thus learn something of their origins and of the pattern of the universe: the correctness of the design is at least as important as the dance which follows. Certainly, individual expression and artistry are not excluded, but the themes and codes established by tradition must never be violated. Major innovation is out of the question. Hence the painstaking work may take many hours in order to achieve perfection. In some cases, particular patterns are specific to certain parts of the body, and there may even be strict rules about which pigments to use, how to mix and apply them, and the order and number of strokes used.

Lithograph of a 'native festival' by W. Blandowski, a geologist and naturalist who made several expeditions into the hinterland of Victoria and South Australia in the 1850s. His accurate drawings reveal something of the body art in this part of the country.

The 'venus' of Laussel,
Dordogne (France),
44 centimetres
(17½ inches) high,
probably dates to
c. 25,000–20,000 BC).
Although now detached,
it should be classed as
parietal rock art since it was
originally carved on a block of
4 cubic metres (c. 140 cubic
feet). The 'horn' in the woman's
right hand, and the series of
lines engraved on it, have often
been linked with the moon
or menstruation.

painted while the flesh was present – as it decomposed, the colouring was transferred to the bone – while other Neolithic skeletons in Italy seem to have had the bones painted directly. The same applies in Russia, where scholars still hold differing opinions over whether the corpse or the skeleton was reddened. If the whole body was painted at death, or just before, the lumps of pigment placed with the corpse may represent supplies of body-paint for the afterworld. Analysis of skin from Britain's Late Iron Age bog body, Lindow Man, has led some researchers to the conclusion that he had his body painted with a copper-based pigment.

But what of the living? As has already been mentioned, most authorities agree that Stone Age people must have painted their bodies, but the evidence is very limited. One possible clue is that the lumps of pigment in early sites are often shiny, indicating that they were applied to soft surfaces; but while this could be skin it could equally well be animal hide. Another clue – traces of abrasive marks on pigment lumps, indicating that they were used on a rough surface – may simply indicate removal of powder for use in a liquid paste. More persuasive is the fact that some French caves have yielded hollow bone tubes, often engraved, containing powdered pigment, and not all of this material can be linked to cave art. It is perhaps significant that the abundance of pigments in prehistoric sites generally increases through the Upper Palaeolithic period at the same time as other forms of personal decoration such as beads and pendants (see Chapter 4); but, of course, only mineral pigments have survived from those remote times – any biodegradable colouring materials such as those from plants are gone for ever. In fact, the only good evidence for body-painting in the Stone Age is the fact that some of the human figurines, including the famous 'venus' of Willendorf and that of Laussel, were originally painted red but the same is true of most Ice Age portable art and all its bas-relief sculptures, including animal figures!

In later periods, statuettes are clearly decorated with designs which are either abstract or figurative, and it is a fair bet that living bodies were decorated in the same way. However, it is always possible that these designs represent tattoos or scarification rather than paint: for example, infills found on painted human figures in north Queensland, Australia, usually interpreted as decorative patterns, have recently been compared with a neighbouring region's ethnographic records of cicatrization (regular, raised scars, found on both men and women – comprising marks of courage, of initiation or affiliation to social groups) and there does seem to be some degree of correlation.

It is likely that some of this early body-decoration was undertaken simply for aesthetic pleasure. Among many peoples today it merely serves to accentuate their natural traits: for instance, the Colorado Indians of Ecuador paint designs on their face and arms for beautification, while the Nuba of the Sudan do the same to celebrate, emphasize and enhance a healthy and strong body. The motifs tell no stories and there are no action scenes, since this would attract too much attention away from the main point of the practice!

(Opposite) Excavations in 1947 in a burial mound at Pazyryk in the High Altai (southern Siberia) recovered the remains of a chieftain dating to the fifth century BC. Preserved by the permafrost, his skin still bore an abundance of elaborate curvilinear tattoos, produced by deep pricking into which a black colouring substance was introduced. Among the designs can be seen a wild ass, a fantastic winged animal with a feline tail, a mountain ram, and a deer with a bird's beak.

In the seventeenth century, French explorers reported of the Huron warriors of North America that 'they paint themselves various colours, a fashion which seems horrible to us, but so beautiful to them'. Some had the nose and eyes blue, but the eyebrows and cheeks black; others had black, red and blue stripes from the ears to the mouth, or ear to ear across the forehead; others had the whole face black except for the forehead, the point of the chin and circles around the eyes. 'Even mothers paint the children in this way to make them beautiful.'

Despite the total lack of evidence, therefore, it seems safe to assume that prehistoric people also took this kind of simple pleasure in body-painting. However, once they came into contact with literate groups, assessment of the practice becomes far easier, since some early accounts specifically mention the practice of body-painting. Perhaps the most famous is the short passage in Caesar's *De Bello Gallico* (V, 14) of the first century BC: 'All the Britons, indeed, dye themselves with woad, which produces a bluish colour, and thereby have a more terrible appearance in battle.' Some scholars consider this chapter of Caesar's work to be spurious, but in any case other authors such as Pomponius Mela and Pliny relate something similar: Pliny, for example, in *Naturalis Historiae* (XXII, 2) of the first century AD, stated that 'among barbarian tribes the women stain the face, using some one plant and some another ... In Gaul there is a plant like the plantain, called glastum (woad); with it the wives of the Britons, and their daughters-in-law, stain all the body, and at certain religious ceremonies march along naked, with a colour resembling that of Ethiopians.'

These texts serve to highlight two special functions of body-painting – as a signal and as a part of ritual. Clearly, whatever the reasons for the development of this art form, and even if no symbolism was associated with it at first, it would eventually have resulted in group-member recognition and thus contributed to group coherence; distinctions would have arisen which would serve to differentiate groups or tribes, or to denote rank, age, sex or status. This social meaning would be enhanced by the selection of particular occasions when the practice should occur. Thus, some Aboriginal tribes of Australia paint a few spots on their face or body for 'everyday wear', but for solemn occasions such as initiations the whole body may be carefully decorated – though all traces of adornment are removed immediately after the ceremony.

In Australia, ceremonies of this kind tend to be totemic, and a person's totemic clan design might even be painted on the skull after death. In many parts of Arnhem Land, the deceased's whole body was painted with designs representing one of the Ancestral Beings of the clan, and young initiates might have paintings made on their chest which connected them to the deceased. It is generally believed that the designs were created by the creator-ancestors to meet the needs of each ceremony, and thus to recreate the designs is in itself an act of worship, and the motifs are often 'chanted onto' the body, with men 'singing the line' of the dreaming incident which is to be dramatized.

Australian body-painting, therefore, is an extreme example of art in the service of ritual, and ritual expressed through art. In neighbouring New Guinea, this type of self-decoration is likewise more than a cosmetic, being a medium by which to show one's relationship to the ancestral spirits and to make specific statements about one's social and religious values, prestige, wealth and clan solidarity. A 1655 account by a Dutch navigator Schouten concerning South Africa recorded that the herder peoples here used caves or similar places for some sort of ceremony, during which 'with a red stone' they made 'stripes and crosses on each other's foreheads' – thus presumably making statements of a similar kind.

OTHER FORMS OF BODILY ART

Tattooing is a different method of decorating the skin. Although there is possible evidence for the practice in the Ice Age – bone needles from some French sites have been interpreted as being linked to this – and although many of the above-mentioned patterns depicted on Stone Age figurines may be tattoos rather than paint, the earliest definite specimens known are the simple blue lines and a cross found on various parts of the body of the 'Iceman', the 5,300-year-old body found high in the Italian Alps in 1991. Even though these are thought to be therapeutic, for the purpose of relieving arthritis, they at least prove the existence of the practice in the Stone Age.

Perhaps the best known, and among the most spectacular tattoos known from prehistory are those on the frozen Iron Age bodies from the Altai region of southern Siberia – including deer and other animals drawn in sophisticated curvilinear designs. But tattooing was also a prominent and widespread feature in the Pacific Islands when Europeans first arrived there – for example on Easter Island and, most impressively of all, in New Zealand. The practice seems to have been existed there throughout prehistory, since the distinctive bone 'needles' and 'chisels' (actually finely toothed combs that made a series of perforations in the skin rather than a cut) occur in sites of all periods. By the time of the European arrival in New Zealand, there was great regional variation in styles, in designs and in the parts of the body tattooed – in some areas, for instance, women were decorated on the breasts, necks and bellies, while men bore tattoos on their buttocks and thighs.

(*Right and opposite*) Eighteenth-century engravings by Sydney Parkinson of the tattooed faces of two New Zealand chiefs, reproduced in his *A Journal of a Voyage to the South Seas*. Note the ornamental head comb worn by one; the other has the 'northern' style of facial tattoo.

Other forms of bodily art, such as hairstyles and scarification, can only be assessed from prehistoric human figurines and images, except for some preserved bodies whose hair is preserved – for example, from the Altai, the European bog bodies or the early Chinchorro mummies of northern Chile. There is more evidence for skeletal modification. For example, it is known that the deliberate deformation of the human skull, by binding the brow of growing infants or applying pressure at regular intervals, thus giving it a high sloping forehead or a broad flat forehead, was widespread: the phenomenon may even exist among the Neanderthals, and seems

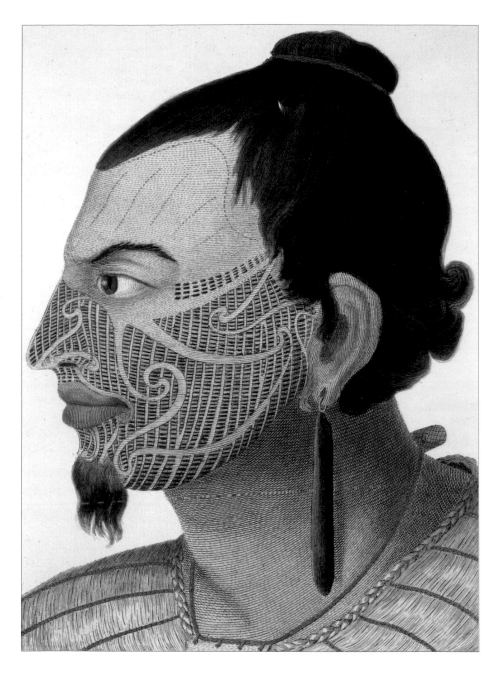

to occur in early Australian skulls such as specimens from Kow swamp, 13,000 years old. The avulsion (extraction) or decoration of teeth was also widespread: in Australia, the Aboriginal custom of knocking out one or two upper incisors as part of male initiation has been found in a burial at Nitchie, New South Wales, dating to 7,000 years ago. The extraction and decoration of teeth – presumably for ceremonial or decorative reasons – was very common around 4,000 years ago in Japan and decorated teeth also occur in the Mesolithic period of India, possibly being engraved while the owners were alive.

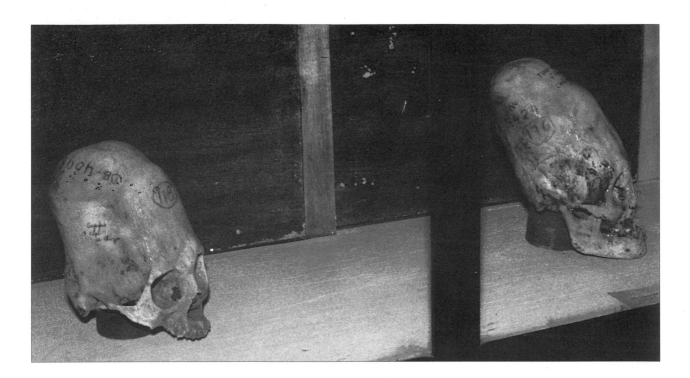

(Above) **Deliberately deformed skulls from the Ica area, Peru. Precise date unknown, probably early centuries AD.**

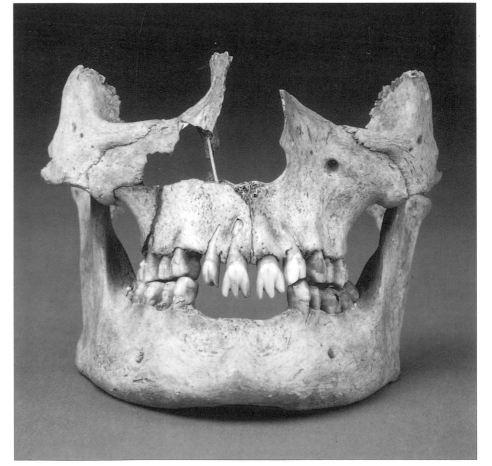

(Right) **Part of an adult female skull and jawbone (probably first millennium BC) from Fuji-idera City, Osaka (Japan), with teeth extracted and decorated – presumably for ceremonial purposes. The practice has been linked with rites of passage such as coming-of-age, marriage, or the death of family members: specific teeth were probably removed at such stages in a person's life.**

In short, it is virtually certain that human skin, bones, teeth and hair were the first and most ubiquitous canvases for artistic expression. One need only reflect on how much prominence, even in modern, supposedly sophisticated societies, is still given to make-up, hairstyles, body-piercing and tattoos to realize that the deep-seated urge to decorate the human form has never left us.

Objets d'Art

> In art, objects are not represented for their own sake, but as vehicles of feelings
> and meanings whose origins are personal, social and religious.
>
> Max Raphael, *The Body Beautiful*

Portable art objects, while not the focus of this book, are nonetheless of great importance – not only for their abundance and the variety of their materials, but also for the diversity of the contexts in which they are found (which can provide some clue to function and meaning). By and large, portable art has been easier to date than art on rocks and cave walls.

CATEGORIES OF PORTABLE ART

Virtually every naturally occurring material available has been used for some kind of portable art: bone, antler, ivory, teeth, horn, hides, mollusc- and egg-shells, and feathers; wood, textiles, coal and amber; stone, stalagmite, coral, and minerals of all kinds. In Polynesia, *tapa* (the beaten bark of the paper mulberry) was turned into figurines; while on America's north-west coast, objects were even carved from the fruiting body of a wood-destroying fungus known as the 'bread of ghosts' and accredited with supernatural powers.

CHAPTER 4

(Opposite) The tiny mammoth-ivory head from Brassempouy, Landes (France), 3.5 centimetres (1½ inches) high, found at the end of the nineteenth century, is traditionally seen as that of a woman and is one of the few Ice Age depictions with facial features and a detailed hairstyle. It may be extremely early, more than 30,000 years old. However, doubts have been expressed recently about its authenticity, especially as little is known of its provenance and it emerged in a site where the workers were rewarded for finds.

(Left) Two of the five Roos Carr wooden figures and their animal-headed 'boat', which were discovered in about 1836 near the River Humber, England. Samples of the yew wood have produced AMS radio-carbon results in the first millennium BC, around 2,500 years ago. The figures are about 40 centimetres (*c.* 16 inches) high, and have stone inserts for eyes. Peter Sweeney, Conservation Officer at Hull Museum, has recently found that what were hitherto thought to be (and fitted as) detachable stubby arms actually fit better as downward-curving penises.

As early as the Ice Age, people began to produce synthetic materials – fired clay, or terracotta, and eventually pottery vessels. These then became another vehicle for artistic expression, and pottery was also used for a wide range of objects and figurines in many parts of the world. The growing expertise with the uses of fire then led to the working of other materials – faience (a kind of 'pre-glass') and, later, glass were produced; copper was worked in various ways; and this was followed in some areas by bronze, gold and silver and, later still, iron and steel.

There have been countless experiments and analyses to discover exactly how these objects were made – the temperatures achieved, how the decoration was incised or applied, etc., and how metal objects were cast. There have also been experiments in the production of other kinds of portable art – such as the carving of ivory figurines. The technological aspects of engraving of bone and stone with stone tools have received a great deal of attention since the pioneering experiments of the French researcher Louis Leguay in the 1870s, who tried engraving on bone with original Palaeolithic tools and found it could be done quickly with a little practice. In recent years, a great deal has been learned from the microscopic observations of Alexander Marshack, but far more from the experimental engravings on bone and stone by Italian researcher Francesco d'Errico, whose microscopic technological analyses have established firm criteria for recognizing the direction of incisions, the order of super-impositions, the number of tools used, the number of artistic episodes, and even whether the engraver was right- or left-handed.

Engraved stones

Although engraved stones probably occur in every prehistoric culture in the world, they achieved a major importance in the Ice Age of Western Europe. Here, the small slabs (or plaquettes) of sandstone, limestone, slate or stalagmite are sometimes found in large numbers – the Spanish cave of Parpalló had over 5,000 decorated

Tracing by Marylise Lejeune of an aurochs (wild ox) and deer engraved on a plaquette from Trou de Chaleux (Belgium), probably dating to *c.* 15,000–10,000 BC. The total width of the plaquette is 80 centimetres (*c.* 31 inches).

specimens, the French cave of Enlène had over 1,000. The incisions on these stones are sometimes deep and clear, but in many cases they are so fine that they are almost invisible, and only under a strong light coming in from the side can one see the lines at all.

Researchers in the early part of the twentieth century, when hunting magic ruled supreme (see Chapter 8), were inclined to see evidence of ritual in everything, and since many of the plaquettes were broken it was supposed that the breakage was purposeful. The fact that some plaquettes had been burned and most were found with the engraved face downwards, seemed to be further evidence that they had formed part of a ritual. However, many are engraved on both sides and the face-down 'rule' is by no means the norm. Moreover, while breakages may sometimes be purposeful, it should be remembered that people and animals trampling around on cave or rock-shelter floors can have drastic effects on any material lying there. Some plaquettes may also have been shattered by thermal tension, since heated sandstone plaquettes are known to have been used by French peasants in historical times as bedwarmers.

Several tonnes of schist plaquettes were brought to the German open-air camp of Gönnersdorf (c. 10,500 BC), probably as elements of construction and as foundations

Detail of one of the engraved plaquettes from Gönnersdorf, Germany (c. 10,500 BC), showing an extremely tiny figure of a mammoth – the pencil tip provides the scale.

Early art

Just as the earliest crude stone tools are notoriously difficult to differentiate from natural flaking (the difference between artifacts and geofacts), so it is very easy to make mistakes in recognizing early 'art'. Many archaeologists in the past have been led astray by apparently engraved lines on bones or shell which were actually natural (root marks, etc), or by perforations in bones and shells which were thought to have been made by humans but which, on closer examination, proved to have been made by carnivore gnawing (bones) or by oceanic carnivores (shells), or by other factors such as an inherent weakness of an object at a certain point, which therefore frequently breaks in the same way in the same place, making the damage seem purposeful. On the other hand, it is a fair bet that natural perforations were not only found useful by early prehistoric people, who thus had ready-made beads available, but were also a source of inspiration for them, leading them to make their own.

It now seems self-evident that 'art' (however it may be defined) by no means began with the period we call the Upper Palaeolithic (around 40,000 years ago) or

This handaxe, about 13 centimetres (*c.* 5 inches) long, found in 1911 at West Tofts in Norfolk (England), and probably several hundred thousand years old, was carefully made so as to preserve a fossil shell of *Spondylus spinosus* at its centre, indicating the existence of a keen aesthetic sense at this time. The very care put into the symmetrical shaping of this superabundant tool also goes far beyond what was required for its presumed functions of bashing and cutting.

even with what we call 'modern humans' – both of them highly artificial concepts in any case. New examples of pre-Upper Palaeolithic 'art' are accumulating, though many of them are still a source of contention. Many scholars in the past have pointed out that the symmetry and 'beauty' of many Lower Palaeolithic (Acheulian) handaxes, hundreds of thousands of years old, went far beyond what was technically required of the tool, whatever its uses; and more specific examples of Acheulian art are appearing now that people are becoming more receptive to the idea – a classic example of 'I would not see it if I did not believe it'!

Two petroglyphs (rock carvings) – a large circular cup mark (cupule) and a pecked meandering line – have been found in Auditorium Cave, Bhimbetka (India), which were covered by, and thus at least as old as, an occupation layer containing stone tools of Acheulian age. There are bones from the Lower Palaeolithic open air site of Bilzingsleben, Germany, of about 300,000 years ago, which bear series of what seem to be patterned and non-utilitarian parallel incisions.

However, the real breakthrough in this subject has come about recently through analyses by American researcher Alexander Marshack of new or hitherto neglected pieces of evidence from the Near East: in particular, a piece of flint from the Israeli site of Quneitra, dating to 54,000 years ago, which is incised with four semi-circles and other lines; and, from the nearby Acheulian site of Berekhat Ram, a small, shaped piece of volcanic tuff that dates to somewhere between 233,000 and 800,000 years ago.

There is also evidence that a natural likeness to a human was noticed far earlier, since in 1925 a pebble was found in the South African cave of Makapansgat which Australopithecines (fossil hominids of two to three million years ago) had brought from at least 32 kilometres (20 miles) away, presumably because of the extraordinary resemblance to a human face on one side.

The reasons why there is so little solid evidence for 'art' before the Upper Palaeolithic period are simple. Firstly, it has been a long-standing dogma among archaeologists and anthropologists alike that

no such thing could exist before then. Earlier occurrences were simply dismissed as utilitarian marks, contamination from later levels, copying from or imports from Upper Palaeolithic neighbours (who thus brought 'beads to the natives'!) or freak one-offs (such as the famous cup marks associated with a Neanderthal burial at La Ferrassie, France) – with the result that many examples in the archaeological record have probably been missed or ignored. Secondly, there is the fundamental role of taphonomy (the processes by which material disintegrates or becomes part of the archaeological record): 'the severity of taphonomic distortion of archaeological evidence increases with its age'. In other words, we should expect much less evidence of artistic activity to have survived from the Middle Palaeolithic period than from the Upper, and far less again from the Lower. The earliest abundance of any form of archaeological evidence (especially of perishable kinds, such as the much touted beads and shells of the Early Upper Palaeolithic) should never be interpreted automatically as the earliest occurrence of a phenomenon. The further back in time we look, the more truncated, distorted and imperceptible will the traces of 'art' appear. But they are there, and now that we are beginning to recognize them, it is certain that many more will surface. As the history of archaeology shows repeatedly (the discoveries of open-air, Palaeolithic-style engravings since 1980 being merely the most recent case in point), once a phenomenon is accepted as real, it starts to be looked for and to be found.

(Above) A view inside Auditorium Cave, Bhimbetka (India), where the world's earliest known petroglyphs – a cup mark and a meandering line – have been found, probably dating to several hundred thousand years ago. The rock paintings visible at top right in the photograph are far more recent, though probably prehistoric.

(Right) The female figurine from Berekhat Ram (Israel), the oldest known figurative carving in the world – *c.* 233,000–800,000 years old. The fragment of tuff bears a natural resemblance to a female, and seems to have grooves around its 'neck' and along its 'arms'. Much rested on the question of whether these grooves were natural or humanly made; but microscopic analysis by Alexander Marshack has now made it clear that humans were responsible. In other words, this was an intentionally enhanced image and indisputably an 'art object'.

Among the best known painted stones in the world are those which characterize the very end of the Ice Age in Western Europe, the small 'Azilian pebbles' named after the huge French Pyrenean cave of Le Mas d'Azil where they were first identified in the 1880s by Edouard Piette. Of the nearly 2,000 known, more than 1,400 are from that one cave. Most are only a few centimetres in length. The motifs, usually in reddish ochre, are simple (mostly dots and lines) and seem to have been applied with the finger. Suggestions of their function range from 'art for art's sake' to totemic symbols or markers for a game.

for structures, but only 5–10 per cent of them were engraved and these seem to be distributed at random among the others. This suggests that the engravings lost all value once the ritual had been performed and they had been broken or dispersed; or simply that the engravings never had any ritual significance, and were done simply to pass the time, for practice, for storytelling, or perhaps even to personalize one's private bedwarmer!

Although it is the fine figurative examples which tend to be reproduced in publications, it should be stressed that – as with parietal art (see Chapter 5) – there are far more which are indecipherable, either because they are tiny fragments or because they are non-figurative. Some have a confused mass of superimposed lines, but experiments with the Gönnersdorf slabs show that a fresh engraving is very visible, owing to the presence of white powder in the incisions. When this is washed off, the effect is like wiping chalk off a slate, and a new engraving can be made (the incisions can be made quickly and easily). This suggests strongly that some of these engravings had significance for only a very brief time, and the 'associations' of superimposed animals on a given surface are not necessarily meaningful. On the other hand, there were plenty of stones available and each figure could easily have had one to itself if desired, so the superimpositions may indeed have had some significance.

The development of pottery

Contrary to the traditional view, pottery was not invented by the first farmers, in the Neolithic period. The principle of hardening clay by fire must have been observed a million times before then – indeed, every fire lit on a clay floor in a cave would have hardened the surface around it. The reason for the absence of pottery vessels before the Neolithic period in most parts of the world is simply that mobile hunters and gatherers do not, on the whole, have much use for heavy, fragile vessels, but rather need light containers made of organic materials. Pottery goes hand in hand with sedentism. Nevertheless, we now know that pottery did exist in the Ice Age in some areas – in Japan, it goes back to 14,000 BC on present evidence.

This Bronze Age (*c.* 1000 BC) grave group from Kinneff, Kincardineshire (Scotland), consists of a pottery food vessel decorated with impressed motifs, and two bronze armlets. Although simple in comparison with the impressive metal-work hoards and elaborate pottery from some sites in this period, such finds nevertheless serve to remind us that the rich graves of Wessex or elsewhere, usually used to illustrate this period, are highly exceptional, and that the vast majority of graves were more modest in their contents.

The oldest known ceramics – terracottas – date to about 26,000 years ago. Comprising, small, well-modelled figurines of animals and humans, they have been found at the open-air sites of Dolní Věstonice, Pavlov and Předmostí (Czech Republic). Recent analysis has revealed that they were modelled in local, wetted loess soil, and fired at temperatures of 500°–800° C (932°–1472° F) in special kilns away from

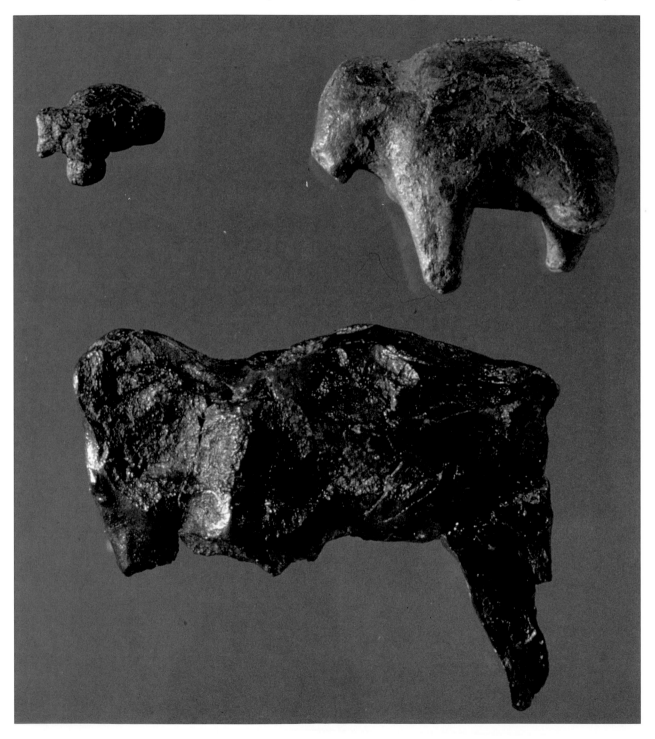

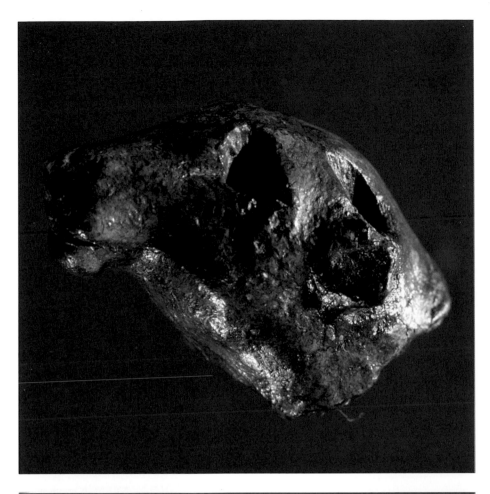

Small fired clay figurines of animals (about 26,000 years old) from Dolní Věstonice (Czech Republic). *(Opposite)* Probable mammoths, and *(this page)* heads of big cats. Fragments of clay animal figurines, of similar age, have recently been found at Krems-Wachtberg (Austria).

Baubles, bangles and beads

Most known Palaeolithic beads (over 13,000) are ivory specimens from the three burials of Sungir, Russia, which date to about 25,000 years ago – that is, to the Streletsian, a culture of Middle Palaeolithic origin. They were arranged in rows across the forehead and temples, across the body, down the arms and legs and around the ankles. Rather than being sewn onto garments one at a time, it is far more likely that they were strung on lengths of sinew, which were then attached to clothing. It has been estimated that each Sungir bead would have required about forty-five minutes for its manufacture (cutting the tusk, drilling the hole, etc.), which means that each body had about 2,625 hours of beadwork buried with it.

This female figurine in limestone, found at the Russian site of Kostenki in 1988, is by far the biggest such object known from the Ice Age. The height of the surviving fragment is 13.5 centimetres (5.5 inches). It is noteworthy not only for its massive size and the prominent navel, but also for the bracelets on either wrist, which are joined together at the front like a set of handcuffs.

Huge quantities of shell beads are also commonly found with burials of much later prehistoric cultures, for example in Polynesia; while at Khok Phanom Di, a necropolis in Thailand dating to the second millennium BC, a female skeleton nicknamed the 'Princess' was buried with more than 120,000 beads.

A great deal of experimental reconstruction of beads of different kinds has been done, mostly to learn more of the particular techniques employed and the time required.

An awareness of self?

A bizarre view, much promoted in recent years, is that the 'awareness of self', as evidenced in bead decoration, arose in the Upper Palaeolithic period in Europe – notably in the Dordogne region of France – in other words, that there is a European origin for art, language, social complexity and personal decoration. This theory is flawed in a number of ways. First, there is no evidence that the Early Upper Palaeolithic beads were for personal adornment, rather than part of the decoration of collective objects (such as hides or emblems) associated with a burial or accidentally dispersed through a site. Second, the Eurocentric presumption that the Dordogne beads were the earliest form of decoration does not stand up to the evidence: features on Upper Palaeolithic figurines suggest that decorations, presumably made of perishable materials – twined thongs, belts, aprons, bracelets, armbands,

headbands, anklets, etc – were far more common than beads. Most forms of body ornamentation are unlikely to be detected by archaeology: tattoos, body-painting, cicatrices, infibulations, deformations, hairstyles, and most forms of decorative objects. And third, there is no solid correlation between early beads and modern humans. There is no evidence that anatomically modern humans in Africa, the Near East or Asia produced bone or ivory beads, although they presumably had language, ritual, personal decoration and social complexity. Conversely, since it is now known that the Neanderthal occupants of the northern French cave of Arcy-sur-Cure had beads (objects incised with a groove around the top), it is sheer prejudice to insist that they did not make these themselves. So the Neanderthals could certainly understand the concept, production and use of beads. The Dordogne's 'transition' or 'revolution' therefore has only a very limited regional and archaeological validity – it is by no means evolutionary or universal.

(*Opposite*) Necklace from Mount Stuart, Bute (Scotland), an example of the spacer-plate jet necklaces of the northern British Bronze Age (*c.* 1000 BC), thought to have been prestige goods made in Yorkshire and distributed from there to other regions. This specimen, like others, displays considerable signs of wear and refurbishment. The necklace, comprising numerous beads interspersed with decorated spacers, was discovered in a burial.

the living area. Almost all terracottas are fragmentary and the shape of their fractures implies that they were broken by thermal shock – that is, they were placed, while still wet, in the hottest part of the fire, and thus deliberately caused to explode. In other words, rather than carefully made *objets d'art*, they may have been used in some special ritual.

Baked clay figurines are also known from later in the Ice Age at a number of sites in North Africa, the French Pyrenees and Siberia. However, it is certainly in the Neolithic period, or its equivalent in other parts of the world, that ceramic figurines and vessels become superabundant. Quite apart from its wide variety of shapes, the decoration also spans a wide spectrum of possibilities, from simple finger marks to incisions and indentations, appliquéd work and of course painted designs. Among the most spectacular productions of the potter's art are the fifth-century BC Lydenburg heads of Southern Africa, the vessels of the Mimbres culture of the south-west United States, the colourful ceramics of Peru's Nasca culture, and, of course, the amazing array of detailed and often very realistic depictions in the Moche pottery of Peru.

It took some time for it to be realized that prehistoric pottery vessels were a relic of ancient peoples. For example, in some parts of Europe during Medieval times, pots (probably Late Bronze Age cremation urns of *c.* 700–1200 BC) which were ploughed up or unearthed by burrowing animals were often seen as 'magic crocks' which had either grown in the ground or been made in mines by gnomes! In more recent times, there have been two major focuses to the study of prehistoric pottery. The first is typology – that is, arranging these extraordinarily abundant, ubiquitous and durable relics of the ancient past into different categories, based on their shape, fabric and decoration, and trying to assess their relative ages. Innumerable chronological sequences of pottery types have been created: these have sometimes almost seemed like an end in themselves but their real use has been as a tool for further research. (Pottery was a major means of dating later prehistoric cultures before the radio-carbon revolution after the Second World War brought the prossibility of obtaining direct dates from organic material.)

The second focus of study has been on the technology required to produce the vessels – the source of the clay, its preparation and tempering (with, for example, plant material, sand, shell or mica), the shaping of the vessel (whether handcoiled or wheelthrown), its firing, and its decoration. Experiments have produced many valuable insights into these processes, as has ethnoarchaeology – the on-the-spot study of how modern-day 'primitive' peoples make their pottery vessels.

Such ethnographic studies are also shedding great light on the social or symbolic aspects of pottery production and decoration. For example, American archaeologist Donald Lathrap has worked among the Shipibo-Conibo Indians of the Upper Amazon (eastern Peru), whose modern ceramic styles can be traced back into their prehistory in the first millennium AD. He found that most of the women are potters, each producing vessels primarily for her own household, not only for cooking but also for storage. The pots are handcoiled with local clays, with a variety of materials (including ground-up potsherds) as tempers, but other minerals and pigments are imported from neighbouring regions for decorative work.

Metal work

Although nothing much is known of the earliest discoveries and exploitation of different metals, the development of this new technology – at different times in different parts of the world and employing a variety of metals (primarily copper, bronze, iron, gold and silver) – swiftly brought new opportunities not only for functional tools and weapons, but also for personal adornment and the expression of wealth and status. Many of the most intricate and dazzling pieces of artwork from the prehistoric world are those of metal – jewellery, ornaments, figurines and decorated vessels.

Quite apart from its qualities of toughness or sharpness, which could often be rivalled by stone or pottery, metal also had one important virtue which these other materials lacked: if broken, it could be recycled – melted down and re-used. In addition, gold had one outstanding quality among metals: while copper and bronze turn green, iron rusts and silver becomes dull and distorted, gold remains incorruptible. It appears to last for ever and this explains its widespread use as a material of display and of symbolic prestige in many ancient cultures.

As with pottery and other materials, early finds of metal work served mainly to produce chronological and classificatory schemes based on type, shape, style, decoration and relative age. Attention also focused on the evidence for trade and on the technological development of metallurgy. The simplest and earliest use of metal appears to be the cold-hammering and shaping of nuggets of native copper – for example, in the 'Old Copper' culture of the northern United States and Canada (2000–4000 BC) or at early farming sites in Turkey and Iran before 7000 BC. Subsequently, annealing – the heating and hammering of copper – was followed by the smelting of brightly-coloured copper ores, the casting of copper in open moulds and two-piece moulds, and its alloying with tin to make the far stronger bronze. Some prehistoric cultures achieved amazing prowess in far more complex processes: for example, filigree work (involving wires and soldering), granulation (the soldering of grains of metal to a metal background), and plating (where different metals are bonded together). It is now known that the ancient Peruvians used methods of electrochemical plating of precious metals which were thought to have been invented in Renaissance Europe!

One ingenious technique for casting metal was the lost-wax or *cire perdue* method, which could produce complex shapes and which reached a high level of perfection in the New World. This technique involves modelling the desired form in wax and then encasing this model in fine clay, leaving a small channel to the exterior. When the clay is heated, the melted wax can be poured out. The clay thus becomes a hollow mould, and molten metal can be poured into it. Once the clay

casting is broken away, one is left with a metal copy of the original wax model. Naturally, each mould could only be used once.

Apart from metal art objects as such, other objects, such as vessels, tools, weapons and accessories, were also decorated, making them art objects in their own right – from safety-pins to daggers and swords, from razors to mirrors. The Benin brasses of Nigeria, the gold work of the Scythians and that of many prehistoric cultures of South America (see Chapter 9), are just a few of the innumerable examples of breathtaking metal portable art produced. Much of the decoration may have been simply that; yet, as with pottery, ethnography and ethnoarchaeology suggest that the particular shapes or motifs and patterns chosen will have conveyed messages of different kinds – such as group identity or religious symbolism. The immense variety of possible messages is mirrored in parietal art (see Chapters 7 and 8).

The size of images or motifs in portable art is, of course, limited and often defined by the shape of the object and the space available. The smallest include tiny beads or engraved images so small that they are scarcely visible to the naked eye. But 'portable art' is a relative term; for while the vast majority of objects are indeed easy to move around, there is a whole class of objects – stone blocks, small statues, etc. – which are extremely heavy,

A brass cock from Benin City (Nigeria), probably dating to the eighteenth century AD. About 51 centimetres (20 inches) high, it was probably used to decorate a shrine at the Queen Mother's court, and is a fine example of this culture's skill in working brass, which was also used for heads and a series of remarkable wall plaques featuring people in a variety of scenes.

although they could be moved. The largest, inevitably, are so big and heavy that they take us into the other main category of prehistoric imagery – parietal or rock art.

Art on Rocks and Walls

CHAPTER 5

Petroglyphs are the elementary thought of mankind.

Adolf Bastian

Parietal art – predominantly on walls and rocks but also on ceilings and floors – is still precisely where the prehistoric artists put it and meant it to be. This is a factor of major importance in the study of its content and significance, not only in terms of landscape but also from the point of view of where on the rock it was placed. In northern Australia, it is known that sorcery paintings – made, for example, to kill someone – are placed as high as possible to increase their potency. In Europe's Ice Age cave art, the incorporation into images of natural rock or stalagmite forms is common – most famously in the bulging bison bodies on the Altamira ceiling or the spotted horse panel of Pech Merle – while all over the world one can see rock art fitted to natural rock surfaces of different shapes and sizes and images continuing over edges or around corners or linked to cracks and cavities in different ways.

Innumerable different factors may have influenced the placing of rock art. Some are physical: the choice of rocks (smooth surfaces, hardness, shape), the inclination and orientation of the rock faces, the accessibility of the site, and links with trails or water. Others are phenomenal – attributes which stimulate visual responses such as prominent locations, auditory responses such as sound effects, aesthetic responses, and spiritual responses (good or bad places and places associated with creation stories or vision quests).

HUMAN OR NATURAL MARKINGS?

The first step in any study of parietal art is to be sure that it was produced by humans. This may seem a ridiculous point to raise when faced with the animals of

(Opposite) **Boulder bearing several petroglyphs of big-horn sheep in the Big Petroglyph Canyon, Coso Range, California (United States), showing its context in the landscape and its visibility from far off. Date probably before 1000 AD.**

This mark, about 22 centimetres (*c.* 9 inches) long, on the ceiling of Robertson Cave, South Australia, resembles an engraving – yet it was actually produced by the claws of an extinct species of animal, probably *Thylacoleo carnifex*. Date unknown.

Prehistoric paintings in the rock shelter of Perna 4, Piauí (Brazil). The ladder-like motif at the right is actually the remains of the nest of mud-daubing insects.

Lascaux Cave or the rock carvings of Utah, but just as some portable 'engravings' have been proved to be natural (see Chapter 4), so it is all too easy to attribute patches of colour or apparently engraved lines on rocks or in caves to humans when in fact they are entirely natural: minerals occurring on, or emerging from, the surface; cracks, circles or grooves in the rock caused by fossil inclusions, etc; or marks made by animals. Deep scratches made by cave-bear claws are a common phenomenon in European caves, for example, and can resemble simple non-figurative engravings (indeed, some motifs in caves in France and Australia are thought to incorporate animal scratches, while others appear to imitate them). Some clusters of tiny, very finely engraved lines, found in European caves, which seem to form shapes resembling mammoths and schematic female figures, were actually produced by bat-claws! In Brazil and elsewhere, mud-daubing insects leave reddish 'motifs' – ovals with internal parallel barring – on rock-shelter walls and these often closely resemble paintings.

TYPES OF PARIETAL ART

Parietal art forms a continuum with portable art through the intermediate category of stone blacks, stelae (upright slabs or pillars), totem poles and statues which were large and heavy but could be moved around. As with any other category of

archaeological evidence, untold quantities of parietal art have disappeared for ever – for example, any works in snow or sand, most paintings in the open air, all kinds of images through weathering, etc. – and we are left with the small fraction which has survived and the even smaller fraction of that which has been discovered.

The simplest form of marking a surface is with the finger, and innumerable examples are known of apparently non-figurative finger tracings in the soft layer of clay on cave walls and ceilings – for example, there are enormous expanses of such marks in several caves in Australia. In some caves such as Pech Merle in France and the Mud Glyph Caves of Tennessee the tracings also include apparent figures of animals or people.

Finger tracings in Koonalda Cave, South Australia. They cover at least 75 square metres (c. 810 square feet) in this cave, and seem to follow or emphasize the topography of the walls. Such marks exist in numerous caves in this region, always underlying (and hence predating) any engraved marks on the walls. Date unknown.

Engravings and petroglyphs

Engraving – cutting the rock with a sharp tool – is by far the most common technique employed in the European Ice Age caves and ranges from extremely fine lines (which are almost invisible except when lit from the side) to broad, deep lines, as well as scratching and scraping. Virtually any sharp-edged flint could be used, with stone picks employed for deep engravings and bas-reliefs.

For petroglyphs (carvings pecked or hammered into rock), found in rock shelters and on rocks in the open air all over the world, stone picks and grinders were

(*Above*) One of the twenty-three engraved and carved vertical megaliths, around 2 metres (*c.* 6 feet) high, lining the passage grave of Gavrinis, Brittany (France). Late fourth millennium BC.

(*Right*) The Three Kings petroglyph panel at Dry Fork, Ashley, Utah (United States), is located very high up in a position dominating a valley and can be seen from far away. The life-size central figure has been referred to as the Sun Carrier, but it is the 'negative' figure to the right, carved in bas-relief, which gives this group its special impact. Date unknown, but estimates vary between 700 and 1200 AD.

(Right) The headless clay bear of Montespan, Haute Garonne (France) is over 1 metre (3 feet) long, 60 centimetres (24 inches) high, and comprises about 700 kilos (1,500 pounds) of clay. Most of the surviving clay work in these Pyrenean caves probably dates to *c.* 14,000–11,000 BC.

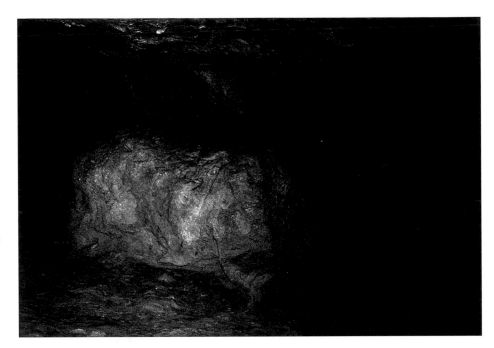

(Below) The central horse in the sculptured frieze at Cap Blanc, Dordogne (France) is about 2 metres (*c.* 7 feet) long, and dates to *c.* 15,000–10,000 BC. Note the two deer heads above it.

used, with metal tools sometimes adopted, where available, in later periods. The depth and type of mark depend on the hardness of the rock and of the tools used, as well as on the degree of weathering, and of course on the artists' motivation. In many cases, patination as well as lichens have made the petroglyphs difficult to see except in oblique light, since they are the same colour as the surrounding rock, whereas elsewhere – for example in the deserts of America or Australia – the petroglyphs still often stand out as very light images contrasting strongly with the dark rock surface into which they are pecked. In a few cases such as the Three Kings' panel in Utah, or a serpent at Horseshoe Tank in Arizona, the rock varnish was removed from around the design until the desired image was achieved. Petroglyphs vary widely from simple, small cupules (cup marks) – virtually a universal motif and of great antiquity – to highly complex and sophisticated figurative and apparently non-figurative images.

Clay and stone sculptures
Work in clay is best known – that is, it has mainly been discovered or has survived – in the Ice Age caves of the French Pyrenees. It ranges from fingerholes and engravings in the cave floor or in artificial banks of clay to bas-relief figures, haut-relief figures (the most famous of which are the two bison in the Tuc d'Audoubert), and even a fully three-dimensional statue in the form of the headless, sphinx-like bear of Montespan. Perhaps the best known clay works in later cultures are the intricate adobe bas-reliefs at Chan Chan and other sites of the Chimú culture in northern Peru.

This fine carved stone, about 1 metre (*c.* 3 feet) long, from Pierowall, Westray (Orkney) was found during quarrying in 1981. It was originally associated with a Neolithic chambered tomb, and may have been its entrance lintel. The motifs were first pecked and then smoothed into V-section grooves. Probably fourth to third millennium BC.

Parietal sculpture in stone began in the Ice Age, with the bas-reliefs of central France and the Dordogne, where the limestone could be shaped. All known examples are in well-lit sites, either in shallow rock shelters or in cave mouths. Some of the friezes are of considerable length and depth – for example, at Cap Blanc, where figures reach a depth of 30 centimetres (*c.* 12 inches) in places. Most of the French bas-relief sculptures seem to have originally been painted. In later periods there are innumerable examples, from the geometric and zoomorphic friezes of the Maltese temples to the complex bas-relief sculptures of Tiwanaku, Bolivia.

Large free-standing sculptures are rarer in prehistoric times, though examples are known in a wide variety of cultures, from the megalithic statue-menhirs of south-west Europe or San Agustín, Colombia, to the 'Lanzón' in the main temple at Chavín, Peru – a 4.5-metres (*c.* 15-foot) tall, slender, knife-shaped stone, carved with a low relief of a 'smiling' or 'snarling god' with snakes for hair. Even the Celts could produce work of this kind, as shown by the recently unearthed statue of an aristocrat from Glauburg, Germany.

(Opposite left) **Statue of an aristocrat from Glauburg (Germany). Dating to** *c.* **500 BC, this remarkable statue was discovered in 1995. It is about 2 metres (6 feet) high and weighs about 230 kilos (500 pounds). Note the beard and the bizarre 'leaf crown', already known from several other Celtic carvings.**

(Left) **By far the best known and most spectacular statues from prehistory must be the** *moai* **of Easter Island. Within the short period from about the eleventh to the sixteenth centuries, this tiny, isolated island culture produced around 1,000 of these stone giants, carved in soft volcanic tuff with thousands of hard basalt hammerstones. Hundreds remain unfinished in the Rano Raraku quarry, displaying clearly their method of manufacture; many others stand, buried by sediment up to their necks, on the volcano's inner and outer slopes; while hundreds of finished statues were transported and erected on numerous great platforms around the coast. Facing inland, these ancestor figures – all variations on a theme, and ranging from about 2–10 metres (***c.*** 6–32 feet) in height – watched over the villagers.**

Cave paintings

The final major category of parietal work is that of pictographs – that is, paintings, involving the application of primarily mineral pigments (usually obtained locally) as well as charcoal. Occasionally, other organic materials were used: for example, the images in the Bulgarian cave of Magura appear to have been executed with

Part of the great painted sandstone rock shelter known as Magnificent Gallery, in the Laura region of Queensland (Australia), showing human figures, kangaroos, etc. It was rediscovered in 1977 by rock art specialist Percy Trezise, who had seen it from the air, and proved to contain about 450 paintings, often superimposed. Excavations in the shelter in 1989 revealed a period when pigments were used around 8,000 BC, and a second beginning 1,200 years ago and continuing up to the European contact period (1875 AD).

thick, dark brown bat guano; powdered ivory has been detected in white paint in
Angolan rock art; red cochineal is known in Andean sites; while 'beeswax' images
are known in northern Australia. (For the latter, the small pellets pressed onto the
rock-shelter walls to make abstract designs or figurative silhouettes were collected
from the nests of the local stingless bee, and consist not only of bee-secreted wax

but also of organic material – resins, gums, saps – collected by the bees as they construct their hives.) In rare instances, colour was not applied but discarded – some Norwegian caves and rock shelters contain images made by removing deposits of iron oxides to make a contrast with the surrounding colour.

There is a tremendous variety in types of painting – simple lines and outline-images, prints and stencils, monochrome silhouette figures, outlines with infill, and sophisticated bichromes and polychromes. Very few clues have survived as to how the paints were applied to the rock. The simplest method was obviously to use the fingers, and this was certainly the case in some French Ice Age caves, for example. Normally, however, some kind of tool was employed, although few have survived. These include specimens from the Peruvian site of Toquepala, a cave decorated with red figures of animals and hunters which yielded two small 'brushes' of wood with tips of wool impregnated with red ochre, stratified in levels dating to almost 10,000 years ago. It is known from ethnographic testimony that the Chumash of California used the little point of a badger tail for painting fine details and dots. In addition, organic fibres have been found within paintings: for example, in the Laura region of Australia's Cape York peninsula about 21 per cent of paints analysed have proved to contain fibrous strands and splinters of wood, which may derive from a binding agent but could also have become detached from brushes during the artistic production. Vessels and mortars are known from many areas and periods, and where these contain crushed pigment they provide insights into the techniques employed. However, many hollows assumed to be for pigment may be nothing of the kind: for example, some present-day Australian Aborigines have explained that ochre was mixed with water in wooden dishes or boab nut containers; whereas the grinding hollows in rock shelters were for processing plant foodstuffs and sometimes animal parts, but only rarely for the preparation of ochres.

Painted panel at Nanguluwurr, Northern Territory (Australia). At bottom right is a dolphin, 1.3 metres (c. 4 feet) long. Note the imprints at left made by bunches of paint-soaked grass being pressed or thrown against the rock. Date unknown.

In many areas, depending on the geology, the freshly applied paint stained the rock surface and seeped into its microscopic pores. As the natural weathering gradually evaporated the water or organic binder it was mixed with, the pigment actually became part of the rock. This helps to explain how painted images could survive millennia of burial (see Chapter 6) and, even more amazingly, how some haematite paintings in the Laura region of Queensland have survived being inundated after heavy rain each wet season.

Stencils and prints

The simplest way of leaving the mark of an object on a wall is to smear that object with paint and then bring it into contact with, or throw it at, the wall. Hence, in Australia's Northern Territory and the Kimberley, one finds the traces of what seem to be grass-bunches in red on some shelter walls, as well as objects of string or perhaps pieces of paperbark and even animal tails. Some were pressed against the rock, while others were thrown onto surfaces up to 8 metres (26 feet) above the ground in Arnhem Land sites. In the Kimberley, however, some enigmatic prints of objects have been found more than 20 metres (65.5 feet) up on inaccessible, sheer walls, yet the fine detail visible on them indicates that they were pressed onto the rock, not thrown. In several Patagonian shelters the prehistoric occupants made circular red dots – some of which even have a concentric design – on high ceilings, apparently by throwing ochre-soaked balls or bolas up there, presumably for amusement.

Red spots high on the ceiling of Cueva de las Manos, Patagonia (Argentina), made by throwing paint-soaked balls or bolas up there – either for amusement or perhaps for some more symbolic purpose. Date unknown.

Red hand prints at the Fate Bell rock shelter, Seminole Canyon, Texas (United States). Such marks are abundant in this region, where they are thought to post-date 600 AD. Note the nested arc motif on the hands which, curiously, is also prominent in the numerous hand prints of Southern Africa.

In Australia, it is thought that images were purposely put in difficult or 'impossible' positions so that they would appear to have been made by spirits rather than by humans. Elsewhere – for example at Huashan, China (see Chapter 1) – the explanation may simply be akin to modern graffiti artists placing their tag in guarded or dangerous places as a rite of passage or perhaps just as a matter of bravado and ego.

By far the most common object to leave its mark in this way was the human hand. Hand prints, usually in red, are found in many cultures, from a few of the Ice Age decorated caves of France and Spain to late prehistoric sites in North America and elsewhere. For example, at the site of Clavelitos in southern Baja California, Mexico, there are thousands of hand prints on rocks at heights of 6–7 metres (c. 20–23 feet) above the ground, which, in places, have been superimposed on and obliterate all previous paintings: their height limit appears to be the maximum distance reachable by one person standing on another or using natural ledges. Hand

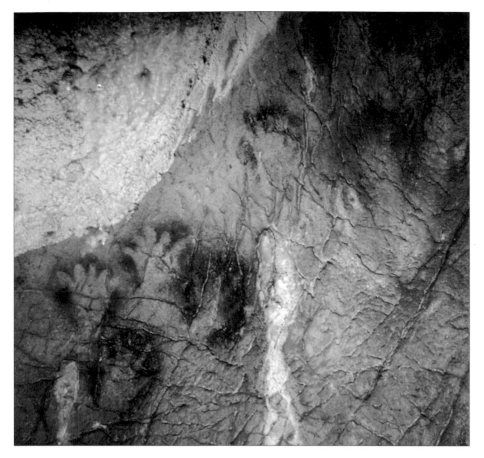

prints are also known in about 250 sites on Southern Africa, such as Elands Bay Cave, some of them decorated with curved lines (just like some North American examples). It has been found that right-hand prints are twice as common as left and that most belong to children and teenagers.

More complex, but also far more frequent, are stencils – primarily of hands (sometimes with forearm attached) but also occasionally of feet and even objects. In most cases, the paint for stencils seems to have been sprayed, though at the French Ice Age cave of Gargas close-up photography and detailed investigation have recently revealed that a pad was used for many of the site's more than 230 hands, while a white specimen in the same cave apparently had white material crushed around the fingers.

It has traditionally been assumed that, because most stencils (unlike prints) are left hands, this denotes predominantly right-handed people. Although this is likely to be correct, the stencils are poor evidence for it, since paintings might have been done by mouth rather than by the dominant hand or the hands might have been stencilled palm-upwards.

Dates from the French caves of Gargas and Cosquer suggest that the practice of making hand stencils goes back at least 27,000 years. However, by far the most

Hand stencils, Cueva de las Manos (Argentina). In Patagonia, enormous clusters and superimpositions of stencils – sometimes hundreds of them – in a wide variety of colours can be found in rock shelters such as Cueva de las Manos and Los Toldos, where they are claimed to date back to *c*. 7300 BC. Occasionally, one finds stencils of human feet and also of the feet of the *ñandú* (the rhea, the local large flightless bird) among the hands.

spectacular collections of hand stencils are to be found in Patagonia (Argentina) – in rock shelters such as Los Toldos and Cueva de las Manos – and in Australia. (Curiously, hand stencils appear completely absent from the rock art of Southern Africa, where hand prints are so common.) In Australia, one finds not only hands, and occasional emu tracks, but also objects such as boomerangs and axes. Undoubtedly the most impressive arrays of stencils are to be found in Queensland, especially in Carnarvon Gorge where they are accumulated on the white walls of major shelters like Art Gallery and Cathedral Cave.

Although, as mentioned earlier, some purists would deny that a stencil is 'art', since it involves merely the mechanical reproduction of an object, most researchers would class the phenomenon as art, and the groupings of them in Patagonia, Queensland and elsewhere are so colourful, striking and beautiful as to have an overwhelming aesthetic impact. But what do hand stencils mean?

In the absence of the original makers, we do not know. There are many possible explanations: they could be signatures, property marks, memorials, love magic, a wish to leave a mark in some sacred place, a sign of caring about or being responsible for a site, a record of growth, or a personal marker – 'I was here'. The specific reasons for making such marks only seem to be remembered for a couple of generations.

A corner of Art Gallery in Carnarvon Gorge, Queensland (Australia). Here, whole series of boomerangs, axes and nets can be found stencilled on the white sandstone, with compositions involving hands with forearms, sometimes crossed over each other. The main panel is 62 metres (c. 204 feet) long, with 1,343 engravings and 646 stencils and paintings. Date unknown. At least a dozen stencils of full humans – mostly children but also of adults – as well as of small animals are also known in central Queensland and elsewhere in Australia.

Geoglyphs – drawing on the landscape

Not content with producing images of modest size scattered around their environment, prehistoric people sometimes undertook the decoration of hillsides or even entire landscapes – a category of art known as ground drawings or geoglyphs. Among the most famous are the giant hill figures of southern England, images made by removing turf above chalk to make a bright white line against a green background. These figures require regular scouring to maintain their whiteness and to prevent them from being overgrown. The Long Man of Wilmington and the very phallic Cerne Abbas Giant are of unknown age and controversy still rages over the date of the latter in particular; but there is no doubt that the Uffington Horse is prehistoric.

In the north-east United States there exist large prehistoric earthen mounds, some of which were built in animal shapes. The best known of these is the Great Serpent Mound of Ohio, dating probably to the final centuries BC, which is almost 390 metres (1,280 feet) long, 6 metres (c. 20 feet) wide and 1.5 metres (5 feet) high. It has the form of a curved serpent which seems to hold an egg in its jaws. In Arnhem Land and neighbouring areas, Aborigines make sand or earth sculptures during mortuary or healing rites – human-like forms, images of giant fishtraps, and so forth. It is very probable that such ephemeral art forms also existed in prehistory.

More durable are 'desert intaglios' made in rocky or desert areas by moving aside stones coated with a natural dark varnish to expose the lighter-coloured soil beneath. These exist in Australia, Chile, Arizona and California – in fact, about 300 figures of various large sizes are known in the deserts of the American south-west, and radio-carbon dating (see Chapter 6) of organic material growing on gravel in figures near Blythe, California, has led to claims that they were created in about 890 AD. To the local native Americans, the images are living shrines made by their remote ancestors; but at least one has been used for ceremonial purposes fairly recently, with offerings of feathers, coins and buttons being deposited in small piles of stones around a stick-figure in Arizona. In northern Australia, in historic times, large designs were observed on the surface of the plains. They were made in the dry season, while the ground was still damp, by pounding the earth with stones to make it smooth. These images, unlike the true desert intaglios, were impermanent, but it is probable that they were also made here in prehistoric times.

By far the best known examples, however, are the spectacular and gigantic figures on the plain at Nasca, Peru. Best visible from the air, these images – birds, a monkey, a spider, whales, etc, up to about 200 metres (650 feet) in size – are found amidst geometric shapes such as trapezoids of about 3 kilometres (2 miles), as well as numerous straight lines of up to 10 kilometres (6 miles). Some believe that these lines are ceremonial pathways, while others see a great deal of astronomical involvement in the whole Nasca layout, with the images perhaps representing constellations. After the dark, well-varnished cobbles were moved aside to make the pictures, organic material accumulated on the lighter cobbles beneath and was encapsulated in new rock varnish. Radio-carbon dating of this organic matter provided results from 190 BC to 660 AD, a timespan which has been claimed to be a minimum age for the geoglyphs.

A different kind of surface image is known from Canada. Petroforms, instead of involving the removal of stones, are made by setting out small stones to form large outline figures or geometric shapes. In the deserts of the American south-west, there are long, twisting lines of boulders, laid out side by side in abstract patterns. On the northern plains of North America, prehistoric inhabitants constructed 'medicine wheels' by this method – stone alignments in the form of radiating spokes. Some may be as much as 5,500 years old and they probably had many different purposes: memorials, boundary markers, calendars, or locations linked with ceremonies or vision quests (see Chapter 8).

Aerial view of the white horse at Uffington (England), about 110 metres (c. 360 feet) long and about 40 metres (c. 130 feet) high. Long assumed to be of Iron Age date, through comparison with stylized horses on coins of the period, this chalk figure was recently claimed, through optical dating of silt in its lowest levels, to be 1,000 years older and to belong to the Bronze Age (c. 1400–600 BC).

(Left) Aerial view of desert intaglios near Blythe, California (United States). The giant human, about 29 metres (94 feet) from head to toe, is thought by some to represent evil. The circular patterns around it were caused by off-road vehicles. Date uncertain.

(Below) The enormous figure of a monkey at Nasca. The animal figures on this desert plain in Peru resemble designs painted on pottery dating to 1–400 AD. Their outline usually comprises a single line which never crosses itself. Entrance and exit points were provided so that these lines could be used as (presumably ceremonial) pathways.

to produce satisfactory results, but when he used a sharp granite flake he produced good results with the greatest of ease.

Elsewhere, such as in the Canary Islands, there was great debate as to whether the petroglyphs had been produced with metal tools or with a hard stone point of obsidian or basalt. As mentioned earlier (see Chapter 2), it was Dr Bonnet, in the Sahara, who in 1889 noticed the abundance of worked flints close to three petroglyph sites and wrote that it was probably 'with a fragment of flint' that the hunters had engraved this 'gigantic page of their history'. Although he noticed that most of the flints were broken and he was unable to find one with a shape and size that seemed perfectly suited to the engraved lines, his experiments with different types of flint gave identical positive results.

In the twentieth century such studies became more rigorous and scientific. A major pioneer was the geologist G-B-M. Flamand whose lengthy 1921 study of the rock engravings of a region in Algeria included an investigation into the technology of their production, which included making numerous cross-sections of the engraved lines to show their differing shapes, depths and directions. Flamand also undertook a detailed examination and comparison of patinas on the rock surfaces and on the engravings, involving chemical, macroscopic and petrographic (thin section) analyses, to establish their composition and how they were formed.

After Flamand's work, it took some time for the technology of parietal engraving to return to the forefront of rock art studies, but in the 1980s a French couple, Brigitte and Gilles Delluc, undertook a detailed investigation into the production of

This large figure of a crocodile, over 2 metres (7 feet) long, was pecked and incised into rock at Wadi Mathendush, at Messak Settafet, Fezzan (Libya). Note the baby under its tail. This animal is extremely rare in Saharan art, and shows that water must once have been abundant there. Date unknown.

In a pioneering experiment carried out on Easter Island in the 1950s by the expedition of the Norwegian adventurer Thor Heyerdahl, the islanders were asked to produce the outline of a *moai* (statue) in the quarry of Rano Raraku, using the same basalt picks as their ancestors. Six men outlined a 5-metre (16-foot) statue on the quarry wall, by first measuring it out on the rock face in arm- and hand-lengths and then bashing with picks, each blow raising a bit of dust. The rock was frequently splashed with water to soften it (the spongy tuff absorbs it), yet the picks quickly became blunted and had to be sharpened or replaced. It took three days for these unpractised men to produce an outline, shown here, from which it was (somewhat riskily) deduced that it would have taken twelve to fifteen months to complete the statue. Experiments were also carried out by the same expedition in the transportation and erection of a giant stone statue. Research into these problems continues to this day, using facsimile statues of cement.

the engraved lines in Ice Age caves and rock shelters and on stone blocks. In particular, they began to produce cartographic representations of images, encoding the different types of lines. Other researchers, emulating the methods used by Marshack and d'Errico on portable engravings (see Chapter 4), have investigated the superimpositions and direction of finger markings in caves.

Where petroglyphs and sculptures are concerned, there has been less work, although the French team which has undertaken a long-term investigation of the carvings of Monte Bego has examined the technology of the petroglyphs through microscopy and experimentation. They have found, for example, that the contours of some dagger images were probably made by incising around a real dagger using a fine point.

In the area of pictographs, however, a wide variety of studies have been carried out. The outstanding pioneer in experimental painting is the French specialist Michel Lorblanchet whose deep knowledge of Ice Age art, coupled with a familiarity with the techniques of the Australian Aboriginal artists, have given him unique insights into the production of cave paintings. In his first major experiment, he memorized every mark in the Black Frieze of the cave of Pech Merle. (On this panel, measuring 7 by 2.5 metres/23 by 8 feet, there are twenty-five animal outlines – mammoths, aurochs (wild oxen), horses, bisons.) He then reproduced the whole thing on an equally smooth panel of similar dimensions in another cave, lit by a lamp in his left hand. Each figure took an average of one to four minutes, so the whole frieze required about an hour, including initial sketching with a stick, a fact which underlines the likelihood that much rock art was probably done in intensive bursts by talented artists.

This stone, found in a burial at the Coldstream Cave (South Africa) in 1911, bears paintings of three people in black, white and red. Many different interpretations have been suggested, but rock art specialist Bert Woodhouse has argued that the central figure is carrying, in the right hand, a fine-pointed quill for producing fine painted lines, and, in the left, a stone palette. If so, this is one of the very few known depictions of a prehistoric artist (presumably a Bushman). Date unknown.

Superimpositions are often difficult to verify: where two painted images overlap, the fainter and more deteriorated image is not necessarily the more ancient. If the older image has the stronger colour, it can easily appear to overlie the younger picture which is actually on top of it. Such cases require very careful field observations and technological assistance. Experiments have been done to investigate problems of superimposition of different paints. In the cave of Lascaux, for example, it was long uncertain whether the red cows were on top of the black bulls or vice versa, because the two pigments had mixed. Infra-red pictures (which make red ochres appear transparent, so that other pigments can be seen beneath them) suggested that the bulls were done first. Experiments using samples of similar pigment found that red on top of black does not mix, but black on top of red does – therefore the bulls were clearly painted after the cows.

Red paint can be deceptive in other ways. For example, one cannot be certain that pictographs have always been red, because it is known that yellow goethite paint can change to red haematite in dry, hot conditions. Moreover, red pigment tends to be more durable than yellow or white and can remain when other colours have disappeared – hence, among the Bradshaws of the Kimberley, some images which

Australian rock art specialist Grahame Walsh's drawing of the largest known complete 'Bradshaw' human figure in Australia's Kimberley, which he discovered in 1991. The painted figure is 1.7 metres (5½ feet) long. Date unknown. Note the broad shoulders, horizontal head-dress and various kinds of tassel. To understand the delicate brush strokes which clearly produced these elegant figures, Walsh has studied the brush types used by oriental calligraphers, their very specific brush strokes, and the brush-holding techniques needed to achieve them – the pressure exerted and the direction of the stroke. All these techniques appear applicable to the Bradshaws, for some of which the artists definitely needed specialist brushes with tapered tips which permitted uninterrupted flows of equally specialized fine paints of high opacity.

Spit-painting – breathing life onto a cave wall

Most hand stencils, and many other images in some parts of the world, were produced by paint being sprayed onto the rock, rather than applied with brush or finger. Where paint was sprayed, a 'diffused halo' resulted around the hand. There are two possible methods of spraying – through a tube or directly from the mouth. If the paint was a dry powder, it can only have been applied through a tube onto a humid wall, or there would have been no adhesion. But if the paint was liquid, blowing it through a tube would concentrate it too much: experiments suggest that spraying from the mouth, about 7–10 centimetres (c. 2–4 inches) from the wall, is the easiest method and one which produces results most closely resembling the original stencils. Pursing the lips slightly projects a spray of fine droplets which form the required halo with diffuse edges. On average it takes about 3 grams of paint and between thirty and forty-five minutes to do each hand in this way, whereas the dry method can be quicker but uses 9–10 grams.

Armed with knowledge of the spitting techniques of the Aborigines, Michel Lorblanchet, the leading exponent of experimental reconstruction of cave paintings, has replicated the spotted horse frieze in the cave of Pech Merle by spitting ochre and charcoal from his mouth: by screening with his hands, he was able to create straight or fuzzy edges, while dots were produced by spitting the paint through a hole in a piece of leather, its distance from the wall determining the size of the dot. The hands and bent thumbs of the frieze were replicated with the stencils technique. This experiment revealed that the whole frieze could be done in thirty-two hours, though it was clearly built up in at least four episodes.

Spit-painting may have had symbolic significance. As Lorblanchet has said, 'Human breath, the most profound expression of a human being, literally breathes life onto a cave wall. The painter projected his being onto the rock.'

(*Above*) French prehistoric art specialist Michel Lorblanchet spitting paint from his mouth to create a stencil of his hand in an undecorated cave in the Quercy region of France. The sound of the soft repetitive spitting resembles the 'put-put' noise of a motorboat far out at sea.

(*Right*) Michel Lorblanchet has also produced a remarkable replica of a bichrome horse of Lascaux type by first sketching it in charcoal, then spitting a red infill with ochre, and finally spitting the mane with powdered charcoal.

seem originally to have been bichrome or even polychrome now consist only of the red parts. For example, complex series of red dots and dotted lines around some humans may be the surviving remnants of bichrome cords or ribbon-like appendages whose less stable colours have vanished.

Infra-red photography, with special cut-off filters, has been used to determine the use of different ochres and mixes of ochre within a single panel or composition: although the ochre itself becomes transparent, any impurities within it do not, so different mixes with different impurities can be detected. Infra-red spectrometry can also make compositions clearer by 'removing' the thin trickles where pigment has run; it can also counteract the effects of changes in humidity and wall conditions, which can make certain painted lines visible on some days and not on others – for parietal paintings 'live' in accordance with atmospheric conditions.

ART AND THE LANDSCAPE

As mentioned at the start of this chapter, one of the most precious aspects of parietal art is that it is located where the artist placed it. This means that its distribution can be examined and something of its relationship with the landscape can perhaps be learned – always bearing in mind that what has survived and been discovered

In some Brandberg shelters (Namibia), such as Ostrich Shelter shown here, ostriches are only represented by white necks and legs, with no indication of any other paint ever having existed inbetween. This suggests that feathers might have been stuck to the rock to form the body. It should never be taken for granted that the colours surviving on the wall were the only ones applied by the artist. Date unknown.

Petroglyphs in their landscape
on sandstone at McKee Springs
Wash, Utah (United States).
Note the flat 'hair' of the main
figure. It is uncertain what
these images are carrying:
suggestions such as shields,
bags or large blades have
been made, while some
researchers think these are
headhunters with trophies.
Probably 700–1200 AD.

(Opposite) View over the Massleberg petroglyph site, Bohuslän (Sweden), next to farmland. Date unknown, probably Bronze Age.

Petroglyphs in their landscape at Monte Bego. In this area of the Alps, about 50 square kilometres (*c.* 19 square miles), there are more than 100,000 petroglyphs at an altitude of about 2,000–2,600 metres (*c.* 6,560–8,530 feet), thought to date to about 4,000 years ago. The subvertical slant of many signs seems to point in certain directions. These signs may have been intended as indicators of the way to follow, showing herdsmen how to reach the higher pastures from the stony ground where the art is located. It is argued that this helps explain the very limited repertoire of the motifs – essentially horns, weapons/ tools, anthropomorphs (human forms), geometrics and dots – which were repeated to make the panels more visually arresting rather than to add information.

may be a tiny or distorted sample of what existed originally, since any paintings in the open air will have gone, as will wood carvings, dendroglyphs (carvings on trees), etc. Naturally, cave art only exists where there are caves and rock art where there are rocks, but within those limitations there is plenty of variation. The long-lasting quality of petroglyphs, and their placement at a few locations selected from the often very wide choice available, point to a deliberate and meaningful attempt to mark the landscape.

(*Opposite*) The Lightning Brothers painted at Ingaladdi, in the Victoria River District of Australia's Northern Territory. The figures are placed for maximum visual impact, since rubble conceals them until the visitor suddenly finds them towering above. The left figure, Yagjagbula, is the older brother, and stands nearly 3 metres (10 feet) high, with a 66-centimetre (26-inch) penis. The right figure, Yabiringi, is the younger brother, and is slightly taller, with a 56-centimetre (22-inch) penis. Both brothers hold a stone axe in the right hand. Note the stripes, and the rayed head-dresses with a pointed plume. These ancestral heroes are said to have travelled here during the Dreamtime. Although the paintings have clearly been retouched over the years, Aborigines claim that it was the two brothers who originally put their shadows on the rock.

association between the petroglyphs and prehistoric settlement sites, and shows that rock art was not always remote and esoteric but closely tied to living areas. It has been speculated that, since these images are not visible from a distance but usually close to the ground, they may have been dedicatory – created when the land was first claimed – or they might represent ritual renewal of boundaries or a link with fertility. Certainly, in some areas there does appear to be a close correlation between rock art and the pattern of settlements which are thought to be contemporaneous with it – thus linking the ritual and social landscapes.

Art and spiritual geography

The mythological landscape was probably an important phenomenon in many parts of the prehistoric world, but it is best documented in Australia where the natural features of the landscape (mountains, springs, etc.) and everything living within it, are thought to have been created by the mythic figures who lived during a period, the ancestral past, the Dreamtime. When the creative activities were over, these beings 'sat down' at the locations where their last acts took place and now remain there as a living essence; many placed themselves on rocks and shelter walls, where they still exist today as images. Hence the location of much Australian rock art is the focus of rites and ceremonies, and the sources of pigments too are often centres of religious significance.

In other parts of the world, too, rock art is still part of the spiritual geography of the indigenous peoples. For the Hopi of the American south-west, deep canyons are dangerous places, symbolic of the underworld, the home of the dead, yet they used to make expeditions into them to collect salt and yellow paint for rites. For example, the site of Tutuventiwngwu (Willow Springs), Arizona, seems to be a prehistoric shrine which the Hopi continued to visit in the historic period. It was a stopping place on expeditions into the inner gorge of the Little Colorado River canyon and the participants placed their clan symbols on sandstone boulders here: images representing twenty-seven clans are carved here in rows and testify to the significance for the Hopi of the place itself and of the journeys made to the shrine.

In Southern Africa, information given to Bleek and Lloyd by Bushman (San) informants (see Chapter 2) suggests that the ritual and legendary significance of certain places in the landscape – such as sites used in rainmaking – was enhanced by rock engravings, which reinforced the existing power of these places. Hence images gradually accumulated around springs and waterholes, though their metaphors and significance doubtless changed over time. Petroglyphs likewise cluster around springs in the Colorado Desert of the American south-west. In large areas of western North America, there may also be an important association between rock art and game migration trails (hunting trails) – for example, in the Great Basin, scratched rock art generally occurs in locations especially suited to big-game drives and ambushes, while at Joshua Tree National Monument the major rock art sites are located along well-established trails, as well as being associated

with water sources. Many of these sites may constitute trail shrines at which ritual activity – including the making of petroglyphs – was undertaken to ensure the safe completion of a journey or a successful hunt. The ownership of sacred places may secure access to subsistence resources, or vice versa.

Petroglyphs of deer and shield-bearing man, Steamboat Butte, Montana (United States). Their location commands impressive views. Date unknown.

Art and visibility

In other cases, however, visibility is definitely a major factor. Some cave art is on open, clear view in large chambers, made to be seen from a distance, whereas much is carefully hidden away in nooks and crannies. The same is true for rock shelters

Art in total darkness

Although the vast majority of prehistoric art was produced and is located in full daylight or in the entrance areas of caves and deep shelters, there is nevertheless an important body of art lying in total darkness within deep caves. The best known examples, of course, are some of the hundreds of decorated caves from the Ice Age of Eurasia, though art from more recent periods of prehistory is also found deep inside European caves – for example, in several caves in northern Norway, about 3,000 years ago – as well as sealed inside the chambers of megalithic monuments. However, the phenomenon is by no means uniquely European. A whole series of deep caves in Australia have been found to contain a profusion of finger markings (such as Koonalda Cave, 15,000–24,000 years old) and engraved motifs. Increasing numbers of decorated deep caves are being discovered in various parts of the United States, most famously the Mud Glyph Caves of Tennessee; and there is a wealth of decorated caves in Cuba and the Dominican Republic.

Because caves appear mysterious and menacing places to us, there has long been a tendency to associate their art with secret, esoteric, exclusive rites redolent of fear and awe. Rock art in the daylight and the open air seems far less 'private'. But it would be simplistic to interpret art of the past in relation to these modern impressions. As we know from Australia, for example, open-air sites can be just as imbued with power and as taboo as anything underground – a prohibition suffices to make them so and, as has often been pointed out, 'locked doors are a late invention'. Indeed some of the art in deep caves appears to be 'public', being easily visible in large, readily accessible chambers. However, a great deal of it is undeniably 'private', in small niches, or chambers only accessible through a long journey or after negotiating difficult physical obstacles necessitating climbs, crawls or tight squeezes. There are cases – as with the famous Ice Age clay bison of France's Tuc d'Audoubert – where the very act of making the journey and of producing the images seems to have been what mattered; the artist(s) never returned to visit their work.

Why should art have been placed in such inaccessible locations? Deep caves are strange environments, bereft not only of light but also of sounds – except perhaps for dripping water or, at times, bats. One experiences utter blackness, total silence, a loss of sense of direction, a change of temperature and a frequent sense of claustrophobia. To enter a deep cave is to leave the everyday world and cross a boundary into the unknown – a supernatural underworld. It is easy to imagine that caves therefore symbolized transitions in human life and could be used for rituals linked with those transitions, especially puberty rites. Or perhaps it was felt that by entering this world one could better commune with or summon up the supernatural forces which dwelt there, and hence the images were made to reach and compel those forces. Cave decoration certainly requires strong motivation, since it involves negotiating such obstacles and taking both equipment and illumination into the site.

We have no ethnographic information from Australia on the use of deep caves, which seem to have been avoided by Aborigines in historical times. However, we can gain some insights into potential motivations by studying the deep caves which were decorated by the Maya of Central America. Since theirs was not a prehistoric culture, and since some of their cave decoration consisted of their glyphs (which were their writing), we can both read the texts and learn from Maya ethnohistory what they were doing in caves. It is certainly clear that, for the Maya, it was the act or production that counted, not the durability of the art. 'Hidden' or private images are sometimes found in especially awkward or even

Deeply engraved circles associated with the extraction of flint nodules in Karlie-ngoinpool Cave, South Australia. These cover a 10-metre (33-foot) width of wall near the cave's entrance. Farther inside, in total darkness, is a tiny chamber covered in engravings, especially circles, which seem to have been of particular significance. Date unknown.

dangerous locations. Their use of caves involved altars and 'chapels', and water was a focus of the rituals here. Caves were considered dangerous and chaotic places, contrasting starkly with the domestic community, and they were visited to make contact with gods and spirits in some way. Sanctity was proportional to spatial remoteness and this factor would certainly help to explain the decorated 'sanctuaries' in remote corners of many prehistoric caves: for example, the Tuc d'Audoubert's clay bison are located at the very furthest point of a 900 metre- (c. 3,000 foot-) long cave, in a chamber reached only after an often uncomfortable and difficult journey. In Maya terms, these bison were left in a sacred location,

The two clay bison of the Tuc d'Audoubert, Ariège (France) probably date to *c.* 15,000–10,000 BC and are 63 and 61 centimetres (25 and 24 inches) long respectively. They probably cracked shortly after being made, as the clay dried. The bison owe their preservation to the miraculous fluke that this chamber has no water dripping from the ceiling to form the stalactites and stalagmites which festoon other parts of the cave.

unsullied through their utter remoteness from daily human life. The realm of total darkness and silence was the greatest contrast imaginable to the everyday human world.

and open-air blocks, where light can also play a crucial role – locations for images could be chosen depending on whether they were in full sunlight throughout the day or lit up at certain times of day or even illuminated at astronomically significant times (see Chapter 8). Many open-air engravings are only clear for a few hours per day, when the light is right, while others are never truly visible. Certain shelter and open-air panels seem to be of particular importance, judging by their high-up locations which makes them visible from a great distance, while some rock art is placed in positions of dominance, from which it commands tremendous vistas. Unusually wide views of the coast and the hills have, in the past, been recognized as a factor in the location of rock art in Galloway, Scotland, and a recent detailed investigation of the area has not only confirmed this phenomenon but also found evidence that the size and complexity of motifs may also be related to location: the simpler ones occur around the edges of lowland near the shoreline, while the more complex lie in upland areas as well as around shallow basins and waterholes.

Such assessments of complexity, of course, come from twentieth-century minds, and are therefore superficial – it is always possible that what seem highly complex motifs to us may have had simple meanings and vice versa. Nevertheless, locational approaches are at least beginning to detect some of the many varied factors involved in the siting of parietal art.

(*Opposite*) **These humanlike petroglyphs with patterned bodies in Renegade Canyon, Coso Range, California (United States) are – like the Three Kings (see page 103) – in a dominant position in the canyon, being visible from some distance away. Date unknown, but probably before 1000 AD.**

CHAPTER 6   *The Appliance of Science*

There has never been much of a problem in studying portable art: if it is made of organic material, it can be dated directly; if not, its stratigraphic position and/or its close associations with other datable material make the dating procedure fairly straightforward. Where art on rocks and walls is concerned, however, there are

tremendous difficulties in obtaining dates. Until very recently, only indirect dates could be hoped for, based on a wide variety of clues of differing reliability.

INDIRECT DATING

Proof of prehistoric age can sometimes be found in the historical content: the depiction of what appear to be animals now extinct (for example, in the Ice Age decorated caves) or long vanished from the region (for example, giraffes and elephants in the

Part of the painted cliff face at Huashan (south-west China), the biggest rock art panel in the world. The circles with stars inside are thought to be bronze drums, a characteristic ancient artifact of the region. These, together with the ring-handled swords, suggest that the Huashan paintings are not prehistoric but must be about 2,000 years old. They have survived owing to protection by the rock overhang, although some areas are badly weathered. Recent radio-carbon analysis of stalactites associated with some of the figures has confirmed this date, placing them between 2,370 and 2,115 years ago. These are the only well-dated rock art figures in China at present.

One of at least seven paintings of mammoths in the cave of Kapova, Urals (Russia), thought to date to around 14,000 years ago, an example of a depiction of a now extinct animal (which provides some indication of the age of the painting).

Sahara), or detailed illustrations of what appear to be tools or weapons known from particular periods (for example, daggers and halberds in Alpine petroglyphs or bronze drums and ring-handled swords at Huashan), see Chapter 1.

Sometimes cave art can be roughly dated owing to changes in its surroundings – as when a cave was blocked during the Ice Age or when wall art is actually covered by (and must therefore predate) prehistoric occupation layers. Occasionally, fragments of decorated wall (known as spalls) have fallen off and become stratified in an occupation layer, so that the date of the layer in question provides a minimum age for the art (which may have fallen years, centuries or even millennia after being produced) – examples include painted sandstone spalls at Pedra Furada in Brazil and the Red Giant painting in Namibia's Upper Brandberg. This figure's body shows numerous signs of flaking and an excavation directly beneath it recovered over thirty paint-bearing granite chips in the top layer, one of which could be fitted back into a small human figure below the 'giant'. A piece of charcoal next to these fragments gave a radio-carbon date of 2,760 years ago, thus suggesting a minimum age for the painting.

A petroglyph of a giraffe in the southern Hoggar (Algeria) in the Sahara, an example of the depiction of an animal which no longer inhabits the region, indicating the antiquity of the art and a change in climate and environment. Date unknown, but certainly prehistoric.

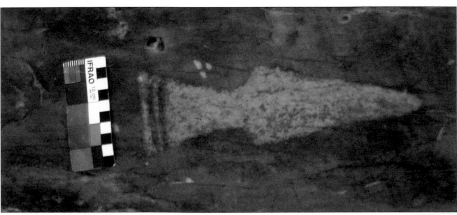

One of the many daggers and other weapons depicted in petroglyphs at Monte Bego and other Alpine sites. They bear a close resemblance to copper and bronze specimens from the European Copper Age and early Bronze Age (third to second millennium BC). Note the attention to detail as shown by the transversal bands across the pommel.

(*Above*) **Fallen fragment of sandstone shelter-wall at Pedra Furada (Brazil). This was found stratified in an occupation layer dating to 10,000–12,000 years ago, which indicates that the human figure painted on it must have been created before that time.**

(*Opposite*) **Painting of a salt-water crocodile in Australia's Northern Territory. Some researchers associate early depictions of this animal with the Estuarine period (1,000–7,000 years ago).**

In other cases, maximum ages can be obtained in relation to known environmental changes: for example, in some Pyrenean caves which could not be occupied before the late Ice Age because of glacial activity, or in Scandinavia where the rocks became available for decoration as sea level fell and the land rose after the Ice Age. In fact, since Scandinavian researchers have usually assumed that most petroglyphs (rock carvings) were 'shore-bound' (see Chapter 5) – that is, originally located in or just above the tidal zone – the position of the rocks in relation to sea level is a traditional, albeit approximate, dating method in the region. Shoreline chronology of a different kind has been proposed in northern Australia (although it is not widely accepted). In the pre-Estuarine period, at the height of the last glaciation, rock art featured non-marine species, including what may be some now extinct. By the Estuarine period, starting 6,000–7,000 years ago, the postglacial rise in sea level had ceased and the encroaching sea water brought the depiction of new species such as the giant perch and salt-water crocodile, while the small marsupials which had once occupied the pre-Estuarine plains moved further inland and disappeared from coastal art, as did the boomerang, the weapon used to hunt them. Finally, the Freshwater period (about 1,000 years ago) brought the development of fresh-water wetlands, and the depiction of waterfowl, lilies and wild rice.

Large boat petroglyph at Bjørn-stadskipet, Østfold (Norway). Some researchers see at least some of these motifs as sledges. Resemblances to images of supposed boats on bronze razors found in graves in Denmark and southern Sweden would date these petroglyphs to *c.* 1000 BC.

If some prehistoric occupation can be detected in the decorated cave, shelter or site, it may provide some clue to the age of the art, especially if there are traces of pigments and objects such as grinders or stone tools, which can be related to the images – as, for example, in several famous Ice Age caves such as Lascaux in France or Altamira and Tito Bustillo in Spain. Portable art can also provide helpful evidence: in some sites which contain both wall and portable images, there are clear analogies between the two in technique and style.

Where no such helpful hints exist, comparisons have been made with motifs from other sites or even other regions. For example, petroglyphs in some parts of

the south-western United States bear strong resemblances to designs on the pottery of the Mimbres culture of 1,000 years ago, while some of the spectacular, gigantic animals and birds drawn on the landscape at Nasca, Peru, are comparable with designs on the pottery of the Nasca culture of the early centuries AD. Some motifs in Scandinavian rock art, notably the 'ships', have been linked with similar designs on razors and other artifacts from the local Bronze Age.

All such stylistic dating is based on an assumption that images which appear similar in style or technique were roughly contemporaneous in execution. While many of the comparisons made are probably broadly valid, there always remains a degree of uncertainty in these subjective assessments. For instance, it is always possible for an artist to be inspired by, or even to copy, works or styles from earlier periods. Relative age can more reliably be estimated where there are superimpositions of different figures – this was the basis for much of Breuil's classification of Ice Age parietal art. And where petroglyphs are concerned, differing degrees of patination can also be a clue: in fact, this phenomenon was noticed in the Nile Valley as long ago as 1820 by Giovanni Belzoni, the notorious strongman-Egyptologist, who speculated about the possibility of establishing a chronological sequence on this basis.

THE ANALYSIS AND DIRECT DATING OF ROCK ART

For many years, rock art specialists dreamed of being able to date parietal images as confidently and accurately as portable art. The techniques of modern science have recently been brought to bear on prehistoric cave and rock art with profound consequences.

Pigment analysis

The analysis of pigments has been carried out since the turn of the century – for example, by French scholars using samples from several Ice Age painted caves such as Font de Gaume and in 1924 in Argentina. But in the past it could only be done in relatively crude ways which depended on chemical reaction. Today, only a tiny amount of pigment is required, and the new techniques which can be applied to it – such as scanning electron microscopy, X-ray diffraction and proton-induced X-ray emission – produce a highly detailed analysis of the paint's content. Similarly, radio-carbon dating could not be applied to cave art in the past, partly because the pigments were not thought to contain organic material, and because even if they did the amount required to produce a date would have removed entire images. However, scientific advances have revealed that organic material (notably charcoal) was used far more often than had been thought, and an estimation of age can be obtained from a mere pinprick of paint thanks to accelerator mass spectrometry (AMS).

New impetus was provided in the 1960s and 1970s by mineralogical and chemical analysis of pigments in many parts of the world. There was particularly pioneering work in Argentina, where Carlos Gradin took samples of paint in Cueva de las Manos, Patagonia, from badly eroded images of animals and hand stencils on

(Following page) **Hand stencils and paintings of guanacos (wild llamas) at Cueva de las Manos, Patagonia (Argentina). Date unknown.**

Fakes

An incidental but nevertheless important contribution of the new scientific techniques is that we are now better able to investigate potential fakes and either expose or authenticate them. Where parietal art is concerned, great progress has been made since the days when the style of the art or the presence on images of calcite (in caves) or lichen (in the open air) seemed to be the only way of deducing that the art had not been done very recently. Methods such as these were imperfect: since calcite and lichen can form fairly quickly, their presence was not necessarily a proof of great antiquity. Naturally, actual testimony is useful – for example, the Sierra Blanca paintings in New Mexico, once thought to be Apache, are now known to have been made by Scouts in 1932 as part of their Indian Lore programme! But recent scientific methods have provided far more reliable guides to authenticity.

In 1991, press photographs of the newly discovered 'Ice Age' art on the walls of the Spanish cave of Zubialde were sufficient to arouse profound suspicions among most specialists. Scientific analysis proved that most, if not all, of its figures were of recent manufacture, since the paint was found to contain highly perishable materials such as insect legs, as well as synthetic fibres from modern kitchen sponges. It was also scientific analysis which brought firm and final proof of the authenticity of Cosquer Cave about which there had initially been doubts, thanks to poor press pictures and the recent Zubialde fiasco. Where specific doubts linger – for example, over a handful of images in the French cave of Rouffignac – such analyses

(Opposite) **One of the painted panels in Zubialde Cave (northern Spain). The (red) dot and plant/ feather-like motif to the right of the dreadful 'hand stencil' were not on the photographs taken by the art's 'discoverer' in 1990, but had appeared by the time cave art specialists began their investigations in 1991. They were found to be of the same pigment as the rest.**

Fake Azilian pebbles from France. There are many of these fakes, since they are remarkably easy to make, requiring only a small flat pebble and some red pigment, and there were great incentives to make them. Not only did nineteenth-century excavators often leave their workers unsupervised and pay them by the find, but collectors and foreign museums quickly began to offer large sums for these objects. By 1929, a veritable commerce in fake pebbles was under way. A systematic attempt by French researcher Claude Couraud eventually established some criteria for weeding out most of the fakes and has exposed large numbers of them in museums in France, Britain and America.

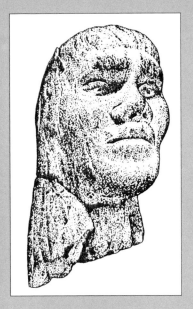

The Dolní Věstonice head,
8 centimetres (3 inches) high.

discovered in the 1860s and again after Azilian pebbles (the small flat pebbles from the end of the Ice Age, decorated with red dots and lines) were discovered in the Pyrenees in the 1880s. Fossil bones and antlers were plentiful in many sites, and fossil ivory also occurred in some, so that the necessary raw materials were readily available.

The analysis of some pieces of dubious Ice Age portable art, such as the 'venus' on a stone block at Abri Pataud (France) or the fossil-ivory Brassempouy head (see page 83), is still beyond current expertise – we have no means of establishing when the figures were produced. Occasionally, however, dating the raw material can expose the forgery. For example, a unique engraving of a mammoth on a whelkshell from Holly Oak, Delaware – supposedly found in 1864 but not made public until 1889 – was long suspected to be a fake based on the mammoth engraving found at La Madeleine, France, in 1864; but argument raged over its authenticity until radio-carbon dating settled the issue by dating the shell to only 1,530 years ago. Since mammoths had become extinct in America about 9,000 years earlier, this was clearly a fake.

An ivory carving of a male human head, said to come from near the Czech Ice Age site of Dolní Věstonice, has no definite provenance, stratigraphic context or date, yet the *National Geographic* put the figure on its cover in 1988, proclaiming it to be the portrait of an Ice Age ancestor. However, the head neither looks nor 'feels' Palaeolithic; there is nothing else like it in the whole corpus of Ice Age art. Uniqueness in itself is no guide to fakery, but this object suggests an ill-informed forger's idea of what an Ice Age man should look like. The problem in proving it a fake is that the raw material is fossil ivory, but in fact the ivory has proved to be so very ancient that the carving must be a forgery.

Some forgeries are patently obvious. A crude pair of heads from the French site of Glozel, 'dug' in the 1920s, produced an amazing hodge-podge of 'Ice Age' engravings

and/or dating should now be able to settle the issue once and for all and either prove them to be recent or confirm their attribution to the Palaeolithic period.

There have been numerous cases of forgery in portable prehistoric art, and it is very likely that many well-known pieces are actually fakes. It is known, for example, that in south-west France a trade in fakes sprang up as soon as Ice Age art portable art was (complete with writing!), 'Anatolian Neolithic' pots complete with eyes and eyebrows, and 'Near Eastern' clay tablets inscribed with 'writing' – all of which most archaeologists dismiss as ridiculous and clumsy fakes. Equally outrageous were the 'Ica stones', a huge collection of black stones from Ica, Peru, engraved with supposedly prehistoric depictions of telescopes, open-heart surgery, dinosaurs, etc. Trumpeted for a while in the 1970s as evidence of extraterrestrial visits to Earth, or of an early super-civilization, they inevitably turned out to have been made by a local peasant, copying pictures from magazines and burying the stones in donkey dung for colouration.

At Mników Cave, southern Poland, in 1880, Gottfryd Ossowski excavated not only bones of Ice Age animals and stone tools, but also an extraordinary array of over 8,000 bone artifacts. Many were in the shape of animals, some were human representations, others were geometric shapes, stars, and even a fork and spoon set. An international controversy broke out, with Viennese and French scholars declaring them to be fakes, while other eastern European scholars thought them genuine, although possibly of later date than that claimed for them by Ossowski. The Mników controversy was not settled until 1929, when workmen admitted

manufacturing the bone artifacts themselves. Ossowski had paid premiums for particularly fine specimens, and since he was on the site for only about an hour each day, the workmen had plenty of unsupervised time to carve the artifacts from unworked prehistoric bone found in the excavations. This phenomenon of workers being paid by the find was common in the early days of archaeology and helps to cast doubt on the authenticity of many art objects which lack clear provenance, such as the Brassempouy head or the 'venus' figurines from the Grimaldi caves on the Italian Riviera.

Tremendous numbers of fake ceramics are made by clever artisans for sale to tourists or gullible collectors in many regions of the world. For example, it is widely believed that many of the stone carvings 'hidden in secret caves', which were sold or given to the Norwegian adventurer Thor Heyerdahl on Easter Island in the 1950s, were modern products. Even some of the most cherished icons of prehistoric art have had doubt cast on their authenticity for reasons of style and technique – most recently Spain's famous Lady of Elche, a sculpted limestone bust of a woman with strange 'cartwheels' of hair, which is traditionally attributed to the Iberian period (Iron Age) but has now been claimed to be a nineteenth-century fake.

The famous, supposedly Ice Age engraving of a horse head on a rib-bone, 'found' by two schoolboys in a quarry at Sherborne, Dorset (England), in 1911, was always considered of doubtful authenticity. Recent analysis has revealed that the engraved lines do not have the same patina as the bone surface, and display none of the features normally visible in experimental lines produced by stone tools on fresh bone, such as sharp edges and multiple parallel striations. It seems clear that the engraving took place on an already weathered bone. A fragment of the piece was eventually dated by AMS to about 610 years ago, in the fourteenth century, proving the object to be a fake.

the walls and compared them with granules of pigment encountered in excavations in the site. X-ray diffraction analysis identified the minerals present in each sample – most notably gypsum, as well as quartz, feldspar and haematite – and showed the different mixtures which the occupants of the site had used for their art. Interestingly, X-ray diffraction analysis of pigments from prehistoric paintings in Monitor Basin, Nevada, in the 1970s likewise showed that gypsum had been the binding agent and that red and yellows had been made by adding various minerals. All the samples were different, suggesting that the paintings accumulated at different times, with different mixtures being used in each artistic episode.

For Ice Age art, this kind of analysis was pioneered by Michel Lorblanchet (see Chapter 5) in the Quercy region of France. It was then taken up by the French prehistorian Jean Clottes and his team in the Ariège (French Pyrenees) and subsequently elsewhere – using scanning electron microscopy, X-ray diffraction and proton-induced X-ray emission. It has also been applied to residues of paint on portable art objects. For example, in the cave of Niaux, Ariège, a number of different mixtures have been detected: there seem to be specific 'recipes' of pigments mixed with mineral 'extenders' such as talc, which made the paint go further, improved its adhesion to the wall and stopped it cracking. In the cave's famous Salon Noir sanctuary, most of the animals were first sketched in charcoal, with manganese paint added on top. This was clearly a special place where the images were carefully planned, whereas the other drawings in the cave were done without preliminary sketches. In other Ariège caves, the paint used has been found to contain oil of animal or plant origin, presumably as a binder.

Analysis of the red and black pigments in Russia's Ignatiev Cave by X-ray diffraction and infra-red spectrometry has revealed that they sometimes contain gypsum, feldspar and clay minerals which are not naturally present in the cave and

Tracing of figures (probably painted by Bushmen) from Sonia's Cave Upper, Boontjieskloof (South Africa). Scale in centimetres. The two human figures in the centre are painted in black, and it was the legs of the right-hand figure which produced the first direct dating of rock art in the world. (After Yates, Manhire & Parkington.)

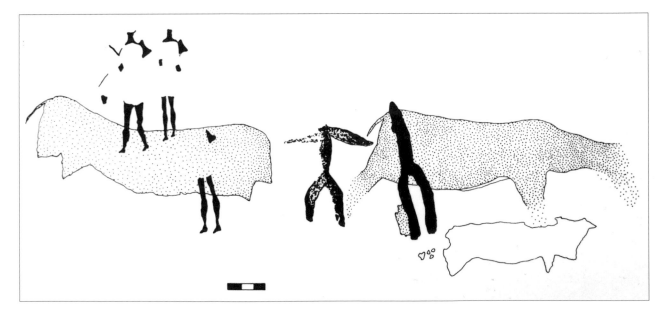

Scientific methods used to date prehistoric art

Accelerator Mass Spectrometry (AMS) A method of radio-carbon dating which counts the actual number of carbon 14 atoms present in a sample, rather than the small number of 14C atoms which decay radioactively during the measurement time. It requires only a tiny sample of carbon, and is a quicker but more expensive method than conventional radio-carbon dating.

Cation-ratio dating A technique based on the fact that the ratio of calcium and potassium/titanium in rock varnish may decrease exponentially with age.

Infra-red spectrometry A technique for determining the mineralogical or chemical composition of a substance or object by bombarding it with infra-red radiation.

Microerosion analysis An optical technique for assessing the age of petroglyphs from their degree of erosion, based on marks of known age.

Proton-induced X-ray emission A technique for analysing chemical composition, since X-rays emitted from the sample have different wavelengths which are characteristic of the elements present.

Radio-carbon dating A dating method which measures the decay of the radioactive isotope of carbon (14C) in organic material to nitrogen. This decay begins as soon as an organism dies, so that a sample's content of 14C is an indicator of the time elapsed since death. (The dates are expressed as a number, followed by a plus/minus sign and then another smaller number. The first number is the age in years before the present; the second is the associated probable error (or 'standard deviation') – and there is only a 68 per cent probability that the true age lies within this range. If the size of the standard deviation is doubled, there is a 95 per cent chance that the true age lies within the range.)

Scanning electron microscopy (SEM) A technique for examining the microscopic and submicroscopic structure of objects up to at least 50,000X magnification. The microscope forms an image as the sample is scanned by a high-energy electron beam.

X-ray diffraction A technique for identifying the mineralogy of crystalline material by exposing it to a beam of X-rays. The different X-ray intensities transmitted after passing through the sample identify the elements present.

which may thus have been added as extenders or to produce different shades. The black pigment is not manganese but a mixture of charcoal, gypsum and calcite; hence it should be possible to obtain direct radio-carbon results from some images.

Direct dating of paint

Direct dating had already been attempted in other regions. In North America, for example, the rock art specialist Campbell Grant tried in the 1960s to date a very eroded Chumash painting in California, but the radio-carbon content was far too small to achieve a result by the methods then available. In South Africa's Drakensberg, a different, biochemical approach was tried in the 1960s by the German scientist E. Denninger and Harald Pager: tiny samples of paint from a number of rock shelters were subjected to dating by paper chromatography, a method

(Above) Pictographs of deer and humans at Cueva del Ratón, Baja California (Mexico).

(Opposite) Excavations at Perna, in the Piauí region of Brazil, exposed small, red paintings of humans, which had survived burial through extreme aridity. Since the occupation layer at their base was dated to almost 10,000 years ago, the paintings must be older than this, as the artists are unlikely to have worked lying down and painting at nose level!

requiring the presence of an albuminoid substance in the paint medium (blood or serum) so that the amino acids – which disintegrate at a constant rate with progressing age – can be quantified. Samples from three eland paintings in Botha's Shelter, Ndedema Gorge, produced ages of 200, 200 and 400 years respectively – results which correspond well with a radio-carbon date obtained recently for art from another site in the region.

The first successful direct radio-carbon dating of a rock painting anywhere in the world was obtained in South Africa in 1987, from fairly recent charcoal pigment: a small black human figure, crudely painted with fingers on top of a faded red animal at Sonia's Cave Upper, Boontjieskloof, gave a radio-carbon result of about 500 years ago. Since then dates have been obtained in many areas: for example, in China, radio-carbon dating of the limestone covering the red paintings of Huashan has yielded results of 2,115–2,370 years ago, while charcoal in the paint of some images at Cueva del Ratón, Baja California, has produced the first clues to the age of that region's remarkable rock art – 5,290 and 4,845 years ago.

could have entered a cave and used charcoal from an ancient hearth to draw on the walls. Thus the charcoal's age merely represents a maximum age for the art. Second, the figures produced by the laboratories – even if they are all accurate and free of contamination (a considerable assumption since even minute contamination can produce great distortion) – are uncalibrated radio-carbon ages, not precise calendar dates. Third, a single date is of little use or reliability and it is unfortunate that some of these dated images can never be redated owing to lack of usable organic material. If just one date of 30,000 had been obtained for the Grotte Chauvet in France, no one would have believed the result; it was the series of dates, together with the later figures obtained for torch marks on top of the calcite covering the art, which convinced everyone despite the universal amazement.

Nevertheless, these uncertainties and caveats concerning radio-carbon dates are, and always have been, equally applicable to the rest of the archaeological record. Because there is only a 68 per cent chance that the true age lies within the span including the plus/minus figure, it is obvious that at least a third of radio-carbon dates may be faulty: some faulty dates are recognized as such immediately, because they are so incongruous, but there are other dates, currently accepted as correct, which are probably wrong as well. The study of the archaeological record by means of the radio-carbon method is still being improved and refined. In the meantime we have to make do with the results obtained, however imperfect and whatever their limitations. Moreover, despite the growing list, the dated images are still only a tiny fraction of the cave art corpus. However, it is certain that in the next few years many more dates will be obtained for images in cave art and these will help specialists to fine-tune their knowledge of how, when and perhaps even why these sites were decorated in this way. It is equally certain that the Grotte Chauvet – so unique, not only because of its size for this region and its early date but also because of its dominant parietal images of rhinoceroses, big cats and mammoths – will play a major role in all future studies of the art not only of Europe but of the world.

STYLE VERSUS SCIENCE?

One overall result of the new analyses and dates – even bearing in mind their uncertainties and pitfalls – is that subjective methods of dating by style alone are beginning to be shown as inadequate. This is not to say that style no longer has a place in studies of prehistoric art – such a proposition would be absurd – but some direct dates have already indicated the imprecise nature of stylistic dating. Conceptions of Palaeolithic art, for example, are rapidly moving away from the linear, ladder-like evolutionary models of the past (from crude, archaic figures at the start to sophisticated realistic figures at the end), as it is realized that two very different periods or widely separated places can produce very similar styles, that a single style can span a very long time or a big area and, conversely, that a single period can produce very different styles side by side, through artistic choice and development, varying function and differing rock surfaces or location.

Nevertheless, most of the radio-carbon results obtained so far have broadly confirmed the ages which had been estimated for the caves on the basis of style and archaeological material. But there have been some surprises – most notably at Chauvet (where initial estimates were around 20,000 but dates came out at more than 30,000 by AMS), though even here the early dates tally well with the sophisticated portable imagery known from portable art in this period in south-west Germany and elsewhere. In France, Cosquer Cave seems to have at least two phases, while the Salon Noir of Niaux (Ariège), previously thought to be extremely homogeneous, also has at least two. In the past, the whole of Niaux's decoration was assigned on stylistic grounds to about 14,000 years ago; however, charcoal from two bison figures in the Salon Noir has now been radio-carbon dated and produced strikingly different results – one bison was dated to 13,850 years ago, as expected, but the other produced a result of 12,890 years ago. In other words, Niaux's decoration seems to have been built up in at least two separate phases, while Cougnac – whose famous Megaloceros (giant deer) panel was confidently thought to belong

Part of a painted panel in the Grotte Chauvet, Ardèche (France). Charcoal taken from the two fighting rhinos produced radio-carbon dates of around 31,000–32,000 years ago.

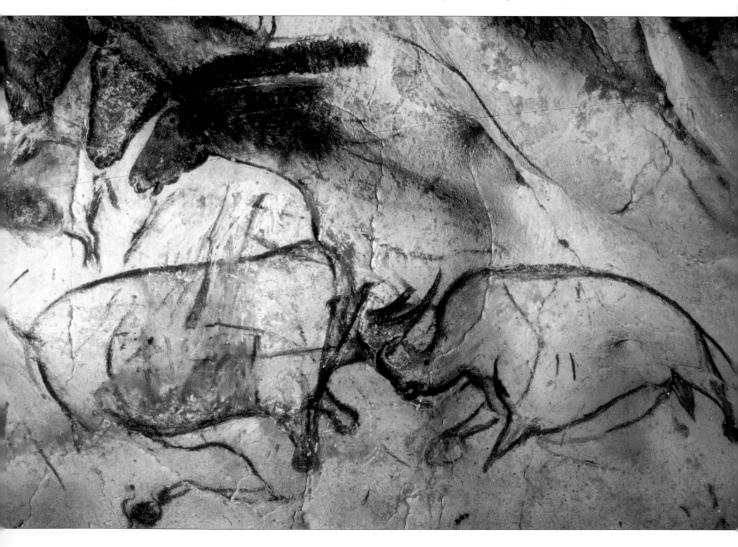

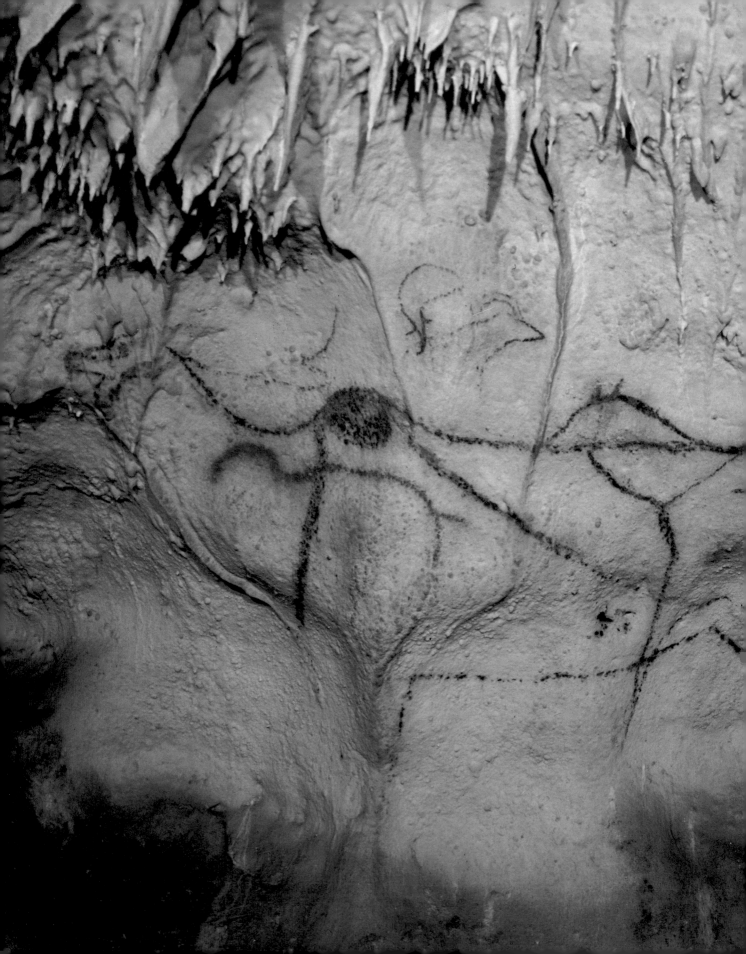

One of the Megaloceros (giant deer) paintings in the cave of Cougnac, Lot (France), whose direct dating has produced results which are difficult to evaluate – do they represent distinct artistic episodes, with retouching of earlier images?

to a single phase – may have at least three or four episodes spanning many millennia, with even its adjacent Megaloceros figures producing markedly different ages. Stylistic studies had assigned Cougnac's art to about 16,000–18,000 years ago but the charcoal in dots on the wall points to a later period, while dates for the images of the extinct giant deer are several millennia earlier –19,500–25,120 years ago.

It must be remembered that most of the radio-carbon estimates obtained for Palaeolithic cave paintings so far have shown that traditional stylistic estimates are not very wide of the mark. Where they have caused surprise this has been due to imperfect knowledge of the age of certain conventions in drawing or to an unhealthy reliance on Leroi-Gourhan's chronological sequence of four successive styles, which had always incorporated some major imperfections – most notably in its ignoring of the great age (more than 30,000 years) of the sophisticated portable carvings of south-west Germany, and of the valuable data provided by the 5,000 decorated plaquettes found stratified in the Spanish cave of Parpalló. The contribution of portable art is crucial to this debate, for while the rock art of most periods and most regions of the world stands virtually alone, with little backup in the archaeological record, the Eurasian Upper Palaeolithic period has a corpus of thousands of images in its portable carvings and engravings which are reasonably well dated and which can be compared with the parietal images. Naturally, this is always a somewhat subjective procedure, unless the two kinds of art are from the same site, but the same applies to any kind of typological scheme, and – as in anything, including direct dating – ultimately one has to rely on the experience and expertise of the practitioner.

As organic material from pictographs and petroglyphs of different cultures and ages is extracted and more dates accumulate, a new, solid and fairly objective chronological framework will emerge. Although it will only ever be possible – for physical and practical as well as financial reasons – to date a tiny fraction of the millions of images in the world, others can be assigned a place in the classifications through the traditional methods of superimposition and careful stylistic comparisons.

In short, both style and direct dating have advantages and flaws, but both have a contribution to make – one should not reject either of them but try to use them together, in accordance with circumstances. The future of prehistoric art studies depends heavily on the judicious balancing of the one with the other, while avoiding a blind faith in the infallibility of either.

(Opposite) Petroglyph of two horses with overlapping heads, at Ribeira de Piscos, Côa Valley (Portugal). Date unknown, but of classic Late Palaeolithic style. The style-vs-direct dating debate came to a head in 1995 over the open-air engravings of the Côa Valley. Every Ice Age art specialist to have seen these images, or even photographs of them, unhesitatingly attributed some of them to the Upper Palaeolithic period, with estimates of age varying from 10,000 to 20,000 years (even 30,000 in one case). Attempts to obtain direct age estimates from a few engraved images (unfortunately much affected by latex moulding, chalking and other damage) using some controversial and experimental methods such as AMS dating of organic deposits and the microerosion technique, produced bizarre results completely at odds with the dating done by archaeologists – ranging from a few thousand years to 200 years ago or even less. While some see this as the last nail in the coffin of subjective stylistic dating, others have pointed out many flaws and uncertainties in the methods used.

CHAPTER 7 ___ *Matters of the Body: Literal Interpretations of Prehistoric Art*

In studying prehistoric art only one thing is certain: nothing is certain!

Kingsley Palmer

Music is just dots and lines on paper until it is played by someone who can read it. And similarly, all prehistoric art is just marks on a variety of surfaces unless it is read. Unfortunately, in the absence of the artists, nobody today can read prehistoric art. Hence a growing number of researchers have decided to abandon the fruitless search for meaning and to focus on other factors which can be investigated with some reliability but do not require any speculation about what the images might signify – we have already mentioned the spatial and distributional aspects of the art,

Petroglyph of an archer and bighorn sheep in Sheep Canyon, Coso Range, California (United States). Date probably before 1000 AD. Apparently simple scenes like this are clearly open to literal interpretations, even if more complex symbolism may lie behind them.

technological analysis and experimentation, the quest for a solid chronological framework, and changes in content through time.

One can certainly learn a great deal from prehistoric art without attempting to 'read' it in any way. However, it is unsatisfying to shrug one's shoulders and dismiss almost the whole of humankind's past artistic output simply as illegible markings, so ever since the discovery of prehistoric art attempts have been made to assess what it depicts.

WHO WERE THE ARTISTS?

It used to be assumed as a matter of course – by the predominantly male scholarly community – that, apart from pottery, jewellery and suchlike, prehistoric art was made by men and for men. For example, the early views of Ice Age art as being hunting and fertility magic led to some researchers seeing it as being entirely about the male preoccupations of hunting, fighting and girls, to the extent that a few have compared Palaeolithic depictions of women with pin-ups in *Playboy* and have grossly exaggerated the importance of the vulva in the art. But of course we do not know the sex of the artists. The carvers of the 'vulvas' and female figurines could just as easily have been female. Much the same applies to other forms of prehistoric art automatically attributed exclusively to men. Ethnographic testimony from various cultures indicates that women do indeed, at times, produce rock art – in some areas of Australia, women make their own sacred rock art, and it is known that women painted as part of some North American Indian puberty ceremonies. Conversely, it is also known that men sometimes make pottery! In short, we cannot make assumptions about the sex of the artists, except where ethnography or ethnohistory give information about the very last prehistoric art production in some areas – for example in Australia (see Chapter 8).

There are, however, some clues in the art itself concerning specific attributes of the artists, such as handedness. For example, the engravings in the caves of Ice Age Europe are often almost invisible when lit from the front, but 'leap out' when lit from the side: this indicates that the artists were right-handed since right-handed artists tend to have their light source on the left, to prevent the shadow of their hand falling on the engraver (or brush). Occasionally, however, one comes across the work of a left-hander. The same is true of portable engravings. As we have seen (see Chapter 5), the predominance of left-hand stencils, assuming they were made palm-down, likewise points to right-handed people.

Trying to work out how many artists there were – that is, whether everyone could create pictures or the phenomenon was limited to a few privileged or gifted individuals – depends on finding criteria for at least tentatively attributing groups of images to the same hand. One such approach is to look for clusters of images which are so similar stylistically and technically that it is very probable that one artist or group was responsible. This is by no means a new approach, and even Sanz de Sautuola in 1880 (see Chapter 2) already saw the Altamira ceiling as a unified work. Leroi-Gourhan on the other hand refused to accept that two adjacent images could be attributed to a single artist. He was obviously correct in so far as it cannot be proved; however, one can make a fairly solid case to support the likelihood of such a claim, if a careful examination is made of details and conventions.

For example, Spanish researcher Juan-Maria Apellániz has for some years been trying to establish firm criteria for recognizing the work of individuals in European Ice Age art. He looks for an original way of drawing – the repetition of idiosyncrasies, peculiarities and details of technique and execution. There are variations, of course, since artists do not repeat themselves exactly and may well have changed style through the years. Such studies are relatively straightforward on portable art, where similar images often form friezes and were almost certainly the work of one artist. In parietal art the situation is similar for panels like the ceiling of Altamira or the black frieze of Pech Merle, but far less clear cut, especially when one tries to compare cave with cave. The criteria used are still rather subjective and intuitive, and involve the assessment of degrees of similarity between images which may be by one hand but which may also simply display the accepted canons and conventions of a particular period and culture. To counteract these problems, Apellániz has developed statistical techniques, using a series of variables and measurements of various parts of animal outlines, and subjecting them to factor analysis (a statistical technique that assesses the variation between types) in order to assess their degree of similarity.

Aboriginal artist Dick Muru-muru at work – producing rock paintings at the first congress of AURA, the Australian Rock Art Research Association, at Darwin in 1988. One of the last great painters of Australian rock art, he was using traditional techniques and paints. Tragically, he was shot dead in a family dispute a few days after the congress.

Vulvas

In many parts of the world, primarily but not exclusively in parietal art, there are motifs which to many researchers look like vulvas. An obsession with sexual interpretations can be traced back to the Abbé Breuil (see Chapter 2) who, in 1911, was consulted about certain deeply engraved motifs found on stone blocks in Early Ice Age sites in the Dordogne. He described these ovoid and subtriangular figures as 'pudendum muliebre', and ever since then most scholars have accepted this view without question. Indeed the 'identification' of so many examples of female genitalia led to ideas about an Ice Age obsession with sex. But such reasoning is circular: the motifs are assumed to be vulvas, from which an obsession with sex is inferred, the evidence for which is the vulvas!

In fact, vulvas are remarkably hard to find in Ice Age art. If one allows that the only definite specimens are those found in context – that is, in full female figures – then they are very few in number. Of the motifs without context, only a few can be identified with any confidence – all the rest are interpretations. Even among the so-called 'venus' figurines of the Ice Age, often seen as proof of an intense interest in female sexuality, very few have the pubic triangle marked and even fewer have the median cleft.

Where vulvas are depicted in context, nearly all are triangles, as one finds in female figures from many other periods and cultures. Yet, as Early Ice Age motifs have a wide variety of shapes, researchers have had to resort to ingenious descriptions in their desperate bid to interpret all these as vulvas: 'incomplete vulvas', 'squared vulvas', 'broken, double vulvas', 'circular vulvas', 'relief vulvas' and even 'trousers vulvas'! More objective observers have simply divided these motifs into descriptive rather than interpretative categories – horned ovals, pear-shaped ovals, arched ovals, etc. Some of these motifs look more like horse-hoof or bird-foot prints, and it would not be surprising if the artists played with such ambiguities of form.

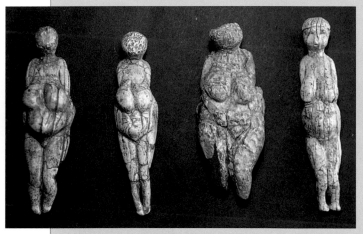

Four of the small 'venus' figurines, about 15 centimetres (*c.* 6 inches) tall and carved in mammoth ivory, from the open-air site of Avdeevo (Russia), dating to about 20,000 years ago. Very few of these Ice Age female statuettes have the vulva marked at all.

There are large collections of such motifs among petroglyphs in other parts of the world – for example, at Río Pachene (north-east Bolivia), San Javier (Baja California) or Carnarvon Gorge (Queensland) – and they are generally interpreted as vulvas. But this remains only an interpretation, except where there are informants to attest to this view. This is the case, for example, on Easter Island, where there are hundreds of *komari*, or vulvas, carved into the rocks, especially around the sacred ceremonial village of Orongo, as well as on portable objects from pillows to skulls. Without such testimony, it is only where the motif is found within full female figures that one can be absolutely 'sure' of its identity.

In parietal art, the vulva is often represented by a natural cavity: female figures drawn or engraved around such cavities are numerous in Australia and have also been found in parts of North Africa, such as Messak, Libya, where the figures are in a 'gynaecological' position.

Petroglyphs on a boulder at Río Pachene (north-east Bolivia), generally interpreted as vulvas, and linked to a fertility cult. Date unknown.

Stencils and petroglyphs at Art Gallery, in Carnarvon Gorge, Queensland (Australia), showing the numerous motifs, interpreted as vulvas, which are a distinctive feature of this region with its soft, easily abraded sandstone. Date unknown.

Small stone pillow with engravings of *komari* (vulvas) from Easter Island. It is known from the islanders that girls had their clitoris deliberately lengthened from an early age and at special ceremonies they would stand on two rocks to be examined by priests, the best being immortalized in stone. However, without the islanders' testimony, we might not even recognize this motif as a vulva, let alone understand why it was so common. Probably eighteenth century.

Female figures painted around natural rock cavities, at Ingaladdi, in the Victoria River District of Australia's Northern Territory. Date unknown.

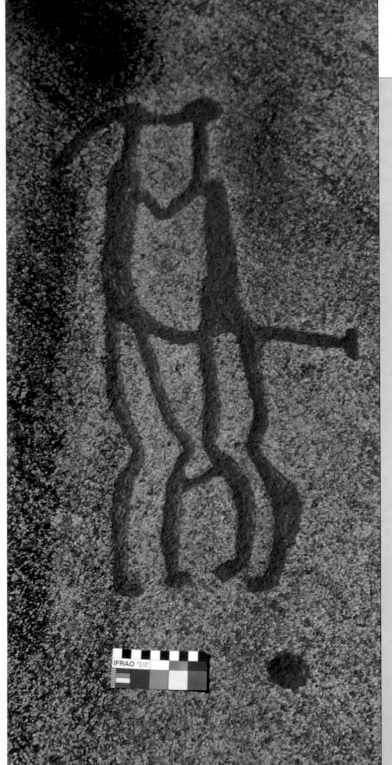

Petroglyph known as The Couple or The Lovers, at Vitlycke in Bohuslän (Sweden). Probably Bronze Age (c. 1000 BC). It appears to comprise a man with a sword scabbard holding hands with, and kissing, a person with long hair, usually seen as a female. It is assumed that the erect penis which also links the two belongs to the person on the right!

Sex

For an activity which looms so large in everyday life, sexual intercourse is surprisingly scarce in prehistoric art – or rather, its presence is extremely patchy. For example, in the thousands of images in Eurasian Ice Age art, whether portable or parietal, there is not a single clear or definite example of human or animal copulation. The rock art of vast areas such as North America, India or China contains very few examples, whereas human copulation is quite frequent in the art of other regions such as parts of Australia and Brazil. In portable art, the most notorious collection of copulatory images is to be found in the pottery of the Moche culture on Peru's north coast, dating to the early centuries AD. Some of these were so pornographic that the later Inca emperors were said to collect

Drawing of some of the unique engraved human figures discovered in the 1980s at Hutubi, in the Tianshan Mountains near Urumqui (north-west China). Located on a vertical red cliff, there are 300 figures ranging from about 10 centimetres (c. 4 inches) to 2 metres (over 6 feet) in height, and many have a penis of exaggerated size. A few clearly female figures, like the one shown here, lie on their backs with their legs spread wide, next to larger males with large penises. Date unknown. (After Wang.) Sexual scenes are very rare in Chinese rock art, as in many other parts of the world.

Painted panel in the rock shelter of Toca do Chico Coelho, in Brazil's Piauí region, known as The Orgy. Note the absence of any specifically female anatomical details. Ascribed to the 'Serra Talhada' phase, 6000–4000 BC.

them. The Moche were not obsessed with sexual matters: it is just that, unusually in prehistoric art, they represented every facet of their world in ceramics, so sexual themes naturally constitute an (albeit small) percentage of the corpus. For some reason, among the ceramics of a sexual nature there are numerous depictions of heterosexual fellatio, anal intercourse and masturbation – perhaps these were the principal methods of contraception in this culture. They also depicted copulations between llamas, felines, mice, frogs, and other creatures.

Drawing of a prehistoric pottery vessel, probably from Peru's Moche culture (1–600 AD), depicting anal intercourse.

Tracing by Harald Pager of a painted scene (date unknown) of two mating Vaal rhebok from Knuffel's Shelter in South Africa's Drakensberg. The scene, painted in red and white, measures about 10 centimetres (c. 4 inches) across. Such depictions are extremely rare in prehistoric rock art.

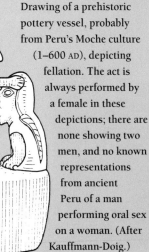

Drawing of a prehistoric pottery vessel, probably from Peru's Moche culture (1–600 AD), depicting fellation. The act is always performed by a female in these depictions; there are none showing two men, and no known representations from ancient Peru of a man performing oral sex on a woman. (After Kauffmann-Doig.)

Tracing of a petroglyph found on a slab in a seventh-century BC burial mound at Byrganov, Khakasia (Siberia). This depiction of a fantastic creature, combining animal and bird features, has been attributed to the Bronze Age (*c.* 1000 BC) and interpreted as a beast-deity symbolizing the Lord of Three Worlds in Okunev mythology. The decorated slab seems to have stood in the open air for some time, after which the small figures of humans and animals were added, and the stone re-used in the mound's construction. (After Pyatkin & Kurochkin.)

However, in the absence of informants about prehistoric images, our own zoological reasoning, our ethnographic analogies and our perceptions of similarities to existing creatures or objects are all we have to go on, despite their inevitable degree of subjectivity. We can only approach this mass of data, like any other, with the concepts of our own culture.

Many images appear to be relatively easy to recognize – they look like humans (anthropomorphs), or animals (zoomorphs), or identifiable objects such as boomerangs and dilly bags in Australia or fly whisks and bows and arrows in Southern Africa. Huge numbers, however, are ambiguous, unfinished or simply unidentifiable – quite apart from the vast quantities of apparently non-figurative motifs. Some designs are interpreted according to personal choice – for example, a simple 'V' with a central line may be described as a 'trident' but interpreted as an arrow, a bird track or a vulva. And of course all or none of these may be correct. Such interpretations are fairly 'literal', but simple motifs can have multiple possible meanings – for example, among Australia's Walbiri people a circle can denote a hill, tree, campsite, circular path, egg, breast, nipple, entrance into or exit from the ground, or a host of other things. 'Translations' of simple motifs in North American art are equally complex, and ethnography serves to underline how bizarre and 'unguessable' the meaning of motifs may be: in Brazil, two triangles drawn apex to apex mean a fish vertebra to the Bororó, while to the Desana they denote a quiver for curare arrows!

Human portraiture

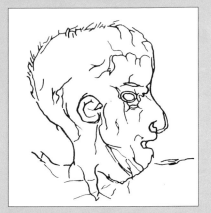 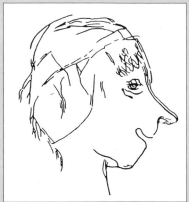 

Portraits of humans date back as far as the Ice Age, with the extraordinary engravings on stone slabs at La Marche, France, more than 14,000 years old. There is also a parietal equivalent, engraved and painted, of a bearded man at the nearby site of Angles-sur-l'Anglin, while the small ivory heads from Brassempouy, France (see Chapter 3) and Dolní Věstonice, Czech Republic (see Chapter 6) – both usually, though unjustifiably, described as females – are also distinctive enough to be probable portraits, if the Brassempouy specimen is authentic.

In subsequent periods, an interesting variant of portraiture has been discovered at Jericho, and later at other sites in the region: here, in the Neolithic period around 7000 BC, human skulls were remodelled with plaster, sometimes with seashell eyes. Some researchers have seen these as portraits, pointing out that each head has a strongly marked individual character, and that plastering a skull in this way and restoring its human features – perhaps those of the individual – may have been a homage to the deceased.

Later prehistory contains innumerable examples of portraiture – such as the clay figurines from Butmir, Bosnia (up to 7,000 years ago), with their neatly combed hair. However, the outstanding examples of portraiture – as of so much else – are to be found in the Moche pottery of Peru, which features numerous heads so realistic and so individualized that they must be accurate depictions of real people.

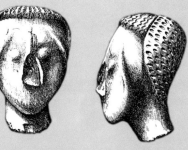

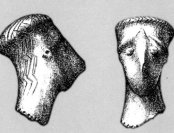

(Above) Drawings of human heads engraved on the small stone slabs of La Marche (France) more than 14,000 years ago. (After Pales & de St Péreuse.)

(Above) Typical pottery head from Peru's Moche culture (1–600 AD). These heads reflect a high degree of realism.

(Left) Drawing of heads of clay figurines from Butmir, near Sarajevo (Bosnia). Dating to the fifth millennium BC, they are 4–5.5 centimetres (1.5–2 inches) in height. Note what appears to be their neatly combed hair.

Some human figures in pre-historic art have exaggerated anatomical details.

(Opposite) Petroglyphs at Fossum, Bohuslän (Sweden), probably dating to the Bronze Age (*c*. 1000 BC), showing the enormously muscular calves and exaggerated penises of the men. The figure on the left is usually interpreted as a woman because of its long hair and the dot between its thighs.

(Bottom left) This typical pictograph from Queensland (Australia) shows a woman with enormous, splayed breasts. Date unknown.

(Bottom right) Petroglyph from Spear Hill (north-western Australia), apparently depicting men with ridiculously huge penises. Date unknown.

In societies without written records, the meaning of things is fluid and will certainly have changed through time, so that any attempt to decipher 'the' meaning of a prehistoric art motif or panel, to read it like a Roman inscription, is not only impossible but absurd. These are messages from other cultures, other worlds, and we know nothing of the artists' original intentions or the transformations in meaning that the art has undergone, so there is no single correct interpretation. However, since it is better to light a candle than to curse the darkness, what one *can* do is to put forward observations, interpretations and hypotheses about the images, which can be evaluated and eventually discarded when something better comes along. This is what researchers have been doing from the beginning, often unconsciously, although many of them, alas, have presented their ideas (and some continue to do so) as certainties – the one true meaning.

CATEGORIES OF IMAGE

Humans

Perhaps the most straightforward category of prehistoric image is the human figure, particularly the portrait, although many are stylized 'anthropomorphs' or even vaguer 'humanoids'. For decades it was thought that depictions of humans were rare in European Ice Age art, and that they were badly done in comparison with animal figures, but 115 quite realistic human figures are known among the engravings of La Marche, France, dating to about 14,280 years ago, including what seem to be portraits.

If some human depictions can be read literally, they may provide information on such features as skin colouring, hair styles and facial hair. However, many are highly stylized – with unrealistic proportions such as the abbreviated head, arms and legs of most Ice Age figurines, or exaggerated anatomical details, such as the

muscular calves in many south Scandinavian petroglyphs, or the impossibly large breasts or genitalia on many humans in Australian rock paintings. There are often differences in the depiction of males and females – for example, a study of 9,000 human figures painted in Namibia's Upper Brandberg has revealed that the males tend to be tall and slim, often very mobile and carrying objects, while the females tend to be short and stout, not very mobile, often involved in communication and gestures, and in co-ordinated groups.

In prehistoric art, another interesting aspect is that whereas males are readily recognizable through the erect penis, females are not always identified physically. In Australia, breasts and vulvas are often depicted very clearly, indeed blatantly; but in other areas these features are rare or absent, and females are inferred from secondary characteristics such as prominent buttocks or long hair. In some rock art, such as the late prehistoric petroglyphs of the Alps and Scandinavia, females are even sometimes inferred simply from a dot between the thighs (extra dots at the sides, for breasts, are sometimes also present). This can make it hazardous to determine the gender of the person being penetrated. Moreover hermaphroditic figures are not unknown in rock art – in Arnhem Land, for example, there is a figure with breasts and a penis, as well as one human and one macropod leg.

These petroglyphs on a great rock at Naquane, Valcamonica (Italian Alps), seem to depict a row of humans. The dots between the thighs have led some researchers to interpret them as females. Probably Iron Age (final centuries BC).

Where primary sexual characteristics are not depicted, it is often necessary to rely on shakier criteria like length of hair, bodily proportions, or even the objects being held – weapons are normally associated with men, although Arnhem Land has a few clear rock paintings of women holding spears. Conversely, bodily ornaments are often associated with women: certainly, in Eurasian Ice Age art,

One of the remarkable human figures in the petroglyphs at Dry Fork, Ashley, Utah (United States), displaying what has been called the 'Vernal style' – note the elaborate head-dress and necklace. Probably 700–1200 AD.

Petroglyph at Three Rivers,
New Mexico (United States),
of a human head wearing
some kind of earrings.
Probably 1000–1400 AD.

bracelets, anklets, belts and necklaces do seem to occur only on female figures. However, ethnography and rock art in other parts of the world reveal countless examples of men wearing neck, arm and leg ornaments, head-dresses, sashes, feathers and earrings.

The later prehistoric art – especially portable figurines – of many parts of the world features countless examples of humans, which provide a great deal of information on every aspect of bodily appearance, clothing and ornamentation – most recently the remarkable discovery of the statue of a Celtic aristocrat or deity, wearing what seems to be armour, and with a necklace and a 'leaf crown' (see Chapter 5).

Occasionally, researchers have chosen to treat human images – especially the female figurines of the Eurasian Ice Age – as if they were scrupulously realistic depictions of individuals, and hence deduce information about their age and appearance, whether or not they are pregnant, how many children they have had, and so forth. However, the fact that the female figurines are highly stylized, and sometimes have tiny heads and limbs, makes it most unlikely that the torso was rendered with photographic accuracy.

Among the most elaborate human figures anywhere are the delicate, elegant, dynamic figures of Arnhem Land and the Bradshaws of the Kimberly (Australia), with their tassels, pompons and other accoutrements – some of which (such as tasselled grass skirts, armlets and fly-whisks) have been compared in detail with ceremonial gear still used by some Aboriginal groups in northern Australia. This painting (height about 120 centimetres/47 inches) at Obiri, by the East Alligator River in the Northern Territory, depicts a man carrying a spearthrower in his right hand, and a number of spears in his left, as well as what has been interpreted as a goosewing fan. Note the elbow ornaments, anklets, pubic cover and a large bag hanging from one shoulder. Aborigines interviewed in the 1940s claimed that the shape of the face indicated he was laughing. Date unknown, but probably within the last 1,000 or at most 2,000 years.

Animals

Where animals are concerned, we can only apply zoological criteria. It is obvious that many of the creatures drawn seem easily 'recognizable' at genus level – some are amazingly detailed, such as some prawns painted in Arnhem Land. Prehistoric art never constitutes a real bestiary and the creatures omitted can be as interesting as those selected for depiction. However, assuming a reasonably accurate interpretation, these zoomorphic images can provide valuable information about which creatures were present in a particular time and place. This becomes of great importance where the animals depicted reveal a major climatic change (for example, reindeer in Ice Age Spain or giraffes and elephants in the Sahara) or where they are now extinct. The best known examples of extinct animals are the mammoths and the Megaloceros (giant deer) of Ice Age Eurasia, but there are also some (albeit controversial) depictions of what may be megafauna in Arnhem Land, such as the long-beaked echidna or the marsupial tapir.

While early attempts to establish exactly which 'races' of horse are depicted in Ice Age art were quickly abandoned as fruitless, since they relied on traits which were subject to artistic whim, recent studies have used more scientific techniques in an attempt to identify species accurately. For example, the hundreds of fish paintings in Arnhem Land (in Kakadu Park they comprise about 76 per cent of all recent X-ray paintings) have been ascribed to different species. Similarly, in the American south-west, researchers claim to have identified twenty species or families of fish depicted accurately on the inside of prehistoric Mimbres pottery from New Mexico: since most of these are sea fish and the pottery has been found at least 500 kilometres (over 300 miles) from the sea, it seems that the artists had been to the coast and were very familiar with these fish. As with human images, some researchers have taken such studies a stage further by calling on specialist animal ethologists to examine animal figures as if they were photographically accurate – for example, bison figures in some French caves have been assessed for age, sex and posture.

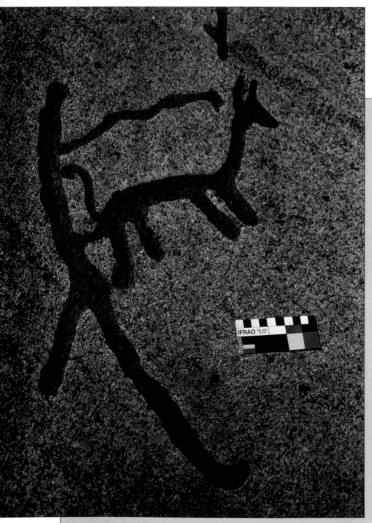

Part of the great petroglyph panel at Vitlycke, in Bohuslän (Sweden), showing what appears to be a case of bestiality. Probably Bronze Age (c. 1000 BC).

Zoophilia

Some of the early commentators on rock art, particularly in North Africa, were shocked or offended by scenes of bestiality – or, to use a less negative term, zoophilia. The phenomenon was accepted in the classical world, but became a capital offence once Christianity took over, and indeed animals were often put to death along with their lovers. It was decriminalized in most of Europe at the time of the French revolution, but England, Germany and America still retain laws against it. Today the practice tends to arouse feelings of awkwardness and laughter rather than disgust, and pity for the abused animal! The phenomenon is by no means rare, even today, and a recent study of the subject estimated that 50 per cent of men in rural areas will have had at least one sexual experience with an animal. Although it is risky to infer humour from prehistoric art, it is impossible not to believe that the artist responsible for the scene from Valcamonica, where the copulator seems to be giving us a cheery wave (see page 209), found this topic amusing. Inevitably, the Moche potters devoted much attention to the practice, particularly involving men and llamas which we know from sixteenth-century chroniclers was a widespread habit in highland Peru. Alas 'cultured persons' are known to have destroyed systematically many of these specimens through the years out of misguided patriotism – attempting to erase evidence for an abominable practice so that others would not 'get the wrong idea' about their ancestors. In rock art, however, clear

Paintings of large fish at Little Nourlangie, in Australia's Northern Territory, in characteristic 'X-ray style' (that is, showing the insides of the animals). Date unknown, but probably within the last few centuries. Some scholars have identified a number of different species in such depictions.

examples can be seen today, not only in the Alps but also in Scandinavia, and especially the Sahara. Normally, the animals being molested seem to be small or medium-sized herbivores, as one might expect, but in North Africa a whole array of unlikely sexual partners can be seen – elephants, giraffes and rhinos (there are even some bizarre pictures which seem to show men ejaculating or urinating into the eye of rhinos).

In the ethnography of many parts of Africa there are descriptions of ritual coitus either with antelopes and ovicaprids or with animals killed in the hunt. However, pictures showing the more bizarre copulations in North Africa may be intended to depict mythical beings, especially as the perpetrators often appear to have animal, or at least non-human, heads; alternatively they may simply be showing the appropriation or domination of these mighty beasts by a symbolic act which was physically impossible or at least highly implausible.

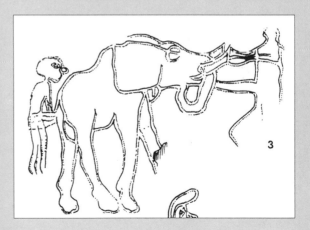

Tracings of rock engravings from Algeria, depicting human copulation with a variety of wild animals – some more plausible than others! (above) With an elephant, at Tel-Isaghen (Fezzan); and (below) with a wild goat, at Ti-Riwekîn (Djerat). (After Jelínek and Lhote.)

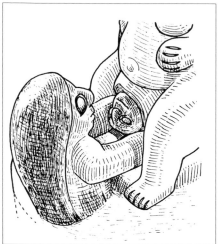
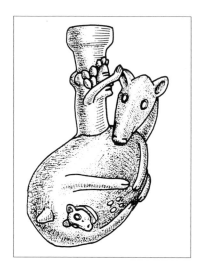

Birth scenes in the pottery of prehistoric Peru. *(Top right)* The vessel in the form of a llama, about 18 centimetres (7 inches) high, is of the Chimú culture (1000–1450 AD). *(Top left and middle)* The human birth is of the Moche culture (1–600 AD). (After Kauffmann-Doig.)

(Below) Tracing by Harald Pager of a red-and-white Bushman painting of two springboks in Shelter A10, Amis Gorge, on Namibia's Brandberg massif. The length of the painting is about 20 centimetres (*c.* 8 inches) and the height about 15 centimetres (*c.* 6 inches). One of the very rare images of suckling young in prehistoric art. Date unknown.

Even if one can be reasonably sure about the identify of an animal, there are still problems: is this a particular bison known to the artist or is it from a special narrative or myth; does it stand for the species as a whole or for an attribute of the animal (strength, courage?) or some other quality of 'bison-ness'? Or is it a metaphor for something else entirely?

Youngsters

For some reason, children do not seem to figure largely in any prehistoric art (they represent 0.1 per cent of the 9,000 human figures in Namibia's Upper Brandberg, for example). Even young animals are not common. Of course, they may be very hard to recognize – how does one tell a diminutive adult figure from a child? Some researchers believe that a few of the engraved Ice Age humans of La Marche, France, are infants on the basis of their proportions, but this is not certain. Occasionally, the context makes the interpretation fairly solid – particularly in what seem to be depictions of giving birth (graphically illustrated in Moche pots not only for humans but also for llamas) or suckling youngsters. In Australian art there are clear pictures of female kangaroos with the head of a joey peeping out of the pouch. Arnhem Land art includes some striking images of what may be Thylacines, the extinct Tasmanian tigers, feeding their young, but there appears to be a total absence of human children in the rock art of that area and children are extremely rare elsewhere. One of the few exceptions are Zimbabwean paintings in which there are babies' heads appearing from the bags in which their mothers carry them.

However, we know from their footprints that Ice Age children did explore the farthest depths of caves in Europe. It has also been found that many of the finger tracings made in the caves of South Australia, especially in their most inaccessible and remote parts, were made by juvenile hands, and some researchers believe that children may have made some of the rock art (in addition to their hand stencils, which actually dominate at some sites).

(Left) Painting of a female kangaroo with a joey in her pouch, at Two Leg Rock, Kakadu, in Australia's Northern Territory. Date unknown.

(Below) Petroglyph at Three Rivers, New Mexico (United States) which may represent a pregnant animal. Date unknown, probably 1000–1400 AD.

only thirty-five seem to have been used; in the ground rock art of northern Norway only five of the sixty-six possible combinations of two motifs are used. A series of researchers in South Africa have likewise shown that certain combinations of motifs in paintings were favoured and others avoided. In other words, prehistoric art is by no means random accumulations of aimless images; it has a syntax, rules and structure.

How can one tell if two or more motifs are deliberately associated or form a 'scene', rather than being accidentally juxtaposed? If they are made with the same technique or pigment or have the same patination, this may denote that they are part of the same artistic episode, but association is really only clear where two images touch or where, for example, one seems to be firing an arrow or throwing a spear at the other. There are very few recognizable scenes in Eurasian Ice Age art, but the art of other cultures and later periods contains numerous examples. However, even if one assumes that one can recognize some association between images, that they constitute a 'scene', it is another step up the ladder to interpret that scene. Even apparently straightforward subjects can be open to any number of interpretations.

Probably the most widespread category of recognizable 'scenes' are those which seem to involve economic activities, such as hunting, herding or ploughing. Among the more exotic are the 'honey gathering scenes', well known from the Levantine art of Spain, as well as from Southern African rock art and farther afield. Scandinavian prehistoric art contains thousands of images of what are normally thought to be boats (or, in some eyes, sledges), many of which carry series of humans, while North African rock art is also known for its chariots and other such vehicles.

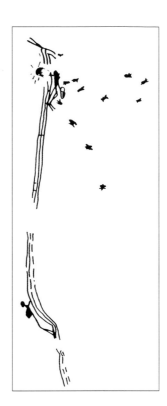

(*Above*) Tracing of a brownish-red rock painting (54 centimetres/21 inches long) of two people collecting honey, at Rock Shelter II, La Araña (eastern Spain). The upper figure, perched on the ladder or ropes, holds some kind of basket, while the lower one also appears to have a bag. Date unknown.

(*Left*) Petroglyph at Three Rivers, New Mexico (United States), depicting a mountain sheep which seems to be pierced by arrows. Note the decoration inside the sheep's body. Date probably 1000–1400 AD.

Violence and warfare

Interhuman violence is surprisingly rare in prehistoric art as a whole. In the whole of Eurasian Ice Age art, for example, only a couple of humanoid figures are shown which may (or may not) have missiles sticking out of them. Even in the Levantine rock art of Spain, where human figures are far more common and 'active' than in Palaeolithic art, this theme of the 'wounded man' represents a very tiny percentage of the whole. In any case, it is by no means a straightforward matter to assess what such figures, apparently pierced by missiles, might represent. Some are isolated, while others seem to be the target of a group of archers, perhaps in an execution or ritual sacrifice. Others seem to be human figures to which 'arrows' were added at some later stage.

Similar uncertainty occurs in other contexts – for example, in what seem to be 'human head-trophies' in the prehistoric rock art of India or the New World. In Brazil's Piauí region, there is an 'execution scene' which has been described as people tied to posts and being clubbed or speared; but whereas this seems a likely interpretation, there is no certainty about what precisely is going on. Since violence involves dynamic action, it is very difficult to convey in a single image, and even harder to interpret with any reliability.

Where 'battle scenes' are concerned, such as a series of panels interpreted in this way in Arnhem Land, one might expect to be on safer ground. However, it has been pointed out that not all paintings showing bows shooting at people are necessarily angry clashes. Bushman ethnography records a 'game' in which men took it in turns to shoot at each other, and were adept at catching the arrows and shooting them back again. Ritual combats (like medieval jousting) are known to take place among many 'primitives' today: these usually non-violent confrontations, involving insults and threats and even simulated combats, appear to help to maintain the fragile co-existence between neighbouring groups and eliminate latent tensions. They sometimes end with the appearance of blood in a participant.

Nevertheless, on the reasonable assumption that most battle scenes depict real aggression, whether narrative, commemorative or mythological, there is some evidence, in Arnhem Land and elsewhere, that such scenes become more frequent in later periods and display changes through time: for example, in Spain's Levantine art, the superimposition of images suggests that the early phases only have very small-scale armed conflicts, which were probably rare and perhaps even limited to ritual combats; but later phases have major conflicts, with depictions of of pitched battles and wounded people. These may have been caused by quarrels triggered by the increasing rarity of game or by the arrival of immigrant groups. At Writing-on-Stone, Alberta, the rock art of the late prehistoric and historical periods reflects known changes brought about by the introduction of horses and guns – most notably a change from large forces of heavily armed pedestrian 'shock troops' – involved in conflicts for territory or women – to small, highly mobile, lightly armed war parties out to get individual war honours. It has proved possible to

Large pictographs of humans with what may be black arrows or spears sticking in them, at the rock shelter of Cueva Flechas, in Baja California (Mexico). The right-hand human, in red outlined in white, is 2.5 metres (8 feet) tall. Date unknown.

obtain some pretty solid readings of this final prehistoric (after 1700 AD) and historic rock art by means of 'ledger art'. These simple drawings (a rudimentary form of picture writing), made in notebooks by native Americans, feature the same subjects and conventions as were painted on hides and engraved on rocks – fairly realistic scenes of horses, humans, weapons and tipis.

(*Above*) Rock engravings at Castle Butte, Montana (United States), depicting two warriors, one of them mounted on horseback: one carries a rifle, the other has a spear. The horse is 71 centimetres (28 inches) long. Note the hooklike hoofs. This panel must date to the eighteenth century or later.

Petroglyphs at Fossum in Bohuslän (Sweden), showing men fighting with axes. Probably Bronze Age (*c.* 1000 BC).

SOUND AND MUSIC

Dance and song leave no material traces in the archaeological record, although some rock paintings, particularly in India and Africa, are often interpreted as dances. Unfortunately, although this may be true for some of them, it cannot be

(Above) Painted human figures in a rock shelter at Perna, in Brazil's Piauí region, which seem to be dancing. Date unknown, perhaps 6000–4000 BC.

(Right) Painted humans in a rock shelter at Bhimbetka (northern India), which have been interpreted as musicians and dancers. Date unknown.

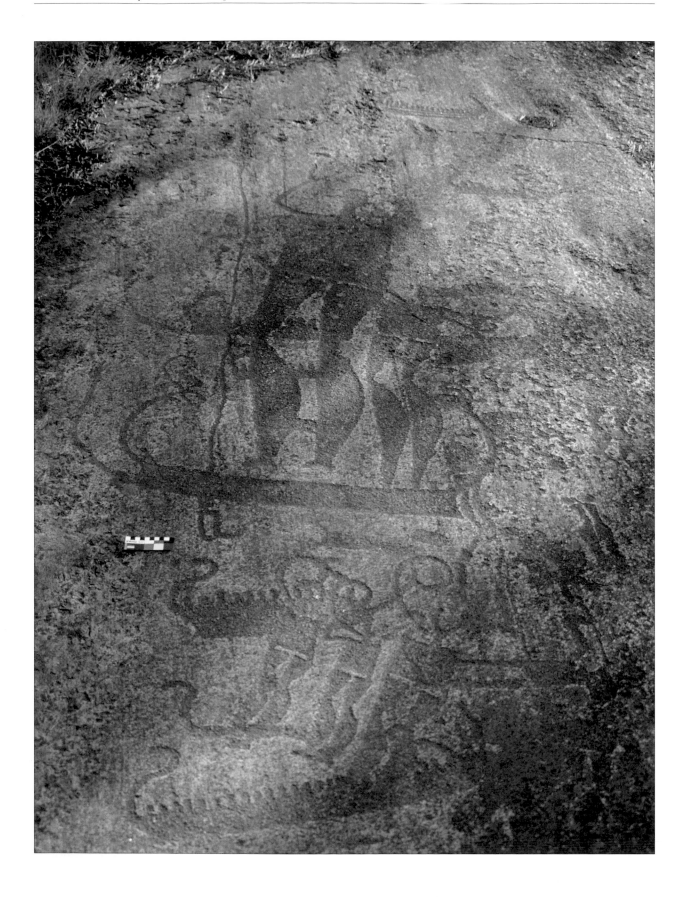

(Previous page) Petroglyphs at Kalleby, in Bohuslän (Sweden), depicting three square-bodied, helmeted people blowing lurer (bronze horns), carved over a boat. Two much larger men and some boats can be seen above them. Probably Bronze Age (c. 1000 BC).

proved: the lively poses of the human figures, with raised arms, or elegantly curving bodies, or interlocked arms, are open to a wide variety of interpretations.

Such things as reed-pipes, wooden instruments and stretched-skin drums will have disintegrated. The majority of definite portable musical instruments to have

survived from prehistoric times are wind instruments such as the great curved bronze 'lurer' horns of the Scandinavian Bronze Age, clay ocarinas from Latin America, or bone 'flutes' which are known from the Ice Age onwards (in Europe there are about thirty of these bone flutes from the last Ice Age, most of them from

Perhaps the best known musical instrument in rock art is that associated with the popular and common 'flute-player', sometimes hunch-backed and sometimes with an erect penis, which is so widespread in the rock art of America's south-west. The erroneously named Kokopelli seems to have been linked with rainmaking, eroticism and human fertility. Date unknown.

France). The French flutes are made from hollowed bird bones, while others from Central and Eastern Europe are of reindeer or bear bone. Bone flutes have between three and seven finger-holes along their length and are played like penny-whistles rather than true flutes. Experiments with a replica by a modern musicologist revealed that, once a whistle-head is attached to direct the air-flow, one can produce strong, clear notes of piccolo-type on a five-tone scale.

A number of oval objects of bone or ivory with a hole at one end, from Europe's Ice Age, have been interpreted as 'bull-roarers' by analogy with modern specimens from Australia – such instruments make a loud humming noise when whirled round on a string. One well-known Ice Age engraving in the French cave of Les Trois Frères depicts a 'sorcerer' with a bison head: it has often been claimed to be playing a musical bow but this interpretation is highly tenuous, since the marks in front of its mouth could be all kinds of things. However, Southern African rock art does, apparently, depict musical bows being played. The rock art of the Sahara likewise contains a few probable representations of instruments being played – lute, trumpet, harp, drum, etc; while a number of paintings in Zimbabwe and South Africa appear to be playing long trumpets resembling didgeridoos or alpenhorns.

Other surviving instruments are of the percussive variety. A number of mammoth bones, painted with red ochre, from the site of Mezin, near Kiev, dating to about 20,000 years ago, have been interpreted as sources of music – a hip-bone xylophone, skull and shoulder-blade drums, etc. (These bones have been played by a Russian orchestra, who cut a record of their jam-session.) However, doubt has been cast on whether there are in fact any marks of percussion on any of these objects and their use as musical instruments is therefore far from certain.

Far clearer examples of Ice Age music-making are to be found in several caves in France and Spain, which contain 'lithophones' – natural draperies of calcite which resound when struck with a hard object (wooden sticks seem to produce the clearest and most resonant notes). In a few caves these lithophones are somewhat battered and are decorated with painted lines and dots. Most are in or near large chambers which could have held a sizeable audience.

In recent years detailed studies of several decorated Ice Age caves have been undertaken in terms of their acoustic properties, and a frequent correlation has been detected between the locations of decoration and the areas of best resonance for men's voices. Most recently, American researcher Steven Waller has tried to extend this idea to the content of rock art, claiming that early artists ingeniously used the acoustics and echoes of caves to conjure up the sounds made by moving herds of hoofed animals. He has found – by yelling, clapping or striking stones together – that in deep caves like Lascaux and Font de Gaume echoes in the painted chambers produce sound levels of between 23 and 31 decibels, whereas deep cave walls decorated with big cats (like Lascaux's Cabinet des Félins) produce sound levels of only 1 to 7 decibels, and undecorated surfaces are often 'totally flat'.

(*Opposite*) Paintings of two musicians in Shelter G1 in Ga'aseb Gorge in Namibia's Brandberg massif. The two men appear to be holding what may be horns or flutes to their mouths. The curvature of the instruments suggests that they may be kudu or eland horns. Date unknown.

Some of Waller's interpretations, linking the acoustics to thundering ungulate herds or to silent carnivores, are less than convincing and fail to fit the data. Nevertheless, studies of this type are valuable in that they are trying to revive something that one might imagine gone for ever – the sound dimension which accompanied whatever rituals may have been carried out in decorated caves and rock shelters. Naturally these studies cannot actually prove anything about something so ephemeral and short-lived; but if a consistent correlation can be found between acoustic quality and 'principal decorated panels', it will certainly provide some indication that sound played an important role. In view of the obvious intelligence of the cave artists, it is extremely likely that, since they took full advantage of the morphology of the cave and especially of particular rock shapes, they would also have utilized any acoustic peculiarities to the full. Echoes are common in and around decorated rock shelters all over the world, as is the equally mysterious and impressive phenomenon of cavities which focus and project sound, so that conversations inside the sites can be heard clearly 50–100 metres (c. 160–300 feet) away – for example, at the decorated shelter of Wikwip or Echo Rock in San Diego County, California. It has even been suggested that some rock art may have been linked with noisy water runs, waterfalls or the crash of the sea.

There are further indications from later periods and other parts of the world that sound was indeed of great importance. For example, at a number of locations in the American far west, open-air rock art is directly associated with rocks which ring like chimes when struck. Many of these primitive 'bells' are simply marked with cupules but occasionally – as at Cocoraque Butte, Arizona, a Hohokam petroglyph site attributed to 600–1450 AD – there are complex motifs pecked into the ringing rocks, which also bear the marks of repeated battering.

Such sites not only link rock art to senses other than the visual, but also suggest that an auditory component might be involved in the actual production of the petroglyphs. Local ethnography in California and elsewhere associated the use of such ringing rocks with puberty rites and also with weather control. Intriguingly, some ringing rocks in Uganda are likewise linked with rainmaking, and certain Ugandan rock gongs are associated with rock paintings – crosses, dots, concentric circles, etc. – in red ochre.

Musical rocks of a different kind can also be found. For example, on Easter Island a slightly phallic-shaped stone called Pu o Hiro (Trumpet of Hiro) has natural holes (as well as some incised petroglyphs of *komari* or vulva forms): according to local legend, blowing into the holes – which produces a sound like a conch shell – causes fish to swim to the shore.

VISUAL HUMOUR

Comedy is an elusive phenomenon which takes many forms; in the present context, of course, we are concerned only with its visual aspects. However, humour changes through space and time: today there are marked variations from place to place in

(*Opposite*) **Petroglyph at Cocoraque Butte, Arizona (United States), pecked into a ringing rock, which displays the marks of repeated battering. Thought to date to 600–1450 AD.**

(*Above*) **Images carved in bas-relief on a block from Roc de Sers, Charente (France), showing a human apparently being pursued round the rock by a bison or (going by the horn-shape) muskox. The block is about 35 centimetres (*c.* 14 inches) thick, and the human is about 50 centimetres (*c.* 20 inches) high. Date *c.* 20,000 BC.**

(*Right*) **There are many examples of the theme of the exaggerated penis from the pottery of ancient Peru, including (*bottom left*) one man with his nose and lips transformed into genitals, and (*bottom right*) another cheerful figure on a vessel from the Moche culture designed so that the only way to drink from it is to use the penis! Probably 1–600 AD. (After Kauffmann-Doig.)**

the type of material considered funny. This problem becomes more acute when the dimension of time is included – nothing dates faster than comedy. What seems topical and witty today will produce a puzzled frown or a yawn tomorrow and this elusive quality of humour increases with time. Inevitably, therefore, there are great difficulties in any attempt to assess the comedy of remote cultures, and especially that of prehistoric times.

All comedy has content and manner: the latter, involving delivery, timing and so forth, cannot survive in art. Prehistoric people undoubtedly laughed uproariously at tellers of funny stories, but all of that side of their humour has gone forever. What we are left with is the content, much of which we cannot recognize – for the simple reason that content draws heavily on contemporary trivia or on shared experiences. There is an added danger that what may seem funny to us in early art was intended to be serious or symbolic.

Consequently, when seeking humour in the art of cultures earlier than our own, and particularly those with no writing to explain things, we are reduced to certain basic categories which seem to be common to all mankind: exaggeration, inversion, satirical caricature, the grotesque/monstrous, scatology and, of course, sexuality. Intermingled with these themes is our apparently fundamental ability and need to laugh at the misfortunes of others – this is the essence of all slapstick humour and explains the global popularity of the silent comedies of old Hollywood. Under the mask of humour, society allows an infinite degree of aggression by everyone against everyone.

For example, an early twentieth-century rock painting in the Largun Shelter in Australia's Northern Territory depicts a man in fright with a snake draped over him. It is known that the story behind this is that a hunter caught a large python and, as a joke, draped it over an old man asleep in camp. When the victim awoke he panicked and leapt into a waterhole inhabited by crocodiles. The incident was

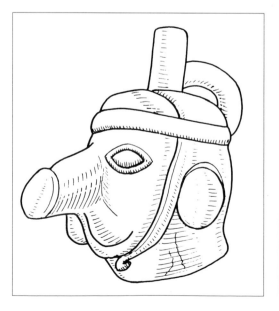

painted by the perpetrator so that people could recall the incident and laugh about it; and indeed the story is still told today in the local Aboriginal community, amid great hilarity. When the people are shown a photograph of the painting they burst out laughing, and children ask for the story to be repeated continually and for the photograph to be handed around. One can be quite certain that there are innumerable examples of this type to be found in the prehistoric art of the world but, without knowledge of the specific story that lies behind them, most, alas, will go unrecognized as being humorous.

Hence, no recognizable slapstick is yet known in the earliest art because of its lack of perceptible narrative, although the bas-relief from the French Ice Age site of Roc de Sers of a human apparently being chased by a bison may conceivably belong in this category.

Inversion, or a topsy-turvy world, can be found in cases where animals are sometimes shown in the guise of human beings: this kind of nonsense world turned upside down is found in other early cultures. Such humour seems to stem from our innate tendency to anthropomorphize animals – endowing them with human abilities and qualities and dressing them up. However, there is no evidence from art that the people of the last Ice Age had this attitude: their rare depictions of what seem to be humans with animal heads are usually interpreted as 'sorcerers'; the animal-headed humans of Saharan rock art are normally seen as hunters in masks or mythical beings; and the therianthropes in the rock art of Southern Africa and elsewhere are currently interpreted as shamans. In any case, in all these prehistoric cultures, the knowledge and appreciation of the real habits of animals were certainly superior to ours, so perhaps they had no compulsion to anthropomorphize in this way. Yet it is probable that some depictions of animals in human-like poses – such as sheep apparently dancing to the flute-player's music in the south-western United States or the bighorn sheep from Three Rivers – were meant to be amusing, and they certainly elicit laughter today.

Where scatology is concerned, the depiction of vomit and faeces is generally subject to taboos, and the humour thus lies in a flagrant flaunting of these rules. At least one case is known from the Ice Age: in the French Pyrenees, a whole series of almost identical antler spearthrowers are known, dating to about 12,000 BC. These show a young fawn or ibex, looking over its shoulder at what appears to be a ridiculously large turd, on

Antler spearthrower showing a young ibex with emerging turd on which two birds are perched, found around 1940 in the cave of Le Mas d'Azil, Ariège (France). The ibex figure is about 7 centimetres (c. 3 inches) long, and dates to c. 14,000 BC.

(Previous page) Petroglyph of an upright bighorn sheep, from Three Rivers, New Mexico (United States). This has a decidedly humorous effect today and was presumably intended to do so. Probably 1000–1400 AD.

which birds are perching, emerging from its anus (some researchers believe this to be a birthing scene, although they cannot explain the birds!). The fact that fragments of up to ten examples have been recovered from different sites, in addition to the two intact ones known, means that scores, if not hundreds, of specimens were originally produced, and this, in turn, implies that this joke – or humorous tale – was extremely popular in this period. What is even more remarkable is that a virtually identical scene (though without the turd) was depicted in Walt Disney's *Bambi*, produced before the discovery of these spearthrowers – thus implying that the image may be deeply embedded in the human psyche.

Erotic humour is by far the most popular of all types, both verbal and visual, and a very high percentage of all jokes are concerned with the sexual impulse. Once again this form of comedy is involved with the flaunting of taboos and, thereby, mocking the authority figures. Perhaps the earliest example of sexual humour occurs in the cave of Le Portel, France, and dates to the end of the last Ice Age. As we have seen, there is very little direct evidence for interest in sexuality as a whole in Ice Age art, and the occasional depictions of male or female genitalia were probably used in a ritual rather than a bawdy context. However, most scholars assume that the Portel figure is a bit of fun: a small stalagmite emerging from the cave wall was surrounded with the painted outline of a man, and a red dot was placed on the end of the 'phallus'. In later periods, humorous images are more readily recognizable. Grossly exaggerated penises can be found in the rock art of many areas, from Australia to Scandinavia, though it is often hard to judge whether the intention is humorous, boastful or mythological.

Tracing of a petroglyph from Valcamonica (Italian Alps), showing a man waving while engaged in copulation with an animal. Date unknown.

There seem to be a few caricatures in the art of the last Ice Age; for, in addition to what appears a realistic portrait, there are a number of depictions of carefully differentiated human profiles on stone slabs from the French cave of La Marche, dating to about 14,000 years ago. It is clear from the remarkable detail in the animal pictures on the same slabs that these people were superb artists who could easily have captured a lifelike human face (even if, as some researchers believe, humans were far more difficult to draw than animals); the fact that they hardly ever did so is generally thought to indicate that there was some sort of taboo operating on accurate portraiture at this period. The La Marche heads may be clumsy attempts at portraits, or they may be purposely stylized; but it is equally likely that they are the earliest caricatures, and one or two have features and expressions which make this a particularly feasible explanation.

IMAGES OF INVADERS

The end of prehistoric art in many areas is reflected not only in the rise of actual written inscriptions on rocks, but also in the depiction of new subjects introduced by colonists or invaders – particularly in the New World, Southern Africa and

(Opposite top) Figure of a human drawn around a natural penis-like stalagmite protruding from the wall in the cave of Le Portel, Ariège (France). It is about 38 centimetres (*c.* 15 inches) high, and probably dates to the end of the Ice Age (*c.* 10,000 BC).

(Opposite bottom) Petroglyphs at Fossum, in Bohuslän (Sweden), depicting three men: the outer pair are highly masculine, axe-wielding individuals, while the central one has a leg raised and a hand behind his head, in a decidedly comical pose. Probably Bronze Age (*c.* 1000 BC).

Petroglyphs of 'masks' in the Helan Mountains (northern China). Date unknown, but the chiselled Buddhist texts visible here are much less patinated, proving that the 'masks' clearly predate the twelfth century by a considerable amount of time.

(Above) Huge painting of a horse, about 5 metres (*c.* 18 feet) long, in the Giant Horse site, Queensland (Australia), rediscovered by Percy Trezise in 1967. Excavations indicate that this shelter was occupied from about 4,000 years ago, but the horse painting is obviously very recent, from the European contact period (over the last couple of centuries). The first horses were seen in this region in 1848 AD.

(Right) Painting of a sailing ship, at Nanguluwurr, Kakadu, in Australia's Northern Territory, from the European contact period.

Petroglyphs at Sapagua, in Jujuy Province (north-west Argentina), depicting a rider (perhaps a Hispanic invader fighting a native?). Among the most interesting images are those where an old motif was transformed into something new: for example, on the same petroglyph panel of Sapagua, (below) some llama petroglyphs were apparently changed into horses by having their tails and heads lengthened, and a rider added – that these are later additions can be seen clearly from the marked difference in patination. Dates unknown, but post-conquest.

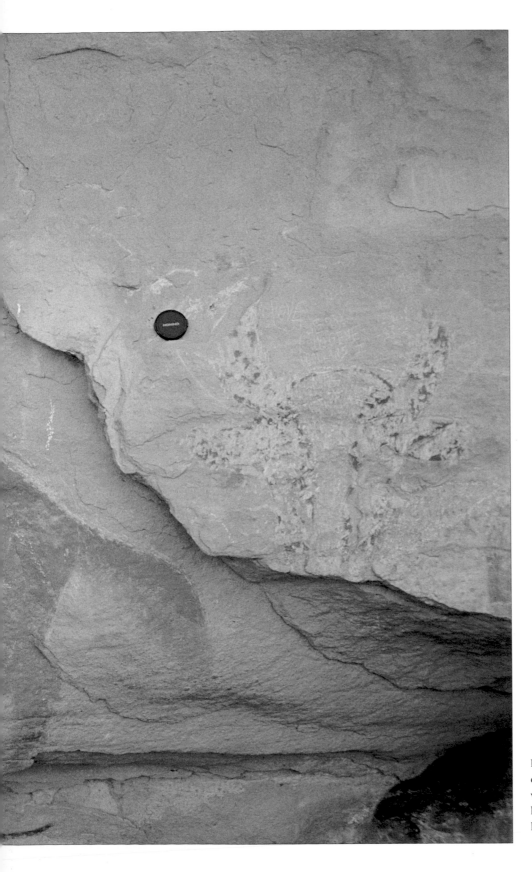

Rock paintings by the Ute
of Colorado, depicting a
white horse and rider, and
hence clearly dating to
historical times.

Australasia – and at times the adoption of new raw materials in art production. The horse and rifle had a major impact in the New World, while in Australia horses, sailing ships and Europeans all appeared in the rock art, especially in the north. On Easter Island, a few depictions of European ships were made on the rocks,

Small Bushman painting of a horse and rider from Steel's Shelter, at Giant's Castle in South Africa's Drakensberg. The rider appears to be leaning back for balance and holds a whip and spears. Date unknown.

including one petroglyph of a sailing ship – with a turtle for an anchor – on the chest of a *moai*. As rock art continued in the historical period, images of the new order came into prominence – for example in Ute rock art in North America, with its horses and cowboys, or, elsewhere, depictions of trains or even cars.

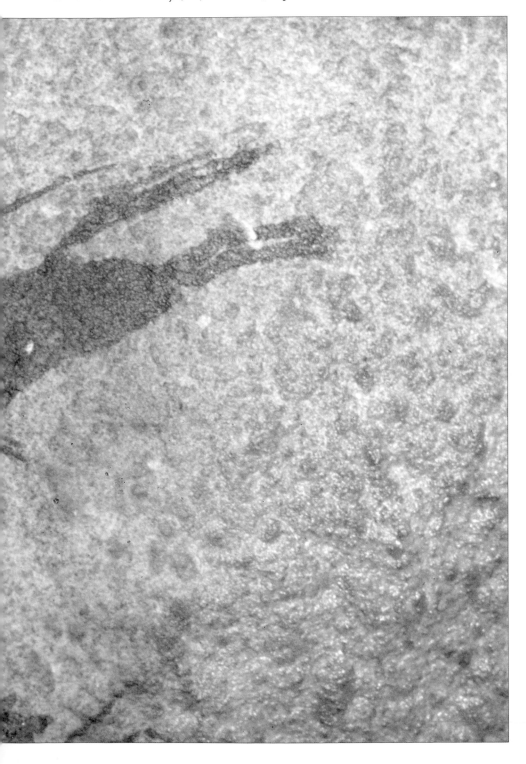

CHAPTER 8

Matters of the Mind: Symbolic Interpretations of Prehistoric Art

I want to suggest as an investigator's rule of thumb that in rock art studies we come to distrust any single context or identification.

William Strange

Meaning is for those who are ready for it, for those who are trained for it. The rest get pretty pictures.

Les Bursill (Aboriginal researcher)

Some of the remarkable paintings of eland in Game Pass Shelter, in South Africa's Drakensberg. This species and this region loom large in recent interpretations of rock art in terms of shamanism and trance phenomena. Date unknown.

To many researchers, 'literal' readings of prehistoric art are unsatisfactory, and certainly we know from ethnographic and ethnohistoric information that the meaning of some art and the motivation behind it are more complex. But similar sources also make it clear that some art is indeed fairly simple or straightforward. So, for the most part, one's approach comes down to personal preference. This can be summed up by the following statements from two present-day researchers working on essentially the same corpus of rock art in Southern Africa: 'Nothing we see today on cave walls is likely to represent quite what it seems'; and 'Where a practical explanation for a rock painting is available I prefer it to a symbolic one, but I accept that other people think differently and prefer "non-real" to real.'

Unfortunately, in recent years some researchers have adopted a rather patronizing view of the 'empiricist perspective' (that is, the literal interpretation of representations) as being somehow naive, trivializing, simplistic or old-fashioned. In fact such views can be just as valid or well founded as the more symbolic or mystical interpretations. Where ethnographic evidence is absent (as in the majority of cases) literal interpretations of prehistoric art are far safer – and at worst may be incomplete rather than wrong. Literal interpretations are also regularly branded 'Eurocentric', even when based on a profound knowledge of indigenous cultures.

As Patricia Vinnicombe's landmark studies in Southern Africa have shown, much of the art is a complex interweaving of the real and the non-real. Separating out the different strands is an impossible task since a group of sites – even a single rock art panel – may include mundane, literal, whimsical, religious and secular, mystical and metaphorical material. Even a single motif may have pluralistic meanings. Or it may not. There are pitfalls in an excessively literal interpretation of ancient art but there are far more in non-literal interpretations, which, at their worst, are mere wishful thinking or flights of fancy.

It has been pointed out that our own psychological needs, as well as the reward structures of academia and society, play a considerable role in promoting exotic interpretations of the past. Unfortunately, some researchers have a tendency to latch onto one idea and present it as the key to all prehistoric art, treating the art of a whole region as a homogeneous lump, and sometimes even assuming that the motivation underlying the art remained essentially unchanged for thousands of years. Such grand schemes – like that of Leroi-Gourhan for Ice Age art (see Chapter 2) – which subordinate the art of millennia or of vast areas to one system of meaning may be stimulating to research or appealing to the media, but they are products of their own time and culture: they inevitably collapse, to be replaced eventually by more realistic theories based on more modest hypotheses fitted to more limited data.

THE USE OF INFORMANTS

Non-literal interpretations depend heavily on local ethnographic or ethnohistoric information in order to obtain some insight into the complex stories or thought processes behind the art: for example, Australian rock art specialist George Chaloupka has been able to use local Aboriginal myths to infer the identity of many of the images in the rock art of Arnhem Land, just as we use classical literature to identify stories and images from Greek and Roman mythology in classical art. However, testimony of this kind is generally derived from one or two individuals and an investigator can easily be given conflicting statements, with equal confidence and detail, about the same motifs by different informants. It is also a well-known phenomenon that some informants will say what they imagine the investigator wants to hear, or will say something, anything, rather than admit ignorance. Informants may be self-contradictory, change their minds or tell untruths. And one always has

(Opposite) **Part of the long frieze at Magnificent Gallery, Queensland (Australia), comprising about 450 rock paintings of spirits, humans, kangaroos, birds, dingoes, etc. Aboriginal use of this gallery began about 15,000 years ago and continued to the late nineteenth century. Aboriginal informants in the region have given researchers numerous legends and stories which seem to relate to at least the younger paintings, and some old Aboriginal men accompanied researchers such as Percy Trezise to some sites and attempted to interpret the paintings based on their knowledge of tribal lore and custom. For example, some figures were 'good' (ancestral heroes, love magic paintings) and others 'bad' (spirit figures or quinkans, sorcery or death magic paintings).**

to bear in mind the difficulties involved in the questions and concepts being trans-lated back and forth, often in obscure languages in which it can be almost impossible to convey what the questioner wants to ask and the informant is trying to explain. We know, for example, that Aboriginal knowledge is imparted incre-mentally – in other words, it is necessary to have a very long period of association with the informants in order to win their trust, and for them to convey, in stages, the complex concepts involved in their beliefs and culture.

Even assuming the ethnographic or ethnohistoric information to be accurate and valid, it is of limited use: for while such information is undoubtedly invaluable for art of the historical periods and the periods immediately preceding them, it is not necessarily applicable to any truly prehistoric art, even in those same areas: in North Africa, for instance, a few recent images evoke elements known from Berber folklore, but for the earliest kinds of Saharan art there is little to help us. Prehistoric art cannot be used to reconstruct prehistoric ideology – instead, we have to assume an ideology based on other evidence, either local or (more often) remote, and then use it to explain prehistoric art.

Getting inside the heads of prehistoric people is probably the most daunting task confronting the archaeologist or the rock art researcher, and it needs to be done with the greatest care, and constant awareness of the flimsy foundations of all our assumptions.

NON-FIGURATIVE MOTIFS

Among the most intractable problems is the interpretation of what seem to be non-figurative motifs. These markings are found all over the world – for example, the great expanses of finger markings in some Australian caves, the innumerable cups, rings and spirals of Europe, and the truly universal cup marks. Some researchers

Some of the numerous circles and cup marks pecked into rocks at Carschenna, in the Swiss Alps, at an altitude of about 1,100 metres (c. 3,600 feet). Date unknown.

believe that such marks are the most ancient surviving in every part of the world, though this remains to be proven. What is certain is that, as one would expect, the simplest shapes are found everywhere – not only cup marks, but also geometric shapes and incised grids (the latter can be seen as far afield as Australia, Utah in the United States, Russia and especially the Paris Basin where they characterize the enigmatic rock art of the Fontainebleau region).

Some of the innumerable grid-like designs engraved in rock shelters in the Fontainebleau region, south of Paris. Date unknown.

This large and striking petroglyph in Washington State known as Tsagaglalal (She Who Watches) is – like similar petroglyphs in the region as well as carved images from burials – thought to be a guardian spirit, carved in the eighteenth century (around the time of the first entry of white people into the Pacific north-west), perhaps in an attempt to ward off the infections and epidemics brought by the newcomers.

These marks may have had meanings to the people of the prehistoric culture which produced them – as mentioned earlier (see Chapter 7), the simplest shapes can have a wide variety of meanings – but to us they seem abstract or at least unrecognizable as objects. In Ice Age art this category of markings was neglected until relatively recently, because it seemed uninteresting or impossible to explain or define. Now, however, thanks to the attention paid to the abstract 'signs' by Leroi-Gourhan who divided them into 'phallic' and 'vulvar' groups (now seen as a simplistic classification), researchers accept that these marks may have been of equal, if not greater, importance to Ice Age people than the 'recognizable' images to which so much attention has been devoted. Non-figurative marks are estimated to be two or three times more abundant than figurative, and in some areas far more. For example, on 1,200 engraved pieces of bone and antler from 26 late Ice Age sites in northern Spain, there are only 26 identifiable animals – all other motifs seem non-figurative.

Paintings known as the Holy Ghost panel in the Great Gallery of Barrier (Horseshoe) Canyon, Utah (United States). Note the heroic size (the main figure is over 2 metres/6 feet tall), the total absence of extremities, the bug eyes, and the mummy-like appearance. They are assumed to represent some kind of supernatural being. Date probably 700–1200 AD.

In Ice Age art, there is a wide range of motifs in this category, from a single dot or line to complex constructions and extensive panels of apparently unstructured linear marks. They can be totally isolated, clustered on their own panels, or closely associated with the figurative. In the past, some shapes were assumed to be narrative or pictographic – that is, to represent schematized objects, based on what they were thought to look like (for example, tectiforms (huts), claviforms (clubs), or aviforms (birds)). Some researchers, on the other hand, see them as 'ideomorphs', representations of ideas rather than objects. In any case, the simpler motifs are more abundant and widespread, as one might expect, since they could have been invented in many places and periods independently, but the more complex forms show extraordinary variability, and are more restricted in space and time, to the extent that they have been seen as 'ethnic markers', perhaps delineating social groups of some sort.

MYSTICAL IMAGES

Perhaps the most basic 'mystical' approach to prehistoric art is to see individual animal or human figures as gods, demons, spirits, ancestors, and so forth. In some cases this is based on good ethnographic evidence – for example, we have clear testimony from the eighteenth-century Easter Islanders that the great stone *moai* (statues) represented powerful ancestor figures with great spiritual power or *mana*.

(*Following page*) This fine Bushman painting of an eland from Game Pass Shelter, in South Africa's Drakensberg, has its body in profile and its head turned forward, though the horns are not shown. An elongated humanlike figure, which is painted in orange and is grasping its tail, has hoofs which, like the eland's hind legs, are crossed. Some researchers believe that this unusual position of the legs, and the hair apparently standing on end, indicate that the animal is dying, and they therefore interpret this frieze as part of a trance scene. Date unknown.

Prehistoric art and astronomy

At the painted rock shelter of Glenisla in the Grampians of South Australia, there are numerous small painted lines, which have often been seen as 'tally marks'. A nineteenth-century settler wrote that the Aborigines counted time by moons, and would draw strokes on the rock representing the number of moons they had been there.

The phases of the moon would have been the principal means available to prehistoric people for measuring the passage of time, the seasons, and the movements of the sun and stars. Since such observations must have been fundamental to every prehistoric culture, it can hardly be doubted that they must be represented in or associated with much ancient art.

The giant figures and many of the geometric shapes and immense lines on the Nasca plain, Peru, have often been linked with astronomical orientations and constellations (see Chapter 5). Patterns of cup marks have often been compared to constellations, and in Britain it has even been suggested that, if they held oil and a floating wick, they could mirror the night sky when lit. In many parts of the world, motifs in rock art have been interpreted as the rayed sun, the phases of the moon, or comets.

It is in North America that the possible links between rock art and astronomy have been pursued most assiduously, with many claims made for solar observatories or calendrical markers. There are numerous examples of motifs, sometimes hidden in dark recesses, which are dramatically illuminated by the sun on a solstice or equinox, often with a shaft of light or 'sun dagger'. Some of these may be accidental – not every spiral is a solstice marker – and in some cases the position of rocks may have changed since the motifs were produced. But it is clear that in many cases the placing, and presumably often the content, of the rock art are directly linked with such celestial phenomena – either to celebrate them, or for calendrical or ritual purposes. In the Navajo area of the south-west, and especially around Canyon de Chelly, small crosses are frequently found painted on the roofs of rock shelters, some low

In the rock art of Australia there are many large collections of short, upright engraved lines, or 'abraded grooves' (as here, at Ingaladdi in the Victoria River District of the Northern Territory). These have been interpreted as the number of participants in a ritual, a link with rainmaking ceremonies, a representation of scarification, etc. But some researchers see possible astronomical significance in their counts.

In Europe, astronomy has been linked with some decorated megalithic monuments, most notably this one at Newgrange (Ireland), where, at dawn on the winter solstice, the sun shines through a specially constructed opening above the door, down the decorated passage, and lights up the chamber at the end for seventeen minutes.

down but others 15 metres (c. 50 feet) up or more with no apparent access. These are generally interpreted as stars, and often seen as possible depictions of constellations.

From the first discoveries of Ice Age portable art, researchers began to look at sets of marks on bones or stones as possible tallies or even proto-mathematics. Repeated multiples of every number from 1 to 10 have been claimed on portable objects from Russia and elsewhere. However, these numbers are quite random, and the discovery of any repetitions in Ice Age engravings is more indicative of a researcher's ability to count than of any number-system in the Palaeolithic period. Claims about isolated sets of marks like these cannot be tested. In the view of pioneering American researcher Alexander Marshack, they are more likely to be notations – that is, sets of marks accumulated as a sequence, perhaps from observation of astronomical regularities. Marshack has tested

linear sets of such marks on Ice Age objects for 'internal periodicities and regularities', particularly as possible examples of lunar notation, with varying degrees of success, though he believes that there are also non-lunar notations.

These studies, whatever the validity of their results, have focused attention on a type of marking previously ignored or dismissed as random; it is now clear that some of these markings are coherent and ordered, and were carefully made over a period of time. Similarly, a study of painted pebbles from the Azilian culture (the very end of the Ice Age in south-west Europe, see Chapter 4) revealed that the 16 signs drawn on them were found in only 41 of the possible 246 combinations, indicating that some form of 'syntax' was employed. There is a predominance of groups numbering from 21 to 29 or their multiples, which may perhaps have some connection with lunar phases or lunations.

Rock painting at Mesa San Carlos, Baja California (Mexico). On the morning of the summer solstice, a triangular wedge of sunlight hits the rock adjacent to one petroglyph: this perfect alignment makes it clear that the positioning of the motif was linked to this phenomenon. The motif, about 30 centimetres (c. 12 inches) high, has been interpreted by some researchers as being house-like, with a doorway. Date unknown

Part of a painted panel, high up on a rock face at Bhimbetka (northern India), depicting what has been claimed to be a giant mythical boar (or possibly buffalo). Large 'deified' zoomorphic beings, composite animals which closely resemble boars, seem to have a prominent place in the religions of the Mesolithic hunter-gatherers of India. By the animal's snout is a little human figure running towards a large crab figure. Date unknown.

Bushman (San) ethnography, especially in the testimony gathered by Bleek and Lloyd (see Chapter 2), makes it clear that the eland was an animal with tremendous power and many meanings, which was central to thought among some Bushman groups (other groups focused on different animals, such as the kudu in the northern Transvaal of South Africa and the giraffe in Zimbabwe) and which they regarded as a link between the material and the spiritual world. It was an all-pervasive symbol in many ritual contexts such as in male and female puberty ceremonies, in marriage and in the control of rain and game animals.

Therianthropes

The therianthropes, with their mixture of human and animal features, are open to a large number of interpretations. It is known, for example, that some Bushmen wore animal masks, and these are unambiguously depicted on some figures. When a celebrated southern Bushman informant, an old woman known as M, was shown reproductions of therianthropes in recent years, she said they were hunting disguises or decorative head-dresses worn by medicine men at dances. Some

Bushman paintings of therianthropes in Mushroom Hill Cave, in South Africa's Drakensberg. Date unknown. These two small figures, part animal and part human, are very elaborate. The left one has an animal head and is finely decorated below the waist; in one hand it holds some kind of stick with a pear-shaped attachment. The other figure, also animal-headed, seems to be wearing a medium-length kaross (cape), and in one hand holds a similar stick with two attachments. Both figures have hoofs instead of feet and so are most likely mythical creatures. Some researchers, however, interpret them in terms of shamanism. Date unknown.

researchers point to the existence of such creatures in mythologies and religions across the globe, and therefore see them as ancestral spirits with the behavioural and visual attributes of animals. Therianthropes are clearly a mixture of the 'real' and the 'non-real' – in Southern Africa a figure with an antelope head and hooves will nevertheless be dressed in a 'real' manner and carry 'real' artifacts. The antelope

Therianthropes – two dog-headed humans, which seem to be consulting together as they follow a rhinoceros to the right. They are carrying what appear to be clubs or sticks. This petroglyph panel, about 1.5 metres (5½ feet) long, is at Wadi Tekniwen, Messak Settafet, Fezzan (Libya). Date unknown.

men or (when they have wings) alites – two different kinds of composite figures – have traditionally been interpreted as spirits of the dead or supernaturals of some kind. Bushman folklore repeatedly and frequently mentions gods, spirits and other mythical creatures, as in the legend that in the beginning all animals were people.

Sorcery figures

In Australia, from Aboriginal informants, we know that – in Queensland, for example – there are sorcery figures and also 'quinkans'. The latter are supernatural spirits or spirits of dead people: capricious and sometimes malevolent, they are similar to 'trickster spirits', a class of being well known in other parts of the world such as South Africa (where the Bushmen had a trickster god known as Kaggen who was mischievous and unpredictable). Some quinkans – tall, thin human beings who can emerge from cracks in the rocks at night – have knobbed penises on which they bound along. Harald Pager, doyen of rock art recorders in Southern Africa, suggested that cracks and fissures in the rocks might have been considered exits for malevolent spirits of the underworld.

Painting of a male spirit figure or quinkan at Red Bluff, Queensland (Australia), showing the knobbed penis on which quinkans bounce around the landscape. Date unknown.

Pictograph of a white figure with a rectangular torso and a 'horned mask' from Hueco Tanks, Texas (United States), sometimes called the Horned Dancer and possibly some kind of spirit or sorcery figure. Date unknown.

Hunting magic?

The relationship between humans and animals was of fundamental importance to both hunting and farming societies and permeates their art, but it is impossible to determine exactly how. For example, the obsession with 'hunting magic' which plagued Ice Age art studies for the first half of the twentieth century (and which has recently reared its head again in the modified form of considering the art to be 'aids for teaching how to hunt') was supposedly based on Australian ethnographic evidence (collected at the end of the nineteenth century) for rock art being used as sympathetic magic, with images being 'killed' to ensure the success of the hunt.

In fact, there is virtually no solid evidence that Australian rock art is produced to influence the hunt magically. On the contrary, we have testimony that a turtle or fish might be painted just to show that someone had visited a shelter or as purely secular records of animals which had been hunted for food. In Kakadu Park, the big fish which dominate the recent art were easy to catch and would certainly not have required hunting magic. In fact, the local Aborigine elders stated that the pictures were usually done after the catch and that usually only food animals were painted. Only good things were painted in the shelters where people lived: fish were a very good subject to paint and, to use what has become an anthropological cliché, also good to think.

Painting of a horizontal wandjina (ancestral spirit) at Mount Elizabeth, in Australia's Kimberley. Date unknown. There is some evidence of a kind of fertility magic in Australia – the Kimberley's wandjina sites are said to be 'increase' places, where, if the images of lizards or fish were retouched, the wandjina would increase the number of these creatures around the site.

Other cultures likewise seem to have depicted the resources which were of economic importance to them, while others emphatically did not. In Eurasian Ice Age art there is no homogeneity: some caves have pictures and bones of the same animals; in other caves the bones are from animals different to those in the pictures. Some North Americans like Plains Indians and Eskimo depicted animals which were of considerable importance to them, but the Susquehannock of the sixteenth-seventeenth centuries did not: deer and elk made up 73 per cent of the meat they ate but they never represented these animals in art. There is a striking scarcity of fish depicted on the central Columbia plateau where salmon fishing played a major role in the Indians' subsistence economy. Similarly, at Alta, in northern Norway, very few fish are depicted in the petroglyphs, yet fish, especially cod, were the main part of the diet in these prehistoric coastal societies. In short, the prehistoric pictures may have been produced purely for pleasure or may have had some direct or indirect link with economic or religious life.

SHAMANISM

Many researchers, particularly in recent years, have turned to the phenomenon of shamanism to explain much (or, in some misguided cases, all) of prehistoric art in some areas. The shaman (a Tungus word from central Asia) is a very important

Highly patterned petroglyphs of humanlike figures in Renegade Canyon, in California's Coso Range. Some scholars interpret all such figures in this region as shamans. Probably before 1000 AD.

Pictograph of an antlered human figure, from Fate Bell Shelter, on the Pecos River, Texas (United States). Some researchers interpret most of this region's rock art in terms of shamanism and trance phenomena. Date unknown.

figure, being a person with spiritual powers who may combine the roles of healer, priest, magician and (sometimes) artist, as well as poet, actor, fortune-teller, weather-controller and even psychotherapist. His most important function is to act as liaison between this world and the spirit world, a task usually performed by means of trances and hallucinatory experiences – either self-induced or using hallucinogenic fungi or other similar substances. Cultures with shamans usually have a zoomorphic view of the world and things are seen and experienced in animal form.

The application of this interpretation to prehistoric art is an old favourite – for example, the German ethnologist Leo Frobenius said in the 1930s that there was shamanistic rock art in Southern Africa – and it has been particularly popular in relation to Eurasian Ice Age art, where the handful of figures combining human and animal features have often been seen as sorcerers or shamans. However, many researchers have also considered them imaginary beings or gods. One theory, based

on Siberian ethnography, suggested that many of the figures in Ice Age art were 'ongones', spirits which took the forms of animals or humans and which were asked to help in hunting, matters of health, and so on. A closely related view, based on concepts widely held among hunting peoples, concerns the 'master of animals' – found, for example, in prehistoric art all over the north-west of South America – and, less commonly, the 'mother of game' who may be depicted in the American south-west. This figure is usually a dead shaman, a humanoid or therianthropic figure who mediates between living shamans and animals and is the animals' life-force. The living shamans derive their own life-force from the animals and then use it in the service of their clients. In this scenario, therefore, the artists were shamans maintaining links with the animals (with which they closely identified) through the 'master of animals'. The power derived from the art came through the act of drawing, not from subsequent viewing.

Obviously we have no evidence to tie Ice Age art to shamanism except as a simple assumption. This also applies, for example, to early attempts to use this interpretation, based entirely on perceived subject matter in the art, for some Nevada petroglyphs in the 1950s and especially for the Pecos River pictographs of Texas since the 1960s. In a few parts of the world – notably South Africa and California (Chumash paintings) – there is some ethnographic evidence that the most recent prehistoric art in these regions may indeed be linked with known practices of medicine men, shamans, healers, trances and suchlike. However, the existence of such practices in a society in no way proves *how* they were tied into the art, and leaves many questions unanswered – whether the shamans were artists, whether they

(*Left*) Nicolaas Witsen's doubtless somewhat inaccurate engraving, published in 1705, of a Tungus shaman in Siberia, with claws, reindeer antlers, furry ears and a drum. It bears an undeniable likeness to the famous 'sorcerer' figure (*right*, in Breuil's tracing) engraved and painted above the 'sanctuary' in the cave of Les Trois Frères in the French Pyrenees. The Ice Age figure, 75 centimetres (about 2½ feet) high, has antlers and other animal parts. But since it dates to *c.* 14,000 BC, any similarity between the two images may be meaningless.

This 88-centimetre-
(34.5-inch-) high petroglyph in
Arizona's Petrified Forest
(United States) has been interpreted by some researchers as
depicting the Mother of Game
– she is surrounded by game
and hunters. According to traditions in the region, animals
'belong' to this deity, who is
responsible for their increase,
and if hunters perform the correct offerings and rituals they
are given the right to hunt her
children. But far from being
benevolent, she is a dreaded
figure whose hideous appearance can make people freeze in
terror. Date unknown.

were the only artists, what the pictures meant, how they were used, and what percentage of the art could conceivably be interpreted in this way.

Unfortunately, in the excitement at finding a possible key to some of the hitherto
enigmatic motifs in the prehistoric art of these areas, some researchers have gone to
extremes and have not only made major assumptions about the content and meaning of prehistoric art in the few cases where there is ethnographic evidence of
shamans, but have also extended the hypothesis to ridiculous lengths. They have
claimed, for example, that Southern African rock art is *entirely* shamanistic (even
that of the Bantu-speakers which has no reference to shamans whatsoever!) while
denying that this in any way affects the diversity of its interpretation. They have
also applied the shaman theory to other bodies of rock art from every period and
continent – naturally Eurasian Ice Age art is targeted, but so is the megalithic art of
Europe, and even North African rock art has not been immune. In answer to such
extremes, one can do no better than to quote Peter Garlake, specialist of Zimbabwean rock art, who maintains that to say that prehistoric art was exclusively
concerned with the representation of different aspects of 'shamanism' is

... too narrow a focus for a full understanding of the art of Zimbabwe. It takes no
account of the large body of paintings there where metaphysical allusions appear
minor or non-existent and where the whole thrust of the imagery is concerned

with delineating people as hunters, gatherers and parents, doing such ordinary things as picking fruit, preparing food, conversing or making love: the great body of material that some describe as illustrating the 'normality' and 'ordinariness' of life and others have described as 'illustrating basic concepts and essentials'.

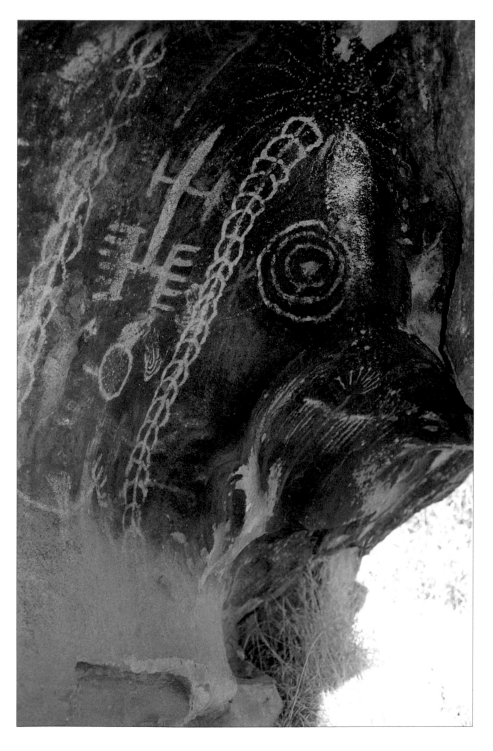

Part of the wealth of Chumash pictographs inside the small shelter of Ventureño (or Burro's Flats) in Southern California (United States), a site which is linked with the winter solstice. Date unknown. The white 'chain' in the centre is about 1 metre (3 feet) long. Above it is what may be a comet, while to the right are some humanoids with rayed head-dresses. Some researchers choose to interpret Chumash paintings primarily in terms of vision quests and altered states of consciousness.

Specialists disagree about how many of the 'entoptic' images derive from the wiring of the human nervous system rather than conscious recalls from things seen in trance. In any case, to seek the source of imagery only in altered states of consciousness and in universal neurophysiology has not produced a cross-cultural 'skeleton key' that unlocks the secrets of prehistoric art. This is no short cut to a universal model. In fact, it reveals no more than that the artists were human beings. It may pinpoint the ultimate source of the imagery but tells one nothing of its meaning: even if one could be sure the imagery resulted from an altered state of consciousness, one would not know of what kind or in what context.

The dangers of blanket explanations

There may, of course, be a degree of truth in some of the assumptions made, but they are so many and so major that one has the impression of a pyramid built upside down. And since we have clear ethnographic evidence that some rock art is not shamanistic in any way, it seems demeaning to prehistoric Bushmen or Californians to pigeonhole all of their artistic production in this way – where every motif, every gesture, is automatically interpreted in a symbolic, metaphorical or mystical way. As Freud said, sometimes a cigar is just a cigar, and we know from Australia, for example, that many rock images have no deep or hidden meaning (see Chapter 7); yet to those afflicted with what has been aptly called 'shamania', a hunting net is a geometric image perceived in trance, arrows are always 'arrows of sickness' and a physical death is always a trance-death. Every other conceivable motif likewise becomes a metaphor of trance – fish, for example, are metaphors for underwater journeying. In the same way, images of flight, fighting, sexual intercouse, marks at the nose (always seen as bleeding) or mouth, standing with the arms back, kneeling, bending forward, fly whisks, pointing, having a raised knee, etc, are all interpreted in oblique ways even when more prosaic explanations are available – for example, arms back may be an imitation of a bird, while bending forward on sticks is a common posture among Bantu diviners who do it when showing respect to ancestors and during training. In order to postulate that all human graphic activity was initiated everywhere and at all times by altered states of consciousness, the explanation is so adaptable that it applies to everything and simply cannot be invalidated. Nothing can be proved wrong; it is just claimed to be as the proponents wish. The animals are all seen as symbols (mostly depictions of shamans who have taken animal form) and the artists are all assumed to be shamans.

Were the prehistoric artists all shamans? Such a hypothesis is both unlikely and restricting. In Australia, for example, we know that the painter was not seen as a person with extraordinary gifts but simply as someone who painted often and with some skill. The artists played a role in ceremonies and in educating the young. It is known from first-hand accounts in the Kimberley that in the late wandjina period male youths were tested for their artistic abilities in order to identify the most skilled, and these then received specialized training by the artist elders to continue the tradition. In Arnhem Land there were no special classes of creators or 'consumers' of the art. And although religion was all-pervasive in Aboriginal culture – and their imagery has complex messages encoded in it, reflecting their belief in the interrelationship of all living things and the shape-changing qualities of the ancestral beings – their art nevertheless contains both religious and secular images. If that is so for the Australians, why should one impose a straitjacket on interpretation of any other body of art? Strict adherence to a single theory is a prophylactic against thought. It limits potential explanations and imposes a bogus, reductionist, utterly hypothetical homogeneity on a vast array of different motifs. It suppresses the consideration of any other motivation such as the human urge to create, and what has been called 'the exercise of the normal, undrugged conscious imagination'.

In South Africa and the western United States – where a few researchers are determined proponents of the shamanism hypothesis – a large number of cumulative assumptions have been made in order to link ethnographic evidence with rock art and to link both of them with shamans and trance. It has been declared that, like the art, ethnographic testimony cannot be taken at face value (except where it fits

Paintings in Shelter G8 in the Ga'aseb Gorge of Namibia's Brandberg massif. Three highly decorated men are walking towards a large giraffe who is apparently being rained upon. The three humans have been interpreted as medicine men: all wear head gear and decorations at the knee, and all hold short curved sticks. The one on the right also carries a bow and arrow, while the other two may be holding fly whisks. The central man is 30 centimetres (12 inches) tall. Date unknown.

the hypothesis) and needs to be analysed and interpreted. Such researchers claim, somewhat patronizingly, that most informants were not capable of articulating – or perhaps did not even know – the deeper meanings of their beliefs, but that they (the researchers themselves) are fully capable of retrieving the metaphors and hidden meanings in this stunted testimony. This attitude smacks of neocolonialism and seems to continue the eighteenth-century practice whereby white Western scholars defined and analysed alien religious sytems.

The Bleek and Lloyd records (see Chapter 2), used by proponents of shamanism as the foundation stone of the whole theory, contain no mention of trance, nor of any practices, dreams or beliefs involving it. And although the old woman M said that her father was a diviner and her sister a rainmaker, she never mentioned trance or hallucinations in any way – for example, she sometimes dreamt of rain, and rain would follow the next day, but she did not regard herself as a shaman or ritual specialist. Yet it has been claimed that there is impeccable ethnographic evidence here for linking 'medicine men' and rainmakers with shamanism, and in turn linking the shamans with the rock art. Nobody denies that the Bushmen sometimes went into trance, usually brought on by prolonged rhythmic dancing, but this was by no means restricted to medicine men; and besides, ritual and dancing among hunter-gatherers do not necessarily involve a trance state. A few paintings may well depict people in this state (in Amis Gorge, Namibia, for instance, only eleven figures out of thousands – 0.2 per cent – are therianthropes), though most others are open to different interpretations. Rainmaking and transformations may certainly be depicted in some pictures. But who painted them?

There is no nineteenth-century ethnographic evidence of the medicine men or 'rain doctors' being the artists, nor of the artists being in a state of trance before or during the making of pictures. Orpen (see Chapter 2) obtained many stories from Southern Bushman folklore, but no information on the sex, age or status of the artists. Bleek and Lloyd did not question their informants about the identity or motives of the artists. They mention 'sorcerers' who, it was believed, could make rain, transform people into animals and vice versa, perform healing, and so on, but there is nothing to indicate that they were more likely to have been painters than were other people. There is a mention from 1917 of one of three painters being a rain doctor, which implies that the others were not. Moreover, the testimony of the old woman M seems to have changed over time. She first said to some researchers that medicine men did the painting in a particular shelter; but later she told another specialist that the art was a record of the way the Bushmen lived, and possibly a form of sympathetic magic. She also stated that, with two exceptions, none of the painters were medicine men! In short, there is nothing in the ethnographic record to prove any connection between shamanism and the execution of the art. None of the few ethnographic accounts of Bushman artists at work refers to them as medicine men or being in any other than a normal state of consciousness. And even if one accepts fully the possibility that the creators of some of the art may have been

influenced by hallucinations, that does not prove that they were medicine men –
unless one calls everyone who experiences an altered state of consciousness a
shaman, in which case we are all shamans, and the word loses all meaning, becoming synonymous with human being!

Yet the proponents of the theory that 'Bushman art is entirely shamanistic' base
their shaky edifice on this evidence, declaring that medicine men were indeed the
painters or engravers. Using a carefully selected portion of the ethnographic and
artistic record, involving a tiny fraction of the hundreds of thousands of figures in
the rock art, they insist that none of the art simply reflected daily life (despite M's
testimony!) or even illustrated myths. As we have seen, their case relies very heavily on tortuous interpretation of ethnography (much of it derived from the modern
Kalahari Bushmen who have no knowledge of any painting tradition and who are
far removed in space and time from the Drakensberg paintings) and on a reading of
the images in the art as being metaphors of trance. Their edifice rises ever higher,
since, having taken it as read that all the art is shamanistic, they can speculate to
their hearts' content about how the making of the art may have been associated with
control within social groups and with hierarchies of power. The inverted pyramid
has risen so high that many have lost sight of its tiny and very wobbly foundation.

Rock paintings at Cueva
Flechas, in Baja California
(Mexico), showing how the
large deer figures are arranged
on either side of a prominent
fissure in the rock face, which
may simply be a matter of composition, but may also have
some significance in terms of
spiritual power linked with
such an interface with the
underworld. Date unknown.

Hand stencils and other paintings at the Coyote Shelter, on the Pecos River, Texas (United States), showing how the snake figure emerges from, or disappears into, a rock fissure. Date unknown.

Even the perfectly reasonable point that the images probably relate to the rock face as much as to each other has been taken to extremes – through the bald assumption that all the rock faces were seen as interfaces between the world of daily life and the spiritual realm, so that any image placed on that interface necessarily had something, no matter how tenuous, to do with beliefs about relationships between the two worlds and with the activities of the shamans who mediated between them. Once again, such absolute, blanket explanations leave no place for discussion. They cannot be tested or proved wrong, and tentative suggestions that maybe some images might have been placed on a rock which was not seen as an interface but which was simply a handy surface for the purpose, are dismissed as naive, simplistic or outmoded. In any case, such divisions between a real world and the spirit world scarcely existed in Bushman life, and so the supposed boundary is simply a construct of Western scholarship. The basic problem appears to be that, in a wholly laudable effort to escape traditional views of the art of indigenous people as worthless, childlike or 'primitive', the pendulum has been swung to the other, romanticized extreme, where every single mark they made has to be deeply spiritual and complex – in either case, their humanity is diminished.

The simple truth, as shown by the far better documented Australian context, is that prehistoric artists, like those of more recent times, were people like ourselves and their art can therefore be expected to reflect every facet of life. To cram even a single corpus into one explanation like shamanism, let alone attempt to fit art from several continents and many millennia into this pigeonhole, is to impose a spurious uniformity on a vast and diverse phenomenon and to do an injustice to the memory and the humanity of these first artists. Just as Leroi-Gourhan's view of Ice Age art as remaining essentially unchanged for 20,000 years has come under increasing fire recently, with the discovery of the very early and remarkably sophisticated pictures in the newly discovered Grotte Chauvet hammering the last nail into its coffin, so it should not be assumed that the historic evidence for shamanism in California or South Africa can tell us anything about the ideology of the local prehistoric populations, which is in any case most unlikely to have remained unchanged for many millennia — for example, the cultures of the Bushmen and Bantu-speakers are known to have overlapped in Southern Africa for almost 2000 years. Instead of a theory which stresses uniformity and continuity in ideology and art, with concepts which were structurally unchanged for thousands if not tens of thousands of years (a scenario that is *a priori* extremely improbable), it should be realized that the art and whatever symbolism may lie behind it represent what has been called a 'complex and dynamic mosaic of beliefs' shaped and changed by contacts with a variety of different cultures.

The realization that motifs and motives in prehistoric art are not easily recognizable has meant that researchers have found it ever harder to move beyond detailed descriptions and well-meant speculations. What it comes down to, basically, is whether one is content to work with the art as a body of markings that cannot be read or whether one wants to have stories made up about it. Since explanations of the meaning of prehistoric art cannot be proved, it has been argued that the use of ethnographic analogy to achieve a 'best fit hypothesis' is a viable and valid enterprise. However, other hypotheses, such as a preoccupation with social health and harmony with nature, can often prove a far better fit for the art than can shamanism even in Southern Africa. More caution and rigour are needed to avoid the abuses of ethnography seen earlier this century, as well as the simplistic, wholesale transfer of specific interpretations from one body of evidence to the other in what has been called 'ethnographic snap'. In twenty or thirty years time, the obsession with trance phenomena will, like hunting magic or structuralism before it, be seen as just another stage in the history of prehistoric art studies, but probably not a decisive one (though certainly a simplistic one, since the basic analogy of trance with shamans is not even in line with current scholarship on shamanism). In all such cases one is left with a few nuggets of useful and sound interpretation; the rest becomes so much verbiage, of only historical interest.

The fundamental problem with such attempts at interpretation is that what begin as signposts become marked tracks, then tramlines, and finally circular roundabouts that take us nowhere. Certainly it is healthy for all paths to be explored thoroughly, and each one contributes some new piece of the jigsaw, but it is vital to avoid asserting that the jigsaw only has one piece!

THE SEARCH FOR UNIVERSALS

A quite different approach to the intractable question of symbolism in prehistoric art has been attempted recently by French researcher Jean-Loïc Le Quellec for Saharan rock art. This involves a return to the history of religion and to a search for, if not universals, then motifs which are widespread in particular parts of the world. According to historians of religion, the sacred has always been structured in universal categories such as solar deities, fertility cults, rites of rebirth, the Earth Mother and the *axis mundi*. The challenge is to find expressions of such entities in prehistoric art. Naturally, the fundamental problem is how to recognize that an image is symbolic – as we have seen, any human, animal or 'non-figurative' motif

Petroglyph at Three Rivers, New Mexico (United States), depicting an animal with a head at either end. Such fanciful depictions are also well known in other areas, such as parts of Argentina and the Sahara. Probably 1000–1400 AD.

may be symbolic, but equally it may not. So the danger, as we have seen with the extremes of shamania, is to choose pansymbolism and see everything, indiscriminately, as a symbol. A dog may be the symbol of a psychopomp (a guide for dead souls, like Anubis or Cerberus), of the guardian of the underworld, or of sexual power; but it may also be a domestic dog or a detail from a hunting scene.

Le Quellec's answer has been to try and detect some universal symbols in the rock art of the central Sahara: his starting point is those images whose contexts or bizarre details suggest strongly that there is some symbolic intent – for example, animals with two heads or two bodies appear to be a theme found throughout Africa, including pharaonic Egypt, over thousands of years. This does not mean that there is necessarily any historical link between these various cultures, since this would be a typical misuse of ethnographic analogy; instead, Le Quellec merely deduces that the image may form part of a kind of African collective unconscious, the same 'imaginary constellation'. Historians of religion interpret such images as part of a mythology expressing divine androgyny and the dangerous powers linked with twins, themes which are found very frequently in modern African beliefs.

This may be a credible explanation for the motifs, but, as ever, it depends on a number of assumptions – first and foremost that the images are indeed symbolic, which dismisses the more banal and functional interpretations such as humour, clan emblems, an aesthetic search for symmetry. And it is heavily dependent on the rather generalizing and subjective opinions of historians of religion. So, once again, it comes down to the fact that if one wants to tell stories about prehistoric images, one has to become subjective and make extraordinary assumptions. All is hypothesis and claim; nothing is proven at all.

ANYTHING GOES

The perhaps inevitable outcome of all attempts to find the meaning of prehistoric art has emerged from the 'post-processual' archaeology of the 1980s, which led to an attitude of 'anything goes' in interpretation. Treating rock art as a 'text' which can be read in every period and thus constitutes a source of diverse meanings, Christopher Tilley has produced a controversial study of the petroglyphs located in the river rapids of Nämforsen, Sweden. What at first sight seems a jumble of elks and boats, together with humans, soles, tools and fish, sometimes occurring in combination, has been broken down into assemblages (the text's 'grammar' and 'sentences') and the design of elks and boats examined. The structural principles linking elks with boats are investigated, leading to the suggestion of a binary system. Where meaning is concerned, ethnohistory is brought in, to check the traditional view that there may be a long-term continuity between the rock carvings and the designs on historically documented Saami drums of the eighteenth century. The beliefs of western Siberian groups relating to shamanism and the spirit world are also highlighted, in particular the notion of a cosmic river mediating between the different worlds of the cosmos.

Examples of offerings being made to rock images in North America today.

(Right) At Medicine Creek Cave, Wyoming (United States), burnt sage can be seen on a small ledge in front of the rock art. *(Opposite)* The great petroglyph known as Tsagaglalal receives numerous small offerings – coins, beads, tobacco, etc. – which are well hidden from view in a crevice.

Tilley concludes that the site does not represent a shamanistic religion, but the reader is left with an open-ended array of imaginative and subjective possibilities 'riddled with contradictions', rather than any unified or coherent interpretation. In this emphasis on the ambiguity of meaning, Tilley's work, which strives to investigate how the images mean rather than what they mean, is undoubtedly more realistic and more truthful than most attempts to explain prehistoric art.

However, there are major problems inherent in seeing 'rock art as text'. For a start, we do not know which images are contemporaneous except in the vaguest way. And even if it seems a fair supposition – based on dating or, far more usually, on technique, size, shape, style or pigment – that some figures are contemporaneous or part of the same episode, we simply do not know whether they were meant to be looked at singly, or in sequence, or as a group. Indeed, this approach seems futile to some, since it has no conclusion – it has been described as 'a strategy of travelling hopefully rather than arriving' – but it does make a notable contribution in providing much food for thought and making more traditional rock art researchers re-examine their assumptions and beliefs.

To sum up, all sensible interpretations of prehistoric art are welcome and potentially valuable, but we need to avoid the adoption of all-purpose, oven-ready explanations which always fail. Instead, the useful portions of each theory need to be retained and amalgamated into a more rounded picture of the artists' meanings and motivations. Or, to use a different metaphor, we need to pick the good cherries and leave the rest for the birds.

THE PRESENT-DAY SIGNIFICANCE OF PREHISTORIC ART

Inevitably, it has become increasingly difficult since the beginning of the twentieth century to obtain good ethnographic insights into the art; only a few regions, such

Distant view of the great cliff face of Huashan (China). As recently as 1985 offerings were made to the God of Water at this site by two local brothers who survived a boat collision and sinking. The principal figures in this great rock art panel have been interpreted as chiefs, sorcerers or warriors, and the site is generally seen as associated with religious dances and divine intervention to ward off disastrous floods or malignant spirits. Dogs are still revered in the region, and the humans' posture may denote frog-gods who would intercede with the Thunder God who commands wind and rain. The local Zhuang people worshipped frog gods, and at festivals still imitate a frog posture in their dances.

as parts of Australia, still have people who produce rock art in the traditional way. In some areas of North America, pictographs were still being made in the twentieth century. But, while such examples of the production of traditional rock art are rare, there are many places where local people still venerate the prehistoric art in different ways – for example, on America's north-west coast where offerings of tobacco, coins and suchlike are still left in front of Tsagaglalal or in Scandinavia where in 1910 Lapps were observed bringing offerings to a prehistoric rock painting at Seitjaur on Kola Island.

Some of the most remarkable examples of persisting veneration for rock art sites have been documented in Latin America: for instance, the Huichol of western Mexico are known to make ritual use of rock art sites, while the modern Maya still use the decorated caves of their region. In Bolivia, the rock at Río Pachene with its numerous 'vulva' carvings (see Chapter 7) is still the scene of religious dances by the Chimane Indians. In other words, although the original motivation and meaning of prehistoric rock art are lost for ever, they can still form an important and active part of traditions and religious beliefs, as a mediator with supernatural forces.

The Christian church has always been aware of this 'competition' and rock art sites were included in the 'Idols Eradication Policy' set up in the City of Kings (Lima) in 1567: the sites were defaced by scratches, incisions, or engraved crosses, sometimes directly on the rock images or prominently placed on the panels (see Chapter 1). At Palmarito, Bolivia, Christian saints were painted on rocks in the nineteenth century and early in the twentieth century, and were worshipped by the

local residents, who still make offerings and perform rites there. The offerings seem to be made to the figures – which are seen as devils or malevolent forces – in order to obtain something in exchange, often related to fertility. In Bhimbetka (India), before the twentieth century, Buddhist hermits used the decorated rock shelters and added their own Buddhist imagery, not so much to eradicate but to adapt and renew the sites' sacredness for their own beliefs.

Prehistoric art – especially the rock and cave art which remains precisely where the artists placed it – retains its impact. It can still embody spiritual power and danger for local peoples; and even in the 'sophisticated' minds of Western scholars it still appeals to a wide variety of emotions, from a simple aesthetic pleasure to feelings of awe and unease.

In Bolivia's high plateau region, near Yaraque, the local Aymara people not only throw chewed coca leaves at zoomorphic figures, but at one site – Korini 3 – villagers have burnt straw in front of the decorated panel and thrown blood over a condor figure. Buried beneath stones at the site is a wooden box filled with bottles of alcohol, as well as woollen tassels and paper strips and flags.

CHAPTER 9   *Current Threats and Future Prospects*

Prehistoric art, especially rock art, has never been more popular, but – in part because of this popularity – it now faces numerous threats to its survival, not only from natural weathering but also (indeed primarily) from the impact of human beings in the form of pollution, accidental damage, excessive tourism and deliberate vandalism. The publication of detailed descriptions of prehistoric art sites can

Petroglyph panel in the Butler Wash area, Utah (United States), showing prominent bullet holes.

increase the likelihood of human damage, while lack of records can make it harder for researchers and public authorities to notice and take steps to prevent threats to the art.

THREATS TO CAVE ART

Cave art faces problems of a special kind. Although attempts have sometimes been made to hack out some Ice Age figures such as the bas-relief fish in France's Abri du Poisson or the bas-relief bison at Angles-sur-l'Anglin, most of the damage has come from natural causes such as microbiological activity, water flow, growth of calcite and bears brushing past. Since the discovery of cave art in the late nineteenth century, it has also fallen victim to the effects of human visits: accidental damage by professionals and tourists alike, deliberate vandalism (one or two Ice Age images in French caves such as Montespan and Gargas have been purposely wiped), and innocent vandalism – most famously the well-meaning French Scouts who, in March 1992, cleaned up the garbage and graffiti in several caves, inadvertently

removing an Ice Age bison painting in the cave of Mayrières with a steel brush! The first Mud Glyph Cave found in Tennessee was permanently sealed five years ago to prevent vandalism to its fragile images. However, the most serious effects have come about through pressure of visitor numbers, and these have had to be reduced over the years, with some caves – most notably Lascaux and Altamira – eventually being closed to normal tourist visits because of the pollution they cause.

Much has been learned over the last few decades about cave climates and the need to maintain their equilibrium as far as possible. Consequently, new discoveries such as the Grotte Chauvet can unfortunately never be opened to the public, while it is accepted that caves still visited by tourists are 'doomed' in the long term, a necessary sacrifice to satisfy the public's legitimate right to see some of its heritage.

THREATS TO OPEN-AIR ART

Rock art in shelters and the open air faces a far wider range of problems than cave art, being more exposed in every way to natural and human damage.

Natural damage

Natural damage ranges from the everyday, such as microbiological activity, rain and wind erosion and temperature changes, to the exceptional such as the shifting of rock strata, rockfalls, lava flows (very destructive to Hawaiian petroglyphs), earthquakes (at least one decorated ceiling in Baja California has been destroyed by a tremor) and lightning. Bird nests and droppings, termite mounds and the nests of certain insects (notably mud-daubing wasps) are very destructive in some places, such as Australia or Brazil. Plants can also be a problem: lichen growth is very widespread; in the Transvaal (South Africa) growth of the rockcracker fig can be a

(Opposite) **The Falling Horse** painted at the end of a gallery in the cave of Lascaux (France), dating to *c.* 15,000 BC. This major site, discovered in 1940, was opened to the public in 1948, but had to be closed in 1963: the excessive numbers of visitors – eventually 2,000 per day in the summer, a total of 100,000 per year – were having a radical effect on the cave's micro-environment and causing a proliferation of algae and bacteria. The biggest factor proved to be organisms introduced on tourists' shoes. These caused a 'green sickness', with algae starting to appear on the cave's walls; and a more serious 'white sickness', with crystals growing on some surfaces. Subsequent treatment has removed the green sickness and arrested the progress of the white sickness, but careful monitoring is required, and the few visitors allowed must disinfect their footwear and may only stay a short time in the cave to avoid adverse effects on the temperature and humidity.

(Left) **Petroglyphs of human-like figures on a huge boulder at Site 5 in the Spear Hill complex (north-west Australia), showing how the rock has split at some time after the art was produced, owing to some natural cause, perhaps lightning. Date unknown.**

A painting of an animal in the sandstone shelter of Roca de Vaca, in Brazil's Piauí region, showing how the back part has already flaked off and fallen – this is exactly how the early painted fragment (see page 146) must have come to be stratified in the occupation layers below. Date unknown.

menace to paintings; foliage may brush against paintings; horizontal decorated rocks in temperate countries can become covered by turf or other vegetation (though this often protects the art rather than destroys it). The intense heat from brush or forest fires can have terrible effects, such as spalling (flaking) of the rock surface, smoke damage, scorching or even total destruction, especially of pictographs, though petroglyphs on friable rocks like sandstone or limestone can also flake off at high temperature. In addition, ash and charcoal from fires can contaminate organic materials used for dating.

Inadvertent damage by humans
Fires, of course, may also be started by people – sometimes, unfortunately, in decorated shelters or close to decorated rocks – but there are far worse and far more common kinds of humanly inflicted damage. In Tanzania, for example, some painted rock shelters are still used as temporary kraals for cattle which are herded into there during the midday heat, rubbing their bodies against the panels. The same phenomenon, involving cattle, sheep and pigs, has smeared paintings in South Africa too, while in New Zealand by 1929 livestock had obliterated many paintings at the Weka Pass site by rubbing against the walls.

Other kinds of inadvertent or thoughtless damage can be seen clearly in Scandinavia, particularly where petroglyph panels occur in farmyards or built-up areas. Farmers have parked machinery on the rocks or dragged it over them; dust and gravel from nearby roads and tracks abrade the surfaces; pollution from car exhausts and from acid rain is causing terrible erosion and spalling on some panels.

Petroglyphs on a panel in the middle of a built-up area in Evjestien, Østfold (Norway), which are constantly crossed by feet and wheels. Probably Bronze Age (*c.* 1000 BC).

Damage caused by a bulldozer to a remote petroglyph pavement at Puako on the Big Island of Hawaii. The large stick figure was run over and several other figures were totally destroyed. Date unknown.

Sign covering rock paintings of deer at Rasmussen or Mummy Cave in Nine Mile Canyon, Utah (United States). Deliberate damage to rock art by landowners is by no means unusual, often designed specifically to deter people from visiting the art.

(Opposite bottom) This now infamous drawing was published by a traveller, Emil Holub, who took over 200 South African engraved slabs back to Vienna with him in 1887, having removed them crudely with hammer and wedge, fire and water. (Ironically, he 'saved' samples of art from one site which was largely destroyed by mining in the twentieth century.)

At the very least there is loss of clarity, detail and depth in the petroglyphs; at worse, whole images or panels disappear or are so badly damaged that covering them up again seems the only long-term solution at present.

A great deal of damage, in Scandinavia as elsewhere, is also caused by people walking on the decorated surfaces wearing shoes, or by raising dust which then consolidates on the rock surface. In desert areas, where the geoglyphs (see Chapter 5) were made by moving dark stones aside to expose the lighter soil beneath, hooves and tyres likewise move the stones aside, leaving light-coloured tracks which are as longlasting as the geoglyphs themselves. Many geoglyphs, in Nasca and the United States for example, are permanently disfigured by swirls of tracks around them (see page 117).

Vandalism and theft

Even this thoughtlessness, however, pales into insignificance when compared with the deliberate vandalism of graffiti, or the even more mindless shooting of rock art in some parts of the United States, where almost any rock figure visible from main roads is sprayed with bulletholes as a matter of course. Theft, too, is a major headache – in Wisconsin, for example, the Gottschall site was recently damaged by would-be thieves armed with a concrete saw in an attempt to remove some of its images, while in 1993 a black rock painting of a human figure, 35 centimetres (*c.* 14 inches) high, was removed from the Cueva de Pumamahay, Bolivia, with chisels. Small boulders bearing petroglyphs have been stolen from a remote site near Hartley Bay, British Columbia.

The legal 'removal' of rock art to museums was once quite common, especially in Southern Africa: for example, a selection of paintings from the site of Ebusingata, Kwa Zulu Natal, now exist on loose slabs of rock, having been quarried and dynamited from the site, probably in 1946 for the benefit of a

(Above) **Bushman painting of elephant at Clifford, in the Newcastle district of South Africa, damaged by rifle fire.**

Do not touch!

It should go without saying that prehistoric paintings must never be touched, since the pigments are often fragile and can rub off, quite apart from the tiny amounts of grease, dirt and sweat that can be transferred to them in this way. Yet some visitors who would never dream of touching pictures in art galleries seem to feel no qualms about prodding the infinitely more delicate and precious images on rocks. Even worse is the suffering inflicted on petroglyphs, especially those on horizontal surfaces, since constant foot traffic makes them lose definition. For example, a foot trail through the petroglyph site of Anaeho'omalu, Hawaii, has worn away many designs, leaving partial figures on either side – and this was done by bare feet!

Taking rubbings of petroglyphs is still a common practice in some areas, particularly China, and makes a fairly accurate copy, but – as can be seen on stelae in Central America or on historical tombstones – it can eventually damage even the hardest rocks, will wear down the edges of glyphs, and may change the chemistry of accretionary deposits which might otherwise prove useful for obtaining a minimum age. Many of the substances (crayons, inks, paints) used for the purpose leave residues on the rock and its petroglyph. This is quite obvious, for example, at the Wrangell petroglyph beach in south-east Alaska, where thousands of tourists every year are actively encouraged to take rubbings, so that the most popular ones are lighter in colour and worn from repeated use. One

(*Right*) **Petroglyphs of animal-like creatures at Nanaimo, British Columbia (Canada). Date unknown. Copies of some of these images, in concrete, are available in this park, from which visitors are invited to make rubbings, to prevent them further damaging the originals.**

(*Opposite top*) **Large 'mask' petroglyph in the Helan Mountains (northern China). Date unknown. Above it can be seen the considerable damage left by the taking of a cast in the 1980s.**

(*Opposite bottom*) **The scraping of petroglyphs is a major problem in some parts of the world: for example, these images at ahu Roai on Easter Island have been destroyed by local amateur guides repeatedly scraping them with stones to make them clearer for tourist cameras.**

solution adopted at sites such as Nanaimo, Canada, the Swastika Stone on Ilkley Moor, Yorkshire, or the Puako petroglyph site, Hawaii, is the provision of concrete replicas of the main motifs, which rubbing aficionados can use. However, some researchers fear that this also serves to give tourists the idea of making rubbings, and enables them to perfect their technique and then apply it to the real petroglyphs. The taking of casts (originally in plaster, but more recently in latex and silicone) is also disappearing because of resulting discolorations or removal of surface material. Perhaps the worst damage of all, short of total destruction or theft, is that caused by scraping.

Rock engravings (an aurochs – wild ox – is particularly visible) at Canada do Inferno in Portugal's Côa Valley. In the background can be seen the dam construction which threatened to inundate the Côa engravings under 100 metres (over 300 feet) of water.

visit of the British royal family in 1947. These slabs are now housed in a museum. The earliest-known such instance occurred in 1878 when members of the Cape Mounted Rifles 'cut out slabs of rock with pictures for sale to museums'. There are many slabs bearing paintings or engravings in museums in Southern Africa (some displaying the holes drilled for dynamite): admittedly the removed art has remained in good condition on the whole, but there are innumerable ugly scars in shelters throughout the country. On one farm in South Africa a rock painting on a sandstone block is built into the wall of a cottage, and engravings are known to be in some private gardens and cemented into fireplaces.

The removal of rock art from its original location can be justified when it is the only way to save it from total destruction by construction, mining, quarrying, road building or flooding. There are numerous examples from places as far apart as the north-western United States, Portugal and Siberia of vast quantities of petroglyphs being lost beneath dam reservoirs. Fortunately, the petroglyphs of north-east Portugal's Côa Valley were saved from such a fate in November 1995 after a vigorous campaign by rock art specialists and archaeologists around the world.

Visitor damage

Obviously, rock art which is remote or difficult of access is far less at risk than sites which are in, or close to, areas of urban development. For example, at South Mountain, a municipal park in Phoenix, Arizona, a new examination was made in 1991 of 401 petroglyph panels which had been surveyed and photographed in 1964. It was found that 77.8 per cent of the panels showed no apparent change, but the rest – almost a quarter – had been damaged: 9.9 per cent had been removed (mostly as whole rocks, but sections of petroglyphs had also been broken off), 4.4 per cent had been vandalized, 3.2 per cent had been developed, 2.7 per cent had flaked off or broken, 1.2 per cent had been hit by gunfire, and 0.4 per cent were under lichen. When location was taken into account, it became clear that easily accessible sites were about three times more likely to be damaged than those which were harder to reach, and development areas had the highest proportion of damaged sites, as one might expect. In 1988, a detailed survey of the thousands of painted figures in shelters in Ndedema Gorge in South Africa's Drakensberg revealed that in the fifteen years since an earlier survey there had been an alarming increase in damage and loss (fading and flaking). This was primarily attributable to large numbers of people camping in the shelters – ironically, they were attracted to this previously unvisited area by the remarkable monograph on its art by Harald Pager. At this rate of loss, in less than 100 years there will be no paintings left in these large and spectacular sites.

Enhancing the images

Most of the techniques developed and used by rock art researchers over the centuries, and particularly in recent decades, for recording the art or to enhance it for photography have now become taboo in most parts of the world, as their damaging

The famous White Lady painting in Namibia is protected by an iron grid, but visitors have thrown beer and cola onto the paintings to try and enhance them.

effects have become apparent. For example, Breuil's 'direct tracing' method (see Chapter 2) for cave art, involving sheets of florist's or rice paper being held onto the wall by assistants while Breuil traced over the lines with pencil or crayon, inevitably damaged the art slightly in some places (as can be seen in modern macro-photographs). This method has now been replaced by that of keeping the (plastic) sheet slightly away from the rock or by tracing from photographs.

In some places, such as the Great Gallery of Barrier Canyon, Utah (United States), shown here, kerosene seems to have been used at some time for photographic enhancement of the painted humanlike figures. The art dates to 700–1200 AD but the application of the kerosene caused a ridiculously high date (32,900 years) to be obtained by radio-carbon analysis of the pigments. Some paintings at Bambata, Matopos (Zimbabwe), were actually obliterated by a coating of what seems to be motor oil, applied in a fruitless attempt to extend their lifespan.

The widespread practice – particularly in India – of wetting rock paintings to make them more visible in photographs is now frowned upon, even where distilled water is used: it will eventually produce opaque coatings over some panels or will activate the numerous soluble salts in the rock so that they react with other salts, or with the pigment, and come to the surface in the form of a white efflorescence. In addition, the moisture can alter the colour of iron-based pigments, or can swell them and cause them to be dislodged. The result, therefore, is paintings that are faded, altered or covered by a film of water-soluble salts.

The chalking of motifs (either outlining faded pictographs or filling in petroglyphs) has been one of the most common and widespread practices, going back to the early nineteenth century at least, but is now forbidden in most parts of the world. The chalk is not only unsightly (and often badly applied – if it cannot be seen well enough to be photographed, it cannot be seen well enough to be chalked) but also contaminates the patina on the engraved surface, thus distorting the dating results obtained by methods such as cation-ratios or radio-carbon. Chalk seems to last forever – some American rock paintings on sandstone that were chalked thirty-five

A 1978 experiment to put an artificial desert varnish on these petroglyphs in Petrified Forest, Arizona (United States), proved disastrous: it was meant to cover defacements and enhance the rock art, but became far darker than the natural varnish around it, acquired a sheen and covered up some motifs. Despite the best intentions, interventions of this type have greater long-term consequences for rock art than the natural deterioration processes which tend to be their *raison d'être*.

years ago still have the marks – and it is virtually impossible to remove from many surfaces. This attracts attention to sites which otherwise would not be noticed.

The application of a white gouache over whole petroglyph panels, although still carried out in some corners of Europe to enhance the motifs, is equally unsightly, and can likewise take a considerable time to disappear, even after being washed off. In any case, the 'degradable' chemicals used may have untold effects on the geo-chemistry of the rock.

Earlier rock art researchers used these methods to conserve and enhance rock art because they did not know any better. Nowadays, it is generally accepted that any conservation measures adopted must be reversible and must be monitored long

Chalked petroglyphs at ahu Roai, on Easter Island. Such damage – intended to make the art more visible – is inflicted by both tourists and by islanders acting as guides.

Walkway at the rock shelter of Cathedral Cave in Carnarvon Gorge, Queensland (Australia). Such walkways afford visitors a clear view of the art while keeping them at a safe distance, prevent the dust that results from walking on the shelter floor, and do no structural damage to the site.

after completion. Simple but effective methods exist for making art panels less accessible to visitors – by installing boardwalks, simply reshaping slopes in front of shelters, or filling in or removing footholds or ledges. Above all, it is crucial that no substance, whether biodegradable or not, should be permitted to come into contact with rock art (with the obvious exception of water in cases where the art is naturally exposed to rain, as on many petroglyph pavements): it is impossible to guarantee

To paint or not to paint?

One phenomenon which is still the subject of some controversy is now largely restricted to Scandinavia – the practice of painting petroglyphs for public viewing. In several major rock art areas such as Bohuslän in Sweden and Alta in Norway, a percentage of the most accessible and most spectacular panels have had their petroglyphs filled with red paint. There are both positive and negative aspects to this practice. The most obvious advantage is that it makes a good deal of first-class rock art accessible and visible to the general public whose eyes are not used to picking out unpainted petroglyphs, or who may not wish or be able to visit the sites in conditions of oblique sunlight or nocturnal illumination, the only times when many of these often shallow and heavily patinated petroglyphs would otherwise be at all clear (although rainfall can sometimes enhance their visibility). Unlike petroglyphs in many other parts of the world, such as North America, which still stand out clearly against the darker rock surrounding them, the unpainted Scandinavian petroglyphs are often virtually invisible in normal light, especially to the untutored eye.

Another advantage of providing the public (including the handicapped who also have the right to see their heritage and who can reach many sites thanks to well-designed wooden walkways) with a limited sample of painted petroglyphs is that it stops them being tempted to enhance the images themselves with chalk, paint or – worst of all – scraping. The Scandinavian philosophy is that by presenting or 'sacrificing' a sample of art to the public, the majority of sites can be left unpainted and largely unvisited – and hence better protected. Most visitors are content with a taste and feel no need to see every example.

One further factor, especially in some areas of Scandinavia such as the Norwegian county of Østfold, is that many petroglyph panels are located within built-up areas, such as farmyards or the gardens of private houses. In most cases, the art was not discovered until after the buildings were erected, precisely because it was almost invisible. It is felt that to have the images painted serves to protect them by underlining their existence, and reminding the locals to treat them with care and respect. This would be effective in an ideal world; but unfortunately, people being what they are, there are always some who persist in walking on the art in built-up areas or, worse, riding over it on bicycles, motorbikes or tractors, etc.

So where damage is being caused or the art is under threat in these circumstances, it is probably wiser to cover the panels with earth after they are recorded.

There are also disadvantages involved in the practice of painting petroglyphs. First, it may provide a false impression of the art since we have no idea whether they were originally painted, or, if so, in which colour. Even if they were always unpainted, it is certainly true that they would originally have been far more visible when freshly pecked into a dark- or even a light-grey rock surface. In any case, we know that Ice Age carvings, Maya stelae, Greek temples and Medieval cathedrals were all originally painted in bright, gaudy colours, but there are no moves to repaint these to make them clearer for today's visitors.

The application of the paint is further cause for concern. Some paints in the past may have harmed the rock and contaminated its patina and as they erode they can pull away the rock surface. In any case the person wielding the brush is inevitably imposing a personal, subjective reading onto the figures – there are often minor errors or examples of incompleteness on the panels. Some specialists fear that the practice might encourage people to paint other sites themselves on the grounds that, if the authorities do it, it must be acceptable.

The Scandinavian petroglyphs were first scrubbed with lichen-killers and painted between the two world wars, at a time when nobody knew any better and nobody foresaw today's analytical methods and dating techniques. The damage is done, so there can be little objection to these sites being repainted at regular intervals for public visibility. However, since there are large numbers of excellent images thus made accessible to tourists, there is no longer any need, and hence no excuse, for more examples or newly discovered petroglyphs being painted. Over the past few years a consensus has begun to develop in Scandinavia that the practice should cease, apart from the retouching of already painted-in sites. A recent booklet about the spectacular large animal engravings at Leiknes in northern Norway ends by stating: 'Many wish to make the pictures clearer by painting them. But those who experience the animals shining in the rock will understand why we have chosen to leave them in stone-age man's original stroke. To paint the drawings can be compared to stuffing an animal to display it. Easier to see – but perhaps something other than seeing a live animal?'

(Opposite) **Petroglyphs of elks at Alta (northern Norway), showing the difference between painted and unpainted images. However, by no means all unpainted petroglyphs are as clear as this. Date unknown.**

(Above) **Petroglyphs of bears at Alta (northern Norway), left unpainted and clearly visible in oblique sunlight. Date unknown.**

that the (albeit tiny) geochemical reactions it might produce will not affect the undoubtedly more sophisticated methods of analysis or dating that will be developed in future centuries.

MASSIVE INTERVENTION

Over the years, some major and well-intentioned schemes to protect rock art have had disastrous results. The worst of these have been massive buildings erected to enclose petroglyph rocks. One example, constructed in the 1960s at Besovy Sledki in Karelia, Russia, is an ugly concrete building which is now in a woeful condition: the windows are broken, the rock inside is dirty and dusty, and vandals have broken in and written graffiti.

Less ugly, but equally destructive, is the building erected in the 1980s around the Peterborough Petroglyph Site in Canada. Inevitably, this building is an intrusion on the site's atmosphere. In cutting the rock off from the outside world, it has rendered it quite 'dead' and made it a museum exhibit. It is clear from this example, as well as from other similar sites, that enclosing a rock art site with a building alters its natural environment dramatically. Shielding a site from natural processes which are perceived to be harmful also cuts it off from natural processes or conditions which would contribute to its preservation or well-being. Worse, an artificial environment is introduced and this may well involve new conservation hazards. We do not know the long-term effects of such massive environmental intervention on rock art which has survived centuries or millennia of natural deterioration and has probably

This ugly concrete structure was built over and around the petroglyphs of Besovy Sledki, in Karelia (Russia), in the 1960s.

existed in equilibrium with its natural environment. Enclosing a site relegates it to the status of a museum object, isolates it from its natural setting, indelibly alters its cultural meaning. The museums become mausoleums.

In 1989 an attempt was made at Aspeberget, in Bohuslän, Sweden, to enclose a petroglyph panel, out of desperation because – unlike the Peterborough site – it was in terrible condition, thanks to pollution from nearby traffic and (probably) acid rain, as well as water flows. A wooden and plastic structure was placed over and around the panel, but this caused serious changes to the site's micro-environment – the place became like a greenhouse, with extensive growth of algae inside. Moreover, the structure prevented the rock being washed clean by rain water: this resulted in a considerable accumulation of soil and leaves but did nothing to stop the flows of acid water. In 1996 the structure was declared a failure and demolished by removing the roof and cutting down the walls. It is likely that, as with another panel at Aspeberget, the only viable long-term solution to preserving this particular art is to rebury it and leave it for the no doubt better-equipped conservators of the future to deal with.

CONSERVING PREHISTORIC ART FOR THE FUTURE

Australian Aborigines used to apply simple but effective methods to protect the art at some decorated sites: in one Kimberley shelter they made a drip line with

This structure was built in 1989 over a petroglyph panel at Aspeberget in Bohuslän, Sweden. It was removed in 1996, having been judged a failure, and the panel was buried until some solution to its ills could be found in the future.

Portable art in danger

(Right) **David Swetnam, one of the American dealers involved in the Sipán affair, poses smugly with one of the golden peanuts looted from the site.**

(Opposite) **Ear ornaments of gold and turquoise from a warrior-priest's tomb at Sipán, depicting a man, a duck and a deer.**

Excavated portable art requires normal conservation procedures and museum curation. It is at risk primarily from thefts-to-order for mad collectors, although museums in war-torn parts of the globe have been ransacked or destroyed, while even in peaceful areas museums are straining for space and resources. However, unexcavated portable art is under constant and ever-increasing threat from looters, grave-robbers and unscrupulous dealers who are active in many parts of the world: the pothunters of North America rifling sites for Mimbres wares and other fine vessels; the huaqueros of Central and South America smashing and discarding archaeologically priceless objects in their lust for gold; the treasure-hunters of Europe, armed with metal detectors; unscrupulous dealers in African and Asian antiquities. The list is endless, and the problem lies squarely with the dealers, the auction houses, the collectors and the museums which trade in and buy this material, thus feeding and encouraging the virus.

The Sipán affair

In 1987 a group of villagers in northern Peru unearthed a hoard of ancient treasures in a royal tomb of the Moche culture of the first to eighth centuries AD. Several sacks of gold, silver and gilded copper artifacts were removed by the looters, as well as some pottery vessels. During the theft many other ceramics were broken and scattered. Immediately quarrels erupted among the looters and one of them tipped off the police. A local archaeologist and museum curator, Walter Alva, was asked by the police to examine a collection of gold

and silver objects seized at the home of a grave robber, including figures of jaguars and warriors, necklaces of big golden peanuts, gold masks and spool-shaped ear ornaments inlaid with turquoise, lapis lazuli and mother-of-pearl. The source of the material was eventually traced to an ancient mud-brick pyramid-mound at Sipán.

Alva had been conducting a ten-year crusade to protect Peru's ancient monuments and was devastated by the ransacking of what was clearly one of the most important archaeological discoveries of recent decades. As yet he was unaware that the find had already triggered a 'Peruvian Gold Rush', and that many of the looted artifacts from the site had already been smuggled out to Britain and the United States where they were sold to wealthy art collectors and dealers (although most appear to be in the hands of a few wealthy and secretive collectors in Peru itself).

United States customs agents began an undercover investigation into the smuggling operation and in March 1988 their armed raids on the homes and businesses of a group of prominent dealers and collectors in southern California and their unprecedented seizure of prehistoric antiquities shook the art world. However, they were not too successful in their efforts to have the stolen artifacts returned to Peru, for while some of those raided co-operated with the customs and did hand over their treasure, others adopted a 'finders keepers' attitude and challenged the legal basis of the seizures as well as the allegations of criminal activity. A controversial decision in the United States courts led to the forfeiture to Peru of only

250 of the almost 2,000 objects seized by the police (a small percentage of which were gold from Sipán).

Alva, meanwhile, despite death threats and fears for his safety, had excavated at the site and found that it was not the burial place of a single Moche, as had been thought, but a necropolis containing a number of lords. At least three tombs, richer in gold and silver than any other in the New World, remained intact, but had to be protected from looters by armed guards.

Despite the unhappy fate of the first finds from Sipán, the affair set an important precedent, raising crucial questions about the private ownership of national treasures and obtain-ing the first conviction in United States history for smuggling prehistoric art. It also sparked a debate about the ethics of knowingly using looted material to obtain information about the past – many archaeologists consider this unethical, but those involved in the Sipán affair feel a duty to record the material despite deploring how it was obtained.

In 1990 the United States customs service announced a ban on the importation of all archaeological artifacts from the Sipán region, and made it clear that it would seize any artifact that was not accompanied by documentation from the Peruvian government certifying that it had left the country legally.

The white elephant of Peterborough

The huge structure of concrete, metal and glass erected in the 1980s around the Peterborough Petroglyph Site in Canada, on the strong recommendation of the Canadian Conservation Institute (CCI), has persistently been presented to the world as the epitome of rock art conservation. Until recently, not a word had been published about the considerable damage it has done.

Not only was there an absence of clear objectives in the planning, but the building – which cost almost 800,000 Canadian dollars – was probably not needed at all. The CCI decided that the site was deteriorating through frost weathering and the growth of several species of algae. It recommended that the main petroglyph site be enclosed in a protective structure to eliminate rain, snow and surface water-flow, and hence abate algal growth. Vandalism was also cited as a danger, although the fence which existed at this remote site had already eliminated this factor. (In any case, no rock art site is entirely safe from vandalism, so why, at a minimally damaged remote site, should it have been deemed vital to enclose it for protection?)

It is hard to believe that the decision to create this building was only undertaken after all other possibilities had been exhausted. It would have been far simpler and cheaper to remove the trees whose shade was encouraging the algae (which grow very slowly in this climate), and to cover the rock in some way each winter to prevent snow cover and frost damage. One has the impression that a deliberate decision was taken to adopt a glamorous, high-tech solution at great expense to send a clear and impressive signal of Canada's commitment to rock art conservation.

Unfortunately, the construction itself damaged the site incalculably. For example, the entire structure rests on the decorated rock itself; yet, incredibly, nothing has been published on the site's ability to support such a massive building weight without detrimental effects – there is no information on the load stresses on the decorated pavement and its geophysical context. It is probable that the weight of the structure is a factor in the marked widening and deepening of a crevice at the north-east end of the site which has become especially noticeable in recent years. Similarly, the waterproofing is inadequate and there is considerable seepage of water and ice in the winter.

During construction, the site was protected by a layer of straw bales covered with plywood sheets which were, in turn, covered with plastic sheeting. However, the straw bales were ignited by sparks from welding torches: the use of fire extinguishers on one fire produced a large white stain, still visible over eight or nine petroglyphs. Many long prominent scratches made by an earth-moving vehicle lie over unwaxed petroglyphs at the north-east end of the rock (most of the petroglyphs

(*Right*) The immense structure which sits on the petroglyph rock at Peterborough, Ontario (Canada).

(*Opposite top*) The scratches left by an earth-moving vehicle on top of some Peterborough petroglyphs can be seen clearly here, as well as the water and ice seeping in from outside.

(*Opposite bottom*) Part of the Peterborough Petroglyph Site, showing the difference between unwaxed images and those which were crayoned in during the 1960s – at the time, nobody knew any better.

inside the building were filled in with wax crayon in the 1960s, long before such practices became taboo).

Visitors, especially in the summer, find the building unbearably stuffy and lacking in fresh air; and amazingly there is no monitoring of the carbon dioxide levels, which might damage the rock surface. The cement walls are cracking in numerous places, salts are leaching through and humidity is getting in. Water drips from leaks in the roof, there is extensive rusting on the metal work, and paint is flaking badly and dropping onto the engraved pavement. The rock gets very dusty all the time and – since there is no natural cleaning by rainfall – the staff have to clean it with soft brushes and a vacuum cleaner.

In short, after only ten years the structure is in poor condition, and there is an ever-growing threat to the art. From the visitors' point of view the situation is even worse: over six years ago, a fine visitor centre some distance from the main petroglyph site – to provide the public with information on the Algonkian culture and on rock art. Meant to house a film theatre (to show a film entitled 'The Teaching Rocks'), cafeteria, gift shop and other facilities, it still remains totally empty, so that visitors have to rely entirely on the hard-pressed park staff and on a few leaflets for their information.

(Previous page) **Even the world's most remote and inaccessible cave art site – the Grotte Cosquer (France), whose now drowned entrance can only be reached by diving 35 metres (115 feet) down into the sea and then negotiating a hugely dangerous (and sometimes fatal) tunnel of about 150 metres (*c.* 500 feet) – was broken into by five people in 1994. Fortunately they only went to look, but they could have destroyed the art or sprayed graffiti everywhere. The photograph shows some of the hand stencils with 'missing' fingers and superimposed paint-marks.**

beeswax to divert rain water from damaging a painting, while in many areas in the wet season they would collect spinifex grass and pile it up above the rock face, with stones on top to keep it in place, to prevent rain water dribbling down the painted surface. Today, protective measures are more sophisticated.

The immediate and the long-term future of prehistoric art studies lies in conservation and recording, and improvements are being made constantly in both areas. Recording is now as full as possible, rather than highly selective as in the past, with images of both portable and parietal art being digitized and stored in databanks. Video cameras and computer enhancement are proving invaluable in the recording and study of rock paintings or in making exact and objective mechanical 'tracings' of portable engravings. For conservation purposes, the most vulnerable or badly damaged sites are being closed or covered up, but others are being protected in more visitor-friendly ways – for example, with walkways or viewing platforms. In a few cases where the public cannot visit the site because of pollution or simple difficulty of access, full-size facsimiles are being produced: a notable example is Lascaux Cave II, in France, which was opened in 1983 and which receives about 300,000 visitors per year. Similar facsimiles of other caves such as Altamira and Cosquer are being prepared, while a virtual-reality version of Lascaux is already available. The new technology will undoubtedly make an increasing contribution to giving the public access to their heritage while relieving visitor pressure on the actual sites. In the same way, accurate three-dimensional replicas of rock paintings and engravings are being produced which draw on stereophotography and electronic survey techniques requiring no contact with the walls: the resulting copies, made of polymers and acrylics, properly coloured and textured, are ideal for bringing the art to museums, galleries and schools in travelling exhibits or permanent displays.

The main remaining problem is probably that of vandalism. While some measures can be taken to protect sites with fences, etc., there is really no protection against the determined vandal.

Graffiti in rock shelters or open-air sites are the subject of some debate. On one hand, they can be physically difficult to remove (and this can damage any art beneath them or affect the site's scientific potential); on the other hand, if their age is known (some are centuries old), graffiti can provide useful information on rates of patination, erosion or weathering, or, depending on their location, on the growth rates of calcite, mondmilch or rock varnish. In general, however, most people would agree that modern graffiti are disfiguring and should be removed if possible. The best remedy is to prevent graffiti from being done in the first place and the key to that lies in education rather than always imperfect site security. Explanatory boards have had positive results in many parts of the world, especially where they stress how precious and unique rock art is. For example, in Utah, some boards forcefully make the point that, just as one would not dream of touching or defacing the pictures in a gallery, so one should have the same respect for the prehistoric Michelangelos and Picassos whose work is on the rocks.

But these are short-term measures. The real answer to the problem is a long-term commitment to conveying the message to people of all ages, especially school-children, that this is a fragile, priceless and irreplaceable resource which needs to be cherished and preserved for future generations, while at the same time showing respect for any indigenous peoples who still regard the art as sacred or highly significant. Many rock art associations, most notably in the New World and Australia, have played and continue to play an invaluable role in this crusade. And the passionate enthusiasm of the local schoolchildren of Portugal's Côa valley in 1995 for the cause of saving 'their' engravings from the dam project was a remarkable and inspiring sign of hope for the future. These youngsters, even some whose fathers were employed on the dam, collected several hundred thousand signatures on a petition, organized a mass camp-out, a concert and other activities, produced campaign posters, badges and T-shirts. In what was the world's first demonstration for rock art, they marched on the town hall of Vilanova de Foz Côa with banners and chants, demanding that their engravings be saved. If even a fraction of this enthusiasm can be aroused around the world for respecting and protecting this common heritage, then, despite all the threats it faces, prehistoric art will have a future.

The children of Vilanova de Foz Côa (Portugal) march on their town hall on 3 February 1995 to demand the saving of the region's newly discovered rock art from the threat of a major dam – the world's first demonstration for prehistoric art.

Epilogue

Not all (prehistoric art) is to be seen as 'sacred' and fraught with spirituality ... (I) caution against seeking religious, sacred, and mythological meaning in every rock art site and element.

Clement Meighan

Prehistoric art cannot be encompassed by any grand, unifying theory or easy, all-embracing explanation. The phenomenon incorporates billions of markings spanning every part of the world and at least 40,000 years (probably hundreds of thousands of years). It includes everything from beads to complex metal work, and from dots or cup marks to Easter Island statues and the Nasca images. Some sites contain one art object or image, others contain thousands. Some art seems private, some public. And it is known from places like Australia that many images were probably multi-functional. The sites with prehistoric art were probably of all kinds – the equivalent of dwellings, churches, shrines, playgrounds, schools, libraries, clubs and meeting places. They formed part of the living societies of ordinary people, embedded in the landscape as significant points, sometimes related to visibility and to occupation sites.

(Opposite) **Imposing petroglyphs on sandstone at Kane Springs Canyon, Utah (United States), depicting an owl, 30 centimetres (12 inches) high, and an almost life-size human, together with birds. Date unknown.**

(Below) **One of the boulders of Cemmo at Capo di Ponte, Italy, with petroglyphs of animals (mostly deer) and actual-size daggers, probably of the third millennium BC.**

The meanings of the pictures are only apparent to those skilled in reading them, which means those from the same culture – who are all long dead. All attempts at interpretation are forced to rely on correlations between modern behaviour and pictures, and on the assumption that similar ancient pictures reflect similar ancient behaviour. Some interpretations seem more plausible than others, or better founded on ethnographic or ethnohistoric evidence. But no hypothesis about the meanings of prehistoric art can ever be confirmed sufficiently to guarantee that it is correct. In any case, over time traditions will have been lost, remade, reinvented and modified for new times.

As the quotation from Clement Meighan reminds us, prehistoric art is not necessarily all sacred and mysterious. Some of it may be games or a celebration of life rather than an awestruck or fearful attempt to communicate with the weather or with spirits. They can be pictures of individuals or groups, they can be narratives or serve as territorial boundaries. In northern Australia, paintings made early in the twentieth century are known to have resulted from memorable personal experiences and many were done while people were holed up, sheltering from the rain for

Large pictograph of a buzzard or vulture, at the shelter of Roca de Vaca, in the Piauí region of Brazil. Date unknown.

days on end. Other paintings are 'memory triggers' for stories or events and for remembering people from the past.

Even within the realm of the spiritual or religious – and, of course, there may have been no clear dividing line between sacred and secular in prehistory – the art may have had a wide range of significance including tribal stories, myths of creation and renewal, sacred beings, journeys from an ancestral Dreamtime, rites of passage such as puberty, death and rebirth, tribal secrets, laws, taboos, love, sorcery and shamanic transformation, prayers for rain and fertility, astronomical markers and animal totems. At the same time it must be borne in mind that 'art' itself was not a distinct component of life: as far as possible, it must always be seen within the eco-logical and social aspects of each period and culture. One Aboriginal elder in the Kimberley said that the rock pictures in that area should not be seen as art at all but as 'images with energies that keep us alive' – in other words, some images were potent entities in themselves.

Most rock art research can only deal in probabilities. In any case, at the time when it was created, prehistoric art will have conveyed a variety of messages: children will not have viewed it in the same way as adults, while men and women may well have seen and experienced it in different contexts. In the present, it is supremely ambigu-ous and can therefore be all things to all people. Prehistoric markings are truly the signs of all times.

Petroglyph of a bird on Gabri-ola Island, British Columbia (Canada), about 1 metre (3 feet) high. Date unknown.

Reference guide to
The Cambridge
Illustrated History of
Prehistoric Art

Glossary

Select Bibliography

Map of Prehistoric Art Sites

Index

Glossary

Acheulian period The part of the Lower Palaeolithic period characterized by the making of bifaces (handaxes), lasting from over one million until about 100,000 years ago.

anthropomorph An object or picture resembling a human form.

aurochs *Bos primigenius*, the wild ancestor of domestic cattle, which became extinct in 1627.

Australopithecus A genus of small-brained, bipedal fossil humans, known from deposits in eastern and southern Africa and dating to *c.* 3.75 to 2 million years ago.

bovid A member of the cattle family, either wild or domestic.

Bronze Age The period of antiquity in the Old World when bronze became the primary material for tools and weapons. In Europe it spans the period from 2000 to about 7000 BC.

Copper Age Term used for a period (mostly in the fourth and third millennia BC) in many parts of the Near East and Europe, when copper metallurgy was in the process of being adopted.

cup mark/cupule Small, roughly circular hollow, pecked into rock.

engraving (Art created by) incisions in the rock face.

gallery A passage in a cave.

Homo erectus 'Upright Man', a species of fossil human in the Old World dating to between 1.8 and 0.5 million years ago.

humanoid A form which bears a vague resemblance to a human being.

Ice Age Term often used to refer to the last cold period when glaciers expanded, lasting from *c.* 115,000 to 10,000 years ago.

Iron Age The period of antiquity in the Old World when iron metallurgy superseded the use of bronze for tools and weapons. Dates differ: in western Europe, it began around 500 BC and ended with the Roman conquest.

Levantine art Prehistoric rock art found primarily in rock shelters in eastern Spain, comprising small, red-painted figures of deer, ibex, humans, etc, including hunting scenes, thought to date to the Neolithic period.

mask A depiction resembling a human face, but often interpreted as representing a mask rather than an actual face.

megalith A large stone (from Greek *megas*, large, and *lithos*, stone). The term is sometimes used to refer to megalithic monuments.

Mesolithic period The Middle Stone Age, a period of transition between the Upper Palaeolithic and the Neolithic periods.

Neanderthals In Eurasia, an archaic form of human dating to between *c.* 150,000 and 30,000 years ago.

Neolithic period The 'New Stone Age', the period of antiquity in the Old World when people first adopted agriculture. Dating is very variable, beginning in the eighth millennium BC in parts of the Near East, but thousands of years later in Western Europe.

Palaeolithic period The 'Old Stone Age', the division of prehistory from the first appearance of tool-using humans to the end of the last Ice Age (q.v.). It is divided into three major periods: the Lower Palaeolithic, the time of early fossil humans and simple pebble tools and handaxes; the Middle Palaeolithic, with more advanced stone tools and the appearance of Neanderthals (q.v.); and the Upper Palaeolithic, the period of full modern humans.

panel A number of motifs or images grouped on the same rock or area of wall.

parietal art Literally art 'on walls', the term is extended to cover prehistoric works of art on any non-movable surface, including blocks, ceilings and floors (as opposed to **portable art**).

pecking The removal of material by hammering or bashing.

petroglyph (Art created by) carving, pecking or bashing the rock face.

pictograph Painting – image made of pigments derived from a variety of organic substances.

plaquette A usually small, flat slab of stone, often bearing engraved designs.

Pleistocene period A division of geological time, beginning *c.* 1.8 million and ending *c.* 10,000 years ago.

rock shelter A natural concavity or hollow in a rock wall, large enough for occupation or activities and providing its occupants with some shelter from the elements.

spall A large flake of rock.

stelae Upright stone slabs, often inscribed or carved in relief, and sometimes painted.

Stone Age The oldest and longest division of prehistory – divided into the Palaeolithic, Mesolithic and Neolithic periods (q.v.).

'venus' A popular but erroneous name given to the small female statuettes of the Upper Palaeolithic period.

Vernal style A style of rock art characterized by the elaborate head-dresses and necklesses worn by human figures.

X-ray art A style of rock art, characteristic of the recent period in northern Australia, in which the skeleton and internal organs of animals and humans are depicted within their outlines.

zoomorph An object or picture resembling an animal form.

Select Bibliography

The following are merely some of the sources which were found of particular use in preparing this book.

Chapter 1 *The 'Discovery' of Prehistoric Art* and
Chapter 2 *The Nineteenth and Twentieth Centuries: Prehistoric Art Comes into its Own*

E. Anati, *Les Origines de l'Art et la Formation de l'Esprit Human*. Paris: Albin Michel, 1989.

P.G. Bahn and A. Fossati (eds), *Rock Art Studies: News of the World I* (Oxbow Monographs). Oxford: Oxbow Books, 1996.

P.G. Bahn and J. Vertut, *Images of the Ice Age* (2nd edition, revised and updated). London: Weidenfeld & Nicolson, 1997.

Chen Zhao Fu, *Découverte de l'Art Préhistorique en Chine*. Paris: Albin Michel, 1988.

W. Davis, 'The Study of Rock Art in Africa', in P. Robertshaw (ed.), *A History of African Archaeology*. London: James Currey, 1990.

G-B.-M. Flamand, *Les Pierres Ecrites (Hadjrat-Mektourat): Gravures et Inscriptions Rupestres du Nord-Africain*. Paris: Masson, 1921.

Jiang Zhenming, *Timeless History: The Rock Art of China*. Beijing: New World Press, 1991.

M. Leakey, *Africa's Vanishing Art: The Rock Paintings of Tanzania*. New York: Doubleday, 1983.

A. Muzzolini, *Les Images Rupestres du Sahara*. Toulouse: Muzzolini, 1995.

E. Neumayer, *Lines on Stone: The Prehistoric Rock Art of India*. New Delhi: Manohar, 1993.

J. Nordbladh, 'Knowledge and Information in Swedish Petroglyph Documentation', in C-A. Moberg (ed.), *Similar Finds? Similar Interpretations?* Gothenburg: Department of Archaeology, University of Gothenburg, 1981.

R. Querejazu Lewis, 'Contemporary Indigenous Use of Traditional Rock Art Sites at Yaraque, Bolivia', *Rock Art Research* 11, 1994.

P. Schaafsma, *Indian Rock Art of the Southwest*. Santa Fe: School of American Research, 1980.

D. Valencia, *El Arte Rupestre en México* (tésis profesional, Escuela Nacional de Antropología e Historia). Mexico City: 1992.

G.L. Walsh, *Australia's Greatest Rock Art*. Bathurst: E J. Brill–Robert Brown & Associates, 1988.

K.F. Wellmann, *A Survey of North American Indian Rock Art*. Graz: Akademische Druck- und Verlagsanstalt, 1979.

A.R. Willcox, *The Rock Art of Africa*. New York: Holmes & Meier, 1984.

Chapter 3 *Body Art* and **Chapter 4** *Objets d'Art*

P.G. Bahn and J. Vertut, *Images of the Ice Age* (2nd edition, revised and updated). London: Weidenfeld & Nicolson, 1997.

W.K. Barnett and J.W. Hoopes (eds), *The Emergence of Pottery: Technology and Innovation in Ancient Societies*. Washington & London: Smithsonian Institution Press, 1995.

R.G. Bednarik, 'Concept-mediated Marking in the Lower Palaeolithic', *Current Anthropology* 36, 1995.

M. Gimbutas, *The Civilization of the Goddess: The World of Old Europe*. San Francisco: Harper Collins, 1991.

B.M.J. Huchet, 'The Identification of Cicatrices Depicted on Anthropomorphs in the Laura Region, North Queensland', *Rock Art Research* 7, 1990.

A. Marshack, *The Roots of Civilization: The Cognitive Beginnings of Man's First Art, Symbol and Notation* (2nd edition). New York: Moyer Bell, 1991.

P.B. Vandiver et al, 'The Origins of Ceramic Technology at Dolní Věstonice, Czechoslovakia', *Science* 246, 1989.

Chapter 5 *Art on Rocks and Walls*

A. Aveni (ed.), *The Lines of Nazca*. Philadelphia: The American Philosophical Society, 1990.

P.G. Bahn, 'Water Mythology and the Distribution of Palaeolithic Parietal Art', *Proceedings of the Prehistoric Society* 44, 1978.

P.G. Bahn and J. Vertut, *Images of the Ice Age* (2nd edition, revised and updated). London: Weidenfeld & Nicolson, 1997.

L. Barral and S. Simone, 'Who's Who in Merveilles? (Tende, Alpes-Maritimes)', *Bulletin du Musée d'Anthropologie Préhistorique de Monaco* 33, 1990.

R.G. Bednarik, 'The Discrimination of Rock Markings', *Rock Art Research* 11, 1994.

Dr Bonnet, 'Les Gravures sur Roches du Sud-Oranais', *Revue d'Ethnographie*, 1889.

R. Bradley, J. Harding and M. Mathews, 'The Siting of Prehistoric Rock Art in Galloway, South-west Scotland', *Proceedings of the Prehistoric Society* 59, 1993.

N. Cole and A. Watchman, 'Painting with Plants: Investigating Fibres in Aboriginal Rock Paintings at Laura, North Queensland', *Rock Art Research* 9, 1992.

J.M. Coles, 'Elk and Ogopogo: Belief Systems in the Hunter-gatherer Rock Art of Northern Lands', *Proceedings of the Prehistoric Society* 57 (1), 1991.

J. Deacon, 'The Power of a Place in Understanding Southern San Rock Engravings', *World Archaeology* 20, 1988.

B. Delluc and G. Delluc, 'Lecture Analytique des Supports Rocheux Gravés et Relevé Synthétique', *L'Anthropologie* 88, 1984.

H. de Lumley, *Le Grandiose et le Sacré: Gravures Rupestres Protohistoriques et Historiques de la Région du Mont Bego*. Aix-en-Provence: Edisud, 1995.

G-B.-M. Flamand, *Les Pierres Ecrites (Hadjrat-Mektourat): Gravures et Inscriptions Rupestres du Nord-Africain*. Paris: Masson, 1921.

A. Forge, 'Handstencils: Rock Art or Not Art?', in P. Bahn and A. Rosenfeld (eds), *Rock Art and Prehistory* (Oxbow Monograph 10). Oxford: Oxbow Books, 1991.

K. Hedges, 'Rock Art in Southern California', *Pacific Coast Archaeological Society Quarterly* 9 (4), 1973.

S. Johnston, 'Distributional Aspects of Prehistoric Irish Petroglyphs', in P. Bahn and A. Rosenfeld (eds), *Rock Art and Prehistory* (Oxbow Monograph 10). Oxford: Oxbow Books, 1991.

M. Lorblanchet, 'Spitting Images: Replicating the Spotted Horses of Pech Merle', *Archaeology* 44, Nov/Dec, 1991.

K. Sognnes, 'Ritual Landscapes: Toward a Reinterpretation of Stone Age Rock Art in Trøndelag, Norway', *Norwegian Archaeological Review* 27, 1994.

J. Steinbring, 'Phenomenal Attributes: Site Selection Factors in Rock Art', *American Indian Rock Art* 17, 1992.

A.J. Stone, *Images from the Underworld: Naj Tunich and the Tradition of Maya Cave Painting*. Austin: University of Texas Press, 1995.

A.J. Stone and P.G. Bahn, 'A Comparison of Franco-Cantabrian and Maya Art in Deep Caves: Spatial Strategies and Cultural Considerations', in J. Steinbring et al (eds), *Time and Space: Dating and Spatial Considerations in Rock Art Research* (Occasional AURA Publications No. 8). Melbourne: AURA , 1993.

J. von Werlhof and H. Casey, *Spirits of the Earth: A Study of Earthen Art in the North American Deserts*. El Centro, California: Imperial Valley College Museum, 1987.

G.L. Walsh, 'Mutilated Hands or Signal Stencils', *Australian Archaeology* 9, 1979.

G.L. Walsh, 'Rock Painting Sizes in the Kimberley and Victoria River District', *Rock Art Research* 8, 1991.

H.C. Woodhouse, 'Utilization of Rock Face Features in the Rock Paintings of South Africa', *South African Archaeological Bulletin* 45, 1990.

Chapter 6 *The Appliance of Science*

P.G. Bahn, 'The "Dead Wood Stage" of Prehistoric Art Studies: Style Is Not Enough', in M. Lorblanchet and P.G. Bahn (eds), *Rock Art Studies: The Post-Stylistic Era or Where Do We Go from Here?* (Oxbow Monograph 35). Oxford: Oxbow Books, 1993.

P.G. Bahn, 'Where's the Beef? The Myth of Hunting Magic in Palaeolithic Art', in P. Bahn and A. Rosenfeld (eds), *Rock Art and Prehistory* (Oxbow Monograph 10). Oxford: Oxbow Books, 1991.

R.G. Bednarik, 'Developments in Rock Art Dating', *Acta Archaeologica* 63, 1992.

R.G. Bednarik, 'Only Time Will Tell: A Review of the Methodology of Direct Rock Art Dating', *Archaeometry* 38, 1996.

G. Chaloupka, *Journey in Time: The World's Longest Continuing Art Tradition: The 50,000-Year Story of the Australian Aboriginal Rock Art of Arnhem Land*. Chatswood, NSW: Reed, 1993.

J. Clottes, 'Paint Analyses from Several Magdalenian Caves in the Ariège Region of France', *Journal of Archaeological Science* 20, 1993.

E. Denninger, 'The Use of Paper Chromatography to Determine the Age of Albuminous Binders and Its Application to Rock Paintings', in M. Schoonraad (ed.), *Rock Paintings in Southern Africa* (South African Journal of Science, Special Publication 2). Johannesburg: South African Association for the Advancement of Science, 1971.

A.M. Iñiguez and C.J. Gradín, 'Análisis Mineralógico por Difracciones de Rayos X de Muestras de Pinturas de la Cueva de las Manos, Estancia Alto Río Pinturas (Provincia de Santa Cruz)', *Relaciones de la Sociedad Argentina de Antropología* 11, 1977.

M. Lorblanchet, 'From Styles to Dates', in M. Lorblanchet and P.G. Bahn (eds), *Rock Art Studies: The Post-Stylistic Era or Where Do We Go from Here?* (Oxbow Monograph 35). Oxford: Oxbow Books, 1993.

M. Lorblanchet et al, 'Palaeolithic Pigments in the Quercy, France', *Rock Art Research* 7, 1990.

T.H. Loy et al, 'Accelerator Radiocarbon Dating of Human Blood Proteins in Pigments from Late Pleistocene Art Sites in Australia', *Antiquity* 64, 1990.

H. Pager, *Ndedema*. Akademische Druck- und Verlagsanstalt, 1971.

J. Russ et al, 'Radiocarbon Dating of Prehistoric Rock Paintings by Selective Oxidation of Organic Carbon', *Nature* 348, 1990.

C. Smith, 'Female Artists: The Unrecognised Factor in Sacred Rock Art Production', in P. Bahn and A. Rosenfeld (eds), *Rock Art and Prehistory* (Oxbow Monograph 10). Oxford: Oxbow Books, 1991.

C.B. Stringer et al, 'Solution for the Sherborne Problem', *Nature* 378, 1995.

N.J. van der Merwe, J. Seely and R. Yates, 'First Accelerator Carbon-14 Date for a Pigment from a Rock Painting', *South African Journal of Science* 83, 1987.

A. Watchman, 'Perspectives and Potentials for Absolute Dating Prehistoric Rock Paintings', *Antiquity* 67, 1993.

A. Watchman and N. Cole, 'Accelerator Radiocarbon Dating of Plant-fibre Binders in Rock Paintings from Northeastern Australia', *Antiquity* 67, 1993.

Chapter 7 *Matters of the Body: Literal Interpretations of Prehistoric Art*

J-M. Apellániz, *Modelo de Análisis de la Autoría en el Arte Figurativo del Paleolítico*. Bilbao: Universidad de Deusto, 1991.

P.G. Bahn, 'No Sex, Please, We're Aurignacians', *Rock Art Research* 3, 1986.

P.G. Bahn and J. Flenley, *Easter Island, Earth Island*. New York: Thames & Hudson, 1992.

P.G. Bahn and J. Vertut, *Images of the Ice Age* (2nd edition, revised and updated). London: Weidenfeld & Nicolson, 1997.

J. Clottes, M. Garner and G. Maury, 'Magdalenian Bison in the Caves of the Ariège', *Rock Art Research* 11, 1994.

J. Coles, 'Boats on the Rocks', in J. Coles, V. Fenwick and G. Hutchinson (eds), *A Spirit of Enquiry: Essays for Ted Wright* (Occasional Paper No. 7). Exeter: Wetland Archaeology Research, 1993.

L. Dams, 'Bees and Honey-hunting Scenes in the Mesolithic Rock Art of Eastern Spain', *Bee World* 59, 1978.

L. Dams, *Les Peintures Rupestres du Levant Espagnol*. Paris: Picard, 1984.

J-P. Duhard, *Réalisme de l'Image Féminine Paléolithique* (Cahiers du Quaternaire 19). Paris: Centre National de la Recherche Scientifique, 1993.

J-P. Duhard, 'Upper Palaeolithic Figures as a Reflection of Human Morphology and Social Organisation', *Antiquity* 67, 1993.

P. Genge, 'The Trumpeters of the Matopos, Zimbabwe', *Pictogram* 1 (2), 1988.

I.P. Haskovec and H. Sullivan, 'Reflections and Rejections of an Aboriginal Artist', in H. Morphy (ed.), *Animals into Art*. London: Unwin Hyman, 1989.

K. Hedges, 'Places to See and Places to Hear: Rock Art and Features of the Sacred Landscape', in J. Steinbring et al (eds), *Time and Space: Dating and Spatial Considerations in Rock Art Research* (Occasional AURA Publications No. 8). Melbourne: AURA, 1993.

A. Hesjedal, 'The Hunters' Rock Art in Northern Norway: Problems of Chronology and Interpretation', *Norwegian Archaeological Review* 27, 1994.

S.C. Jett and P.B. Moyle, 'The Exotic Origins of Fishes Depicted on Prehistoric Mimbres Pottery from New Mexico', *American Antiquity* 51, 1986.

F. Kauffmann Doig, *Sexual Behaviour in Ancient Peru*. Lima: Kompaktos, 1979.

J.D. Keyser, 'Ledger Book Art: A Key to Understanding Northern Plains Biographic Rock Art', in J. Day et al (eds), *Rock Art of the Western Canyons* (Colorado Archaeological Society Memoir No. 3). Denver: Colorado Archaeological Society, 1989.

J.D. Keyser, 'The Plains Indian War Complex and the Rock Art of Writing-on-Stone, Alberta, Canada', *Journal of Field Archaeology* 6, 1979.

J-L. Le Quellec, 'Aires Culturelles et Art Rupestre: Théranthropes et Femmes Ouvertes du Messak (Libye)', *L'Anthropologie*, 99, 1995.

J-L. Le Quellec, 'Les Contacts Homme–Animal sur les Figurations Rupestres Anciennes du Sahara Central', *L'Anthropologie* 99, 1995.

M. Lorblanchet, 'Symbolisme des Empreintes en Australie', *Dossiers Histoire et Archéologie* 90, Jan, 1985.

J. McDonald, 'The Identification of Species in a Panaramitee Style Engraving Site', in M. Smith (ed.), *Archaeology at ANZAAS 1983*. Perth: Western Australia Museum, 1983.

N.W.G. Macintosh, 'Beswick Creek Cave Two Decades Later', in P.J. Ucko (ed.), *Forms of Indigenous Art*. London: Duckworth, 1977.

S. Malaiya, 'Dance in the Rock Art of Central India', in H. Morphy (ed.), *Animals into Art*. London: Unwin Hyman, 1989.

M. Otte (ed.), *Sons Originels: Préhistoire de la Musique* (Actes du Colloque de Musicologie, 1992: Etudes et Recherches Archéologiques de l'Université de Liège 61), Liége: Université de Liége, 1994.

L. Pales and M.T. de St Péreuse, *Les Gravures de La Marche: II, Les Humains*. Paris: Ophrys, 1976.

P. Taçon, 'Identifying Fish Species in the Recent Rock Paintings of Western Arnhem Land', *Rock Art Research* 4, 1988.

P. Taçon and C. Chippindale, 'Australia's Ancient Warriors: Changing Depictions of Fighting in the Rock Art of Arnhem Land, N.T.', *Cambridge Archaeological Journal* 4, 1994.

S. Waller, 'Sound Reflection as an Explanation for the Content and Context of Rock Art', *Rock Art Research* 10, 1993.

G.L. Walsh, *Bradshaws: Ancient Rock Paintings of North-West Australia*. Carouge–Geneva: Edition Limitée, 1994.

D. Welch, 'Material Culture in Kimberley Rock Art, Australia', *Rock Art Research* 13, 1996.

H.C. Woodhouse, *The Bushman Art of Southern Africa*. London: Macdonald & Jane's, 1980.

H.C. Woodhouse, *Conflict, Weapons and Warfare in the Rock Art of Southern Africa* (Paper No. 43). Johannesburg: Institute for the Study of Man in Africa, 1993.

H.C. Woodhouse, 'A Thematic Approach to the Study of Rock Art in Southern Africa', *South African Journal of Ethnology* 19, 1996.

Chapter 8 *Matters of the Mind: Symbolic Interpretations of Prehistoric Art*

A. Aveni (ed.), *World Archaeoastronomy*. Cambridge: Cambridge University Press, 1988.

P.G. Bahn, 'Membrane and numb brain: a close look at a recent claim for shamanism in Palaeolithic art', *Rock Art Research* 14, 1997.

R.G. Bednarik, 'On Neuropsychology and Shamanism in Rock Art', *Current Anthropology* 31, 1990.

G. Chaloupka, *Journey in Time: The World's Longest Continuing Art Tradition: The 50,000-Year Story of the Australian Aboriginal Rock Art of Arnhem Land*. Chatswood, NSW: Reed, 1993.

J. Clottes and J.D. Lewis-Williams, *Les Chamanes de la Préhistoire: Transe et Magie dans les Grottes Ornées*. Paris: Le Seuil, 1996.

J. Coles, 'Rock Art As a Picture Show', in K. Helskog and B. Olsen (eds), *Perceiving Rock Art: Social and Political Perspectives*. Oslo: Novus Forlag, 1995.

P.J.F. Coutts and M. Lorblanchet, *Aboriginals and Rock Art in the Grampians* (Records of the Victoria Archaeological Survey, No.12). Victoria, Australia: Ministry for Conservation, 1982.

P.T. Furst, 'Shamanism, the Ecstatic Experience, and Lower Pecos Art: Reflections on Some Transcultural Phenomena', in H.J. Shafer, *Ancient Texans*. San Antonio: Texas Monthly Press, 1986.

P.S. Garlake, 'Archetypes and Attributes: Rock Paintings in Zimbabwe', *World Archaeology* 25 (3), 1994.

R.N. Hamayon, 'Pour en finir avec la "transe" et l'"extase" dans l'étude du chamanisme', *Etudes mongoles et sibériennes* 26, 1995.

K. Hedges, 'Southern California Rock Art as Shamanic Art', *American Indian Rock Art* 2, 1976.

P. Jolly, 'Southern San Symbolism and Rock Art: Continuity or Change?' *INORA* 11, 1995.

P. Jolly, 'Symbiotic Interaction Between Black Farmers and South-eastern San: Implications for Southern African Rock Art Studies, Ethnographic Analogy, and Hunter-gatherer Cultural Identity', *Current Anthropology* 37, 1996.

J.D. Keyser, *Indian Rock Art of the Columbia Plateau*. Seattle: University of Washington Press, 1992.

E.C. Krupp, *Echoes of the Ancient Skies*. New York: Harper & Row, 1982.

R. Layton, *Australian Rock Art: A New Synthesis*. Cambridge: Cambridge University Press, 1992.

T. Lenssen-Erz, 'Jumping About: Springbok in the Brandberg Rock Paintings and in the Bleek and Lloyd Collection: An Attempt at a Correlation', in T.A. Dowson and D. Lewis-Williams (eds), *Contested Images: Diversity in Southern African Rock Art Research*. Johannesburg: Witwatersrand University Press, 1994.

J-L. Le Quellec, *Symbolisme et Art Rupestre au Sahara*. Paris: L'Harmattan, 1993.

J.D. Lewis-Williams, *Believing and Seeing: Symbolic Meanings in Southern San Rock Paintings*. New York: Academic Press, 1981.

J.D. Lewis-Williams, 'Wrestling with Analogy: A Methodological Dilemma in Upper Palaeolithic Research', *Proceedings of the Prehistoric Society* 57 (1), 1991.

J.D. Lewis-Williams and T.A. Dowson, *Images of Power: Understanding Bushman Rock Art*. Johannesburg: Southern Book Publishers, 1989.

J.D. Lewis-Williams and T.A. Dowson, 'The Signs of All Times: Entoptic Phenomena in Upper Palaeolithic Art', *Current Anthropology* 28, 1988.

J.D. Lewis-Williams and T.A. Dowson, 'Through the Veil: San Rock Paintings and the Rock Face', *South African Archaeological Bulletin* 45, 1990.

L.L. Loendorf, *Nine Rock Art Sites in the Pinon Canyon Manuever Site, Southeastern Colorado* (Contribution No. 248). Grand Forks: Department of Anthropology, University of North Dakota, 1989.

P. McCreery and E. Malotki, *Tapamveni: The Rock Art Galleries of Petrified Forest and Beyond*. Petrified Forest, Arizona: Petrified Forest Museum, 1994.

A. Marshack, *The Roots of Civilization: The Cognitive Beginnings of Man's First Art, Symbol and Notation* (2nd edition). New York: Moyer Bell, 1991.

K. Mulvaney, 'What to Do on a Rainy Day: Reminiscences of Mirriuwung and Gadjerong Artists', *Rock Art Research* 13, 1996.

A. Muzzolini, *Les Images Rupestres du Sahara*. Toulouse: Muzzolini, 1995.

H. Pager, *Stone Age Myth and Magic As Documented in the Rock Paintings of South Africa*. Graz: Akademische Druck- und Verlagsanstalt, 1975.

H. Pager, 'San Trance Performances Documented in the Ethnological Reports and Rock Paintings of Southern Africa', *Rock Art Research* 11, 1994.

F.E. Prins, 'Praise to the Bushman Ancestors of the Water: The Integration of San-related Concepts in the Beliefs and Ritual of a Diviners' Training School in Tsolo, Eastern Cape', in P. Skotnes (ed.), *Miscast: Negotiating the Presence of the Bushmen*. Cape Town: University of Cape Town Press, 1996.

F.E. Prins, 'Southern-Bushman Descendants in the Transkei: Rock Art and Rainmaking', *South African Journal of Ethnology* 13 (3), 1990.

P.S.C. Taçon, 'Art and the Essences of Being: Symbolic and Economic Aspects of Fish among the Peoples of Western Arnhem Land, Australia', in H. Morphy (ed.), *Animals into Art*. London: Unwin Hyman, 1989.

D. Tangri, '!Science, Hypothesis Testing and Prehistoric Pictures', *Rock Art Research* 6, 1989.

J.F. Thackeray, 'Disguises, Animal Behaviour and Concepts of Control in Relation to Rock Art of Southern Africa', in *New Approaches to Southern African Rock Art* (Goodwin Series 4). South African Archaeological Society, 1983.

C. Tilley, *Material Culture As Text: The Art of Ambiguity*. London: Routledge, 1991.

S.A. Turpin (ed.), *Shamanism and Rock Art in North America* (Special Publication 1). San Antonio: Rock Art Foundation, Inc., 1994.

P. Vinnicombe, *People of the Eland*. Pietermaritzburg: Natal University Press, 1976.

D.S. Whitley, 'Shamanism and Rock Art in Far Western North America', *Cambridge Archaeological Journal* 2, 1992.

A.R. Willcox, 'San Informants on the Practice of Rock Art in the Transkei, South Africa', *Rock Art Research* 8, 1991.

H.C. Woodhouse, 'On the Social Context of Southern African Rock Art', *Current Anthropology* 25, 1984.

H.C. Woodhouse, *The Rain and Its Creatures as the Bushmen Painted Them*. Rivonia, South Africa: William Waterman Publications, 1992.

H.C. Woodhouse, *When Animals Were People*. Melville, South Africa: C. van Rensburg Publications, 1984.

Chapter 9 *Current Threats and Future Prospects*

P.G. Bahn, R.G. Bednarik and J. Steinbring, 'The Peterborough Petroglyph Site: Reflections on Massive Intervention in Rock Art', *Rock Art Research* 12, 1995 and 13, 1996.

P.G. Bahn and A-S. Hygen, 'More on Massive Intervention: the Aspeberget Structure', *Rock Art Research* 13, 1996.

R.G. Bednarik, 'About Professional Rock Art Vandals', *Survey*, Anno 4, No. 6, 1990.

R.G. Bednarik, 'Rock Art Conservation in the Upper Lena Basin, Siberia', *Conservation and Management of Archaeological Sites* 1, 1995.

F. Bock and A.J. Bock, 'A Review of an Attempt to Restore Petroglyphs Using Artificial Desert Varnish at Petrified Forest, Arizona', *American Indian Rock Art* 16, 1990.

J.M. Coles, 'The Dying Rocks', *Tor* 24, 1992.

D. Dragovich, 'A Plague of Locusts or Manna from Heaven? Tourists and Conservation of Cave Art in Southern France', *Rock Art Research* 3, 1986.

J.J. Golio and E. Snyder, *Petroglyph Surveys of South Mountain:1991/1964* (San Diego Museum Papers 29 – Rock Art Papers 10). San Diego: San Diego Museum, 1993.

K. Helskog and B. Olsen (eds), *Perceiving Rock Art: Social and Political Perspectives*. Oslo: Novus Forlag, 1995.

J.M. Jacobs and F. Gale, *Tourism and the Protection of Aboriginal Cultural Sites* (Special Australian Heritage Publication 10). Canberra: Australian Government Publishing Service, 1994.

S.D. Kirkpatrick, *Lords of Sipán: A True Story of Pre-Inca Tombs, Archaeology and Crime*. New York: William Morrow & Co. Inc., 1992.

R. Mark and E. Newman, 'Management of Petroglyph Rubbing at Two Pacific Northwest Coast Sites', *American Indian Rock Art* 20, 1994.

D. Morris, 'Conservation of Rock Engravings in the Northern Cape: Getting an Act Together', *Pictogram* 2 (3), 1989.

S-A. Pager, 'The Deterioration of the Rock Paintings in the Ndedema Gorge, Natal Drakensberg, Republic of South Africa', *Pictogram* 2 (1), 1989.

A. Rosenfeld, *Rock Art Conservation in Australia* (Special Australian Heritage Publication Series No. 2). Canberra: Australian Government Publishing Service, 1985.

H.C. Woodhouse, 'Deterioration, Damage, Desecration, Disappearance, and Dynamite: The Depressing Drama of Dozens of South Africa's Rock Art Sites', in *Rock Art – The Way Ahead: SARARA 1st International Conference* (Occasional SARARA Publications No.1). SARARA, 1991.

On rock art in general the following are the principal journals:

Adoranten (The Scandinavian Society for Prehistoric Art). Published since 1969.

American Indian Rock Art: Acts of the Conferences of ARARA (The American Rock Art Research Association). Published since 1974. Emphasis on North American rock art. (Also the newsletter *La Pintura*, published since 1974.)

Ars Praehistorica. Lavish, all-colour Spanish journal, appearing irregularly since 1982.

Boletín SIARB (Sociedad de Investigación del Arte Rupestre de Bolivia). Published since 1987. Most papers concern rock art in South America.

Bolletino del Centro Camuno di Studi Preistorici. Bulletin with worldwide coverage, appearing irregularly since 1964.

Bulletin de la Société Préhistorique Ariège-Pyrénées (formerly *Bulletin de la Société Préhistorique de l'Ariège*). Published since 1946. Annual French journal which has always focused heavily on Ice Age art and, in recent years, on prehistoric art from around the world.

INORA Newsletter (International Newsletter on Rock Art). Published since 1992. Invaluable source of worldwide news.

Pictogram: The Journal of SARARA (The Southern African Rock Art Research Association). Published since 1987. Most papers concern Southern African rock art.

Purakala: The Journal of RASI (Rock Art Society of India). Published since 1990. Most papers concern India.

Rock Art Papers. Papers delivered at the annual one-day conference on rock art held in San Diego, California. Published since 1983. Most papers concern the rock art of North America and Baja California.

Rock Art Research. The journal of AURA (the Australian Rock Art Research Association). The world's foremost journal on rock art (with papers covering the art of whole world as well as general and theoretical issues), published since 1984. (Also the *AURA Newsletter*, published since 1984.)

Sahara. Journal primarily devoted to the art and archaeology of the Saharan region, published since 1988.

Survey. The journal of CeSMAP (Bollettino del Centro Studi e Museo d'Arte Preistorica di Pinerolo), published since 1985. Emphasis on southern Europe, but world-wide coverage.

Tracce (Tracks): On-line rock art bulletin, published since 1995.

Map of Prehistoric Art Sites

Orkney
Bohuslän
Altar
Lake
Onega
Sungir
Newgrange
Gönnersdorf
Kapova
Ignatiev
Uffington
Dolni Věstonice
Yenisei
Butmir
Inner Mongolia
Helan
Mts
Malta
Berekhat
Ram
Altai
Tassili Libya
Chad
Bhimbetka
Huashan
Khok
Phanom Di
Brandberg
Victoria
River District
Kakadu/
Arnhem Land
Kimberley
Queensland
Cederberg
Spear Hill
Carnarvon Gorge
Drakensberg.
Mt Gambier/Glenisla
Sydney
Tasmania

Picture Acknowledgements

Every effort has been made to obtain permission to use copyright material; the publishers apologise for any errors or omissions and would welcome these being brought to their attention.

Paul Bahn: **jacket, half title, title, i**, (vi), **x, xi, xii, xiii, xv, xvi, xvii, xviii–xix, xx, xxi, xxii–xxiii, xxv, xxvi, xxvii, xxviii–xxix, xxx, 1, 2, 3, 4, 22–23, 26–27, 34–35, 50, 51, 52, 53, 61, 62** (top) **63** (both), **64, 65, 68, 80** (top), **87** (top), **93, 98, 100, 101, 102** (both), **103, 104** (both), **105, 106** (right), **107, 108–9, 110, 111, 112, 114, 115, 117** (bottom), **118, 119, 124, 126** (both), **127, 128–9, 130, 131, 132, 135, 136–7, 138, 140, 142–3, 144, 145** (bottom), **146, 147, 148, 150–1, 158, 159, 160, 168, 170–1, 173, 174** (top), **175** (all), **177, 178** (left), **179** (top), **182** (both), **183, 184, 185, 186, 187, 188, 189** (top), **191** (both), **192, 194** (all), **195** (bottom), **196, 197** (both), **198** (both), **199, 200–1, 203, 204 207, 210** (bottom), **211, 212** (both), **213** (both), **214–5, 218–9, 220, 222, 223, 224, 225, 226–7, 228** (both), **229** (top), **230, 231, 233** (both), **234, 235, 236, 238, 239, 241, 243, 245, 246, 248, 250, 251, 252, 254–5, 257, 258, 259, 260** (bottom), **262, 263** (top), **264, 265, 266, 267, 269, 270, 271, 276, 277** (both), **281, 282, 283, 284, 285**

Jean Clottes/ Ministère de la Culture: iii, 165

By permission of the Syndics of Cambridge University Library: **xxxii, 8, 14** (bottom), **15, 16, 17, 18** (both), **25, 38** (both), **39** (both), **41** (both) [Haddon Library], **43, 44** (both), **51** (margin: top and below), **57** (both), **59** (margin: top), **62** (bottom), **156** [African Studies Library], **237** (both), **261** (bottom)

Jarl Nordbladh/Bent Mann Neilson, University of Copenhagen: **5, 6**

The Board of Trinity College, Dublin: 7 (both)

After Robert Bednarik: 9, 163

After Antonio de la Calancha / Library of the Central University, Barcelona: 11

After H. Lewis: 12 (top left)

After William Dennis: 12 (top right)

After Dr Danforth: 12 (middle)

After James Winthrop: 12 (bottom)

Biblioteca Nacional, Madrid: 13

After Martin Vahl: 14 (top)

After Père Laure: 19

Rijksmuseum, Amsterdam: 24

Steven Freers: 30

National Library of Australia, Canberra: 31, 32, 33, 73

Alexander Turnbull Library, Wellington: 36, 37 (both), 78, 79

Giancarlo Negro: 46-7, 122–3

Jan Eric Sjöberg: 54, 55 (both)

Antiquités Nationales (3, 1971): 56

Jean Vertut: 58–9, 74, 82, 113, 166–7, 206 (top), 208, 210 (top), 216–7, 256, 261 (top)

Centro de Investigación y Museo de Altamara: 58, 59 (right)

Altamira y Otras Cuevas de Cantabria Silex, 1979: 59

After Dr Argumosa: 60 (left)

After Marcelino Sanz de Sautuola: 60 (right)

After Henri Breuil: 62 (bottom)

Paul Taçon: 66

Jean Vertut/Michel Brézillon: 67

Montana Historical Society, Helena. Photographic Archives (PAC 74-43.5): 69 (top)

Shirley-Ann Pager: 69 (bottom)

Roberta Simonis: 70

After Sergei Rudenko: 77

Hideji Harunari/Anthropology Dept., The University Museum, University of Tokyo: 80

Andrew Foxon/Hull Museums: 83

After Marylise Lejeune: 84

Francesco d'Errico: 85, 155

Cambridge University Museum of Archaeology: 86

Alexander Marshack: 87 (bottom), 90, 91 (both)

Claude Couraud: 88, 153

National Museums of Scotland, Edinburgh: 89, 92

Werner Forman Archive, London. Courtesy of the Entwistle Gallery: 96

Robert Bednarik: 99, 272

Associated Press, London: 106 (left)

Cambridge University Collection of Air Photographs: 116

Georgia Lee: 117 (top), 121, 260 (top), 263 (bottom), 268

After Henri Lhote: 120

Bert Woodhouse: 125 (top)

After Grahame Walsh: 125 (bottom)

Jean Vertut/Collection Bégouën: 139

Jörg Hansen: 145 (top), 240

Javier Agote, Vitoria, Spain: 152

After Carl Schuster / Edmund Carpenter: 154

Ronald Dorn: **162** (*both*)

Matthias Strecker/SIARB: **174** (*bottom*)

After Marija Gimbutas: **176**, **181** (*bottom left*)

After Wang Bing-Hua: **178** (*right*)

After Harald Pager: **179** (*bottom left*), **190** (*bottom*, courtesy of the Heinrich Barth Institute, Cologne)

After Federico Kauffmann-Doig: **179** (*bottom right*), **190** (*top*), **206** (*bottom*)

After B. N. Pyatkin & G. N. Kurochkin: **180**

After Léon Pales and Marie Tassin de St Péreuse: **181** (*top*)

Christopher Donnan, Fowler Museum of Cultural History, UCLA: **181**, **275**

After Jan Jelínek and Henri Lhote: **189** (*bottom*, upper & lower respectively)

Cahiers du GERSAR (2, 1980): **193**

Lya Dams: **195** (*top*)

Cooperativa Archeologica 'Le Orme dell' Uomo': **209**

Andy Schouten: **229** (*bottom*)

Yves Gauthier: **232**

Roy Querejazu Lewis: **253**

John Coles: **273**

U.S. Customs: **274**

Ministère de la Culture, Direction du Patrimoine, A. Chêné, CNRS, Centre Camille Jullian: **278-9**

Index

Italics denotes a mention in captions

Adamson, Joy xxxi
Alexander, Sir James 38–9, 40
Alfssön, Peder 5–6, 5–6
Alta (Norway) 61, 65, 235, 270, 271
Altamira Cave (Spain) 58–60, 60–1, 99, 148, 163, 172–3, 257, 280
altered states of consciousness 219, 225, 236, 240–7 passim
Alton (USA) 12, 12
Alva, Walter 274
Amis Gorge, Brandberg (Namibia) 190, 244
Ampère, Jean-Jacques 42
Anaeho'omalu (Hawaii, USA) 262
Anafreita (Iberia) 5
Angles-sur-l'Anglin (France) 181, 256
Angola 37, 40, 109
Apellániz, Juan María 173
Araña La 195
archaeoastronomy 228–9, 228–9, 285
Arcy-sur-Cure (France) 93
Argentina 50, 111, 114, 115, 149, 149, 213, 248
Argumosa, José de 60
Arnhem Land (Australia) xxxi, 31, 36, 72, 76, 111, 113, 116, 184–8, 187, 190, 196, 221, 243
Arpan Shelter (Spain) 61
Art Gallery (Queensland, Australia) 115, 115, 175
Aspeberget (Sweden) 273, 273
Auditorium Cave (India) 86, 87
Australia xi, xii, xv, xvii, xx, xxiii, xxiv, xxvii, xxx, 27, 28–9, 31–33, 31–33, 36, 49, 65, 66, 68–9, 71–3, 73, 75–7, 79, 99, 100, 101, 105, 108, 109–11, 110, 113, 115–6, 115, 118, 125, 125, 134, 134, 138, 138, 146, 146, 161, 162, 172, 174, 175, 176–8, 180, 182,

184–5, 187–8, 187, 189, 190, 191–2, 192–3, 196, 206, 209, 212, 216, 221–3, 221, 228, 232, 233–4, 234, 242–3, 246, 252, 257, 257, 269, 273, 281, 283–5
Avdeevo (Russia) 174
Azilian pebbles 60, 88, 153, 154, 229

Backa Brastad (Sweden) 4, 5
Baja California (Mexico) 20–1, 23, 24, 50, 112, 158, 158, 174, 196, 229, 245, 257
Balsfjord (Norway) 14
Bambata (Zimbabwe) 266
'Bambi' 209
Barco, Miguel de 24
Barrier Canyon (Utah, USA) 225, 266
Barrow, Sir John 25, 25, 28
Barth, Heinrich 42, 43, 44
Bastian, Adolf 99
beads 92–3
Bečov (Czech Republic) 71
Bedolina (Italy) 132
Belmaco (Canary Islands) 24
Belzoni, Giovanni 149
Benin (Nigeria) 96, 96
Berekhat Ram (Israel) 86, 87
Berkel, Adriaan van 11
Bernifal Cave (France) 62
Besov Nos (Russia) 163
Besovy Sledki (Russia) 272, 272
Beutler, August Frederick 25
Bhimbetka (India) 50, 86, 87, 198, 230, 253
Bicknell, Clarence 56
Big Petroglyph Canyon (California, USA) 99
Bilzingsleben (Germany) 86
Bize, Grande Grotte de (France) 57
Bjørnstadskipet (Norway) 148
Blandowski, W. 73
Bleek, Wilhelm 41–2, 134, 230, 244
Blythe (California, USA) 116, 117
Boas, Franz 52

body-painting 70–3, 75–7, 93
Bohuslän (Sweden) 4, 5, 14–15, 54, 68, 130, 178, 182, 188, 197, 200, 211, 270, 273
Bolivia 9, 10, 50, 106, 174, 174, 252, 253, 261
Bonnet, Dr 48, 122
Bradshaw, Joseph 36
Bradshaw figures 33, 36, 125, 125, 187
Brandão, Fernandes 8, 9
Brandberg (Namibia) 62–3, 63, 68, 127, 144, 184, 190, 190, 202, 243
Brassempouy Caves (France) 83, 154–5, 181
Brazil xix, 8, 9, 20, 50, 66, 72, 100, 100, 144, 146, 158, 161, 178, 179, 180, 196, 198, 257, 258, 284
Breuil, Henri 62–3, 63, 66, 149, 162, 174, 237, 266
Brunius, Carl Georg 54–5, 55, 57
Burro's Flats (California, USA) 239
Burrup Peninsula (Australia) xx, xxiii, xxiv
Bursill, Les 219
Bushman art xv, 24–5, 25, 28, 38–9, 40–2, 62, 63, 69, 125, 134, 156, 196, 216, 225, 230–2, 231, 240, 242, 244–7, 261
Butler Wash (Utah, USA) 255
Butmir (Bosnia) 181, 181
Byrganov (Siberia) 180

Cabré y Aguilo, Juan 61
Cachão da Rapa (Portugal) xxxi, 13
Calancha, Antonio de 11, 11
Calango (Peru) 11, 11
Calixtus III, Pope 3
Cameroon 66
Canada 13, 19, 19, 52, 95, 116, 196, 261, 262, 263, 272, 276–7, 276, 285
Canary Islands 24, 122
Canyon de Chelly (Arizona, USA) 228

Cap Blanc (France) 104, 106
Carlyle, Archibald 49
Carnarvon Gorge (Queensland, Australia) 115, 115, 174, 175, 269
Carrizo Plain (California, USA) 241
Carschenna (Switzerland) 222
Carvalho da Costa, António 13
casts (stamps) 45, 48, 262
Castillo, cave of El (Spain) 163
Castle Butte (Montana, USA) 197
Castren, Matias-Alexander 45
Cathedral Cave (Queensland, Australia) 115, 269
Cederberg (South Africa) 118, 193
Celts 107, 107, 186
Cemmo boulders (Italy) 283
Cerne Abbas Giant (United Kingdom) 116
Chaffaud Cave (France) 56, 57
chalking 267–8, 268
Chaloupka, George 221
Chan Chan (Peru) 105
Chauvet Cave (France) 66, 164–5, 165, 247, 257
Chavín (Peru) 107
Chile vii, 78, 116
Chimú (Peru) 105, 190
China xxvii, 1, 1, 3, 3, 64–5, 112, 143, 158, 161, 178, 178, 211, 252, 262, 262
Christianity and rock art 3, 9–11, 9, 20, 51, 161, 163, 252
Christy, Henry 57
Chumash 50, 52, 110, 157, 237, 239, 241
Clifford (South Africa) 261
Clottes, Jean 156
Côa Valley (Portugal) 169, 264, 264, 281, 281
Cockburn, John 49
Cocoraque Butte (Arizona, USA) 205, 205
Coldstream Cave (South Africa) 125
Colombia 11, 20, 107

Contador de Argote,
Jerónymo *xxxi*, 13
Coso Range (California,
USA) *99, 141, 171, 235*
Cosquer Cave (France) 113,
153, 165, 280, *280*
Cottonwood Creek (Utah,
USA) *xxi*
Cougnac Cave (France) 165,
167, 168
Couraud, Claude 153
Covaciella, cave of La
(Spain) 163
Coyote Shelter (Texas, USA)
246
Cueva – *see under name*
Cunningham, Allan 33
cup marks 66, 222–3, *222*,
228, 288

dance 198
dating methods 142–69
Debrie *xxxi*
Delluc, Brigitte & Gilles 123
Denninger, E. 157
Devil's Rock (New South
Wales, Australia) 27
Dighton Rock (Massa-
chusetts, USA) 12, *12*
Dolní Věstonice (Czech
Republic) 90, *91*, 154,
154, 181
Drakensberg (South Africa)
xv, 69, 157, 161, *179*,
216, 219, 225, 240, 245,
265
Dreamtime *xvii*, 134, 285
Dry Fork (Utah, USA) *102,
185*
Dry Wash (Utah, USA) *xiii*
Duché de Vancy *36*
Duveyrier, Henri 45, 48

Early Man Shelter (Queensland, Australia) 65
Easter Island 36, 37, *37, 107*,
119–20, *121*, 124, 174,
175, 205, 216–17, 225,
262, 268, 283
Ebusingata (South Africa)
261
'El Gigante' (Easter Island)
119, *121*
eland *219, 225*, 230
Elands Bay Cave (South
Africa) 113
Ellis, William 36
Emory, W.H. 51

engraving 101 (*and see*
experiments)
Enlène Cave (France) 85
entoptics 240, 242
d'Errico, Francesco 84, 124
Escalante, Francisco 21
Evjestien (Norway) *259*
experiments 84, 122–6, *126*,
267
Ezeljagdspoort (South
Africa) *39*

fakes 153–5
Fate Bell Shelter (Texas,
USA) *112, 236*
Ferrassie, La (France) 87
Flamand, G-B-M. 123
Flechas, Cueva (Baja
California, Mexico) *196*,
245
Flinders, Matthew 31, *31*
Font de Gaume Cave
(France) 60, 202
Fontainebleau (France) 223,
223
Fontanalba (Italy) *53*
Fossum (Sweden) *182, 197*,
211
Freud, Sigmund 242
Frobenius, Leo 236
Fuencaliente (Spain) *13*, 14
Fuji-Idera City (Japan) *80*
Fullagar, Richard 66

Ga'aseb Gorge, Brandberg
(Namibia) *202, 243*
Gabon 66
Gabriola Island (British
Columbia, Canada) *52*,
285
Galloway (United Kingdom)
141
Game Pass Shelter (South
Africa) *219, 225*
Gardner, Erle Stanley *xxxi*,
23
Gargas Cave (France) 113,
113, 256
Garlake, Peter 238
Gavrinis (France) *102*
Geiseler, Wilhelm 37, *37*
geoglyphs *vii*, 116–17, 120,
260
Giant Horse Shelter
(Queensland, Australia)
212
Giant's Castle, Drakensberg
(South Africa) *xv, 216*

Gioffredo, Abbé Pietro 6
Gist, Christopher 20
Glauburg (Germany) 107,
107
Glenisla (South Australia)
228
Glozel (France) 154–5
Gönnersdorf (Germany) 85,
85, 88
Gordon, Robert Jacob 24, 25
Gordovaja Stena (Siberia) *15*
Gottschall site (Wisconsin,
USA) 261
Gradin, Carlos 149
graffiti 261, 280
Grant, Campbell 157
Great Gallery (Utah, USA)
225, 266
Great Serpent Mound (Ohio,
USA) 116
Grey, George 32, 33
Grieg, Edvard *xii*
Grimaldi Caves (Italy) 155
Gugu-Yalanji (Queensland,
Australia) *xi*
Guyana 11, 50

Hagar Qim (Malta) *176*
hairstyles 81, 83, 181
Hallström, Gustav 14
Han Fei 1
handaxes *xv*, 86, *86*
Hartley Bay (British
Columbia, Canada) 261
Hawaii 36–7, *260*, 262–3
Head of Sinbad (Utah, USA)
xvi
Helan Mountains (China)
xxvii, 211, 262
Heyerdahl, Thor *124*, 155
Hilfeling, Carl Gustaf 14–15
Hoggar (Algeria) *145, 240*
Holly Oak (Delaware, USA)
154
Holmberg, Axel Emanuel 57
Holub, Emil *260*
Homo erectus xv
honey gathering 195, *195*
Hopi 134
Horseshoe Canyon (Utah,
USA) *225*
Horseshoe Tank (Arizona,
USA) 105
Horstman, Nikolas 20
Huashan (China) 3, *3*, 112,
143, 158, *161, 252*
Hueco Tanks (Texas, USA)
233

Humboldt, Alexander von
20
humour 205–10
Hunsgi (India) 71
Hunter's Shelter (South
Africa) 118, *118, 193*
hunting 195
hunting magic 234–5, 247
Hutubi (China) *178*

Ica (Peru) *80*, 155
Iceman 77
Ignatiev Cave (Russia) 156
In Galguien (Libya) 48
India 49, *50*, 65, 71, 79, 86,
87, 178, 196, 198, *198*,
230, 253
Ingaladdi (Australia) *134*,
175, 228
Ireland 6, 14, 133, *229*

Jacquot, Félix *40, 42*, 48
Japan 79, *80*, 89
Jinmium (Australia) 66

Kaggen 232
Kakadu National Park
(Australia) *xxiv*, 188, *191,
212*, 234
Kalleby (Sweden) *200*
Kane Springs Canyon (Utah,
USA) *283*
Kapova Cave (Russia) *144*
Karlie-ngoinpool (South
Australia) *101, 138*
Khok Phanom Di (Thailand)
93
Kimberley (Australia) 33,
33, 36, 111, *113*, 118, 125,
125, 187, *234*, 242, 273,
285
Kinneff (United Kingdom)
89
Kivik (Sweden) 14
Knuffel's Shelter,
Drakensberg (South
Africa) *179*
Kokopelli *201*
Koonalda Cave (Australia)
138
Korini 3 (Bolivia) 253
Kostenki (Russia) 93
Kow Swamp (Australia) 79
Kuion *33*

La Pérouse, Comte de 36
Largun Shelter (Australia)
206

Lartet, Edouard 57, 57
Lascaux Cave (France) 66, 71, 100, 118, 125, 126, 148, 202, 257, 257, 280
Laura (Queensland, Australia) xi, xxvii, 108, 110–11, 192
Laure, Pierre-Michel 19, 19
Laussel (France) 74, 75
Laval, Lottin de 121
Leakey, Mary xxxi
ledger art 197
Leguay, Louis 84
Leichhardt, Ludwig 36
Leiknes (Norway) 119, 271
Lejeune, Marylise 84
Leon-Portilla, Miguel 21
Lepsius, Karl 42
Le Quellec, Jean-Loïc 248–9
Leroi-Gourhan, André 63, 67–8, 163, 169, 173, 221, 224, 247
Le Vaillant 25
Levantine art 60, 61, 195–6, 288
Lhwyd, Edward 6
Li Daoyuan 1, 3
Lightning Brothers 134
Lindow Man 75
Little Nourlangie (Australia) 189
Livingstone, David 40
Lloyd, Lucy 41–2, 134, 230, 244
Loltun (Mexico) 50, 51
Lope de Vega 4
López de Cardenas 13, 14
Lorblanchet, Michel 124, 126, 126, 156
Lorenzo, Onorato 4, 6
Lukis Granites (Australia) xvii
Lydenburg (South Africa) 94

'M' 230, 244–5
McCarthy, Frederick 68
McKee Springs Wash (Utah, USA) 128
Macintosh, N.W.G. 177
Madeleine, La (France) 57, 154
Madison, James 51
Maggs, Tim 68
Magnificent Gallery (Queensland, Australia) 108, 221
Magura Cave (Bulgaria) 108

Main Caves, Drakensberg (South Africa) xv
Makapansgat (South Africa) 86
Maler, Teobert 50
Mallery, Garrick 53
Malta 106, 176
Maltravieso Cave (Spain) 113
Manos, Cueva de las (Argentina) 111, 114, 115, 149, 149
Mantell, Walter 36
Marche, La (France) 181–2, 181, 190, 210
Mardokhai-Abi-Sourour, Rabbi 45
Marquette, Jacques 12, 12
Marshack, Alexander 84, 86, 87, 124, 229
Mas d'Azil, Le (France) 60, 62, 88, 208
Massleberg (Sweden) 130
Master of Animals 237
Maya 50, 51, 133, 138–9, 252, 271
Mayor, François 57
Mayrières Cave (France) 257
Medicine Creek Cave (Wyoming, USA) 250
medicine wheels 116
megalithic art 6, 14, 56–7, 102, 105, 138, 229, 238
Meighan, Clement 23, 283–4
Mérimée, Prosper 56
Mesa San Carlos (Baja California, Mexico) 229
Messak Settafet (Libya) 48, 123, 232
Messerschmidt, Daniil-Gotlieb 15, 16–17
Mexico 10–11, 19–21, 50, 51 (and see Baja California, Maya)
Mezin (Ukraine) 202
Mimbres (New Mexico, USA) 94, 149, 188, 274
Mitchell, C.C. 38, 40
Mników Cave (Poland) 155
Moche (Peru) 94, 178–9, 179, 181, 181, 188, 190, 190, 206, 274–5
Monconys, Balt. de 48, 120
Monitor Basin (Nevada, USA) 156

Monte Bego (France/Italy) 3, 53, 56, 124, 130, 132, 145
Montespan Cave (France) 104, 105, 256
Montfort, Pierre de 3, 4
Mother of Game 237, 238
Mount Elizabeth (Australia) 234
Mount Stuart (United Kingdom) 93
Moustier, Le (France) 71
Mouthe, La (France) 60
Mud Glyph Caves (Tennessee, USA) 101, 138, 257
Mueller, Gerhard-Friedrich 18, 18
Mummy Cave (Utah, USA) 260
Murrieta Hot Springs (California, USA) 31
Murumuru, Dick 173
Mushroom Hill Cave, Drakensberg (South Africa) 231
music 198–205, 198, 200, 201

Nämforsen (Sweden) 133, 249
Namibia 62, 63, 68, 69, 127, 144, 184, 190, 202, 243, 244, 265
Nanaimo (British Columbia, Canada) 262, 263
Nanguluwurr (Australia) 110, 212
Naquane (Italy) xi, 64, 184
Nasca (Peru) 94, 116, 117, 149, 228, 260, 283
Nauwalabila I (Australia) 71
Ndedema Gorge, Drakensberg (South Africa) 69, 158, 265
Neanderthals xv, 71, 78, 87, 93
New Guinea 28, 36, 77
New Zealand 36, 77, 78, 258
Newgrange (Ireland) 6, 14, 229
Ngarradj (Australia) xxx
Niaux Cave (France) 66, 156, 165
Niebuhr, Carsten 48
Nigeria 96, 96
Nine Mile Canyon (Utah, USA) xxi, xxix, 260

Niola Doa (Chad) 71
Nitchie (New South Wales, Australia) 79
Norway 14, 14, 65, 110, 119, 133, 148, 235, 259, 270–1, 271

Obiri (Australia) 187
Onega, Lake (Russia) 161, 163
d'Orbigny, Alcide 50
Orkney (United Kingdom) 56, 105
Orongo (Easter Island) 37, 37, 174
Orpen, Joseph 41, 244
Ossowski, Gottfryd 155
Østfold (Norway) 259, 270
Ostrich Shelter, Brandberg (Namibia) 127
Oued Djerat (Algeria) 119, 120

Pager, Harald 63, 68, 69, 157, 179, 190, 232, 265
Painted Rocks (Montana, USA) 69
Palmer, Kingsley 170
Panaramitee North (South Australia) 65, 162
Panther Cave (Texas, USA) 119, 161
Parkinson, Sydney 78
Parpalló Cave (Spain) 84, 169
Patagonia 51, 111, 111, 114, 115, 149, 149
Pataud Shelter (France) 154
Pazyryk (Russia) 76
Pech de l'Azé (France) 71
Pech Merle Cave (France) 66, 99, 101, 113, 124, 126, 163, 173
Pecos River (Texas, USA) 118, 119, 161, 236, 237, 246
Pedra Furada (Brazil) xix, 144, 146, 161
Peña Escrita (Bolivia) 9
Perna (Brazil) 100, 158, 161, 198
Peru 11, 11, 20, 80, 94–5, 105, 107, 110, 116, 117, 149, 178, 179, 181, 181, 190, 206, 228, 274–5, 274–5
Peterborough (Canada) 272–3, 276–7, 276–7

Petrified Forest (Arizona, USA) *xii, xxv, 238, 267*
petroglyphs 101 (and *passim*)
Phillip, Arthur 29
phosphene forms 240
Piasa Bird 12
Pierowall (United Kingdom) 105
Pierre aux Pieds, La (France) *193*
Piette, Edouard 60, 62, 88
Pilbara (Australia) *xv, xvii*
Pinon Canyon Maneuver site (Colorado, USA) 241
Pintada, Cueva (Baja California, Mexico) 23
Pisselerand (France) *193*
plaquettes 84–5, *84–5*, 88
Pleito Creek (California, USA) *50*
Poisson, abri du (France) 256
Portel, Le (France) 163, 209, *211*
portraiture 181, *181*
pottery 84, 89–90, *91*, 94–5, 149, 179, *179*, 181, *181*, 188, 190, *190, 206*
Puako (Hawaii, USA) *260*, 263
Pumamahay, Cueva de (Bolivia) 261

'Queen Gooseberry' 27
Quetzalcoatl 10
quinkans 221, 232, 233
Quneitra (Israel) 86

radio-carbon dating 83, 116, *143*, 144, 149, *155*, 157–8, 161, *161, 162, 165*, 168, *169, 266*, 267
rainmaking 228, 244
Ramos Gavilán, Alonso 10
Raphael, Max 83
Rasmussen Cave (Utah, USA) *260*
Ratón, Cueva del (Baja California, Mexico) 158, *158*
Reboud, V. 48
Red Bluff (Queensland, Australia) 233
Renegade Canyon (California, USA) *141, 235*
Ribeira de Piscos (Portugal) *169*

Río Pachene (Bolivia) 174, *174*, 252
Rivière, Emile 56
Robertson Cave (South Australia) *99*
Robinson, George Augustus 33
Roca de Vaca (Brazil) *258, 284*
Roc de Sers (France) *206*, 208
Rochester Creek (Utah, USA) *177*
Rodin, Auguste xiii
Roos Carr (United Kingdom) *83*
Rouffignac Cave (France) 153

Sahara *40*, 42–8, *48*, 122–3, *123*, 144, *145*, 189, 202, 208, 222, 248–9, *248*
San Agustín (Colombia) 107
San Emigdiano (California, USA) *50*
Sandy Creek 2 (Queensland, Australia) 161
Sanz de Sautuola, Marcellino *58–9*, 60, *60*, 172
Sanz de Sautuola, Maria *58*
Sapagua (Argentina) *213*
scarification *75*, 78, *228*
Schoolcraft, Henry Rowe 51–2
Scythians 17, 96
Sefar (Algeria) *67*
Seitjaur (Scandinavia) 252
Seminole Canyon (Texas, USA) *112, 119*
sex 178–9, *178–9* (see also vulvas, zoophilia)
shamanism 20, 208, *219*, 231, 235–8, *235–7*, 240, 242–7 *passim*, 249–50, 285
Sheep Canyon (California, USA) *171*
Sherborne (United Kingdom) *155*
Siberia 8–9, 15–18 *passim*, *15–16, 18*, 45, 54, 77, 237, 249, 264
signs 224–5
Simon, Biddy *60*
Sipán (Peru) 274–5, *274–5*
Skew Valley (Australia) *xx*
Sonia's Cave Upper (South Africa) *156, 158*

sorcery 221, 232, *233*, 236, 244, 252, 285
South Africa *i, xv*, 24–5, *25*, 28, *38–9*, 40–2, 62, 66, 68–9, *69*, 71–2, 77, 86, 94, 113, *118, 125*, 134, 157–8, 161, *179*, 180, *193*, 195, 208, 211, *219*, 220–1, *225*, 230–2, *231*, 236–8, 240, 243, 247, 257–8, *260–1*, 261, 264–5
South Mountain (Arizona, USA) 265
Spear Hill (Australia) *xv, 182, 257*
stamping technique 45, 48
Steamboat Butte (Montana, USA) *136*
Steel's Shelter, Drakensberg (South Africa) 216
stencils xxv, *xxvii*, 113–15, *113, 115*, 126, *126, 149*, 153, 161, 172, 190, *246, 280*
Steward, Julian 65
Stonehenge (United Kingdom) xxi
Stow, George 40–1
Strahlenberg, Philip Johann Tabbert von 15–18, *16*, 54
Strange, William 219
Sturts Meadows (Australia) 192–3
Suhm, P. F. 5, *5*
Sungir (Russia) 92
Swastika Stone (United Kingdom) 263
Sweden xxiv, 4, 5, 14, 54, 68, *130*, 133, *178, 182*, 188, *197, 200, 211*, 249, 270, 273, *273*
Sweeney, Peter 83
Swetnam, David 274

Takiroa (New Zealand) 36
Tanzania 66, 258
taphonomy xx, 87
Tassili (Algeria) 45, 66, *67*
tattoos 75, 77–8, 78, 81, 93
teeth 79, *80*
Tel-Isaghen (Libya) *189*
Terra Amata (France) 71
Thailand 64, 93
therianthropes 230–2, *231–2*, 237, 244
Thompson, Edward *51*
Three Kings (Utah, USA) *102*, 105, *141*

Three Rivers (New Mexico, USA) *186, 191, 195*, 208, *208*, 248
Tiliviche (Chile) *vii*
Ti-n-Tarabin (Algeria) *240*
Ti-Riwekīn (Algeria) *189*
Tilley, Christopher 249–50
Tito Bustillo Cave (Spain) 71, 148
Tiwanaku (Bolivia) 106
Toca do Chico Coelho (Brazil) *179*
Toldos, Los (Argentina) *114*, 115
Tolstoy, Leo xii
Tomskaya Pisanitsa (Siberia) 8
Toquepala (Peru) 110
Torquemada, Juan de 10
Tournal, Paul 57
tracks 192–3, *192–3*
trance – see altered states
Trezise, Percy 212, 221
Trois Frères, Les (France) 66, 202, 237
Trou de Chaleux (Belgium) 84
Tsagaglalal (USA) *224, 250*, 252
Tuc d'Audoubert, Le (France) 105, 138–9, *139*
Two Leg Rock (Australia) *191*

Uffington (United Kingdom) *116*
United States of America *xii–iii, xvi*, xxi, xxiv, *xxv, xxix*, 12, *12*, 19, *31, 50*, 51–3, 65, *69*, 95, 99, 101, *102*, 105, 110, *112*, 116, *117, 119, 128*, 134, *136*, 138, *141*, 149, 153, 156–7, 161, *161, 171*, 177, 178, *185–6*, 188, *191*, 195, 197, 201, 205, *205*, 208, *208*, 215, 217, 223, 224–5, 228, 233, 235, 235–6, 237, 238–9, 241–3, *241*, 246, 247, 248, 250, 252, 255, 257, 260–2, *260*, 264–5, *266–7*, 274–5, 280, 283
Ute art *215*

Vahl, Martin 14
Valcamonica (Italy) *xi*, 61, 64, 132, *184*, 188, *209*

Vallée des Merveilles (France) 3, 4, 6, 56 (*see also* Monte Bego)
Vatsyayan, Kapila xi
Venezuela 11, 20
Ventureño (California, USA) 239
'venus' figurines 74, *74*, 174, *174*, 288
Vernal style *185*
Veyrier Cave (France) 57, *57*
Vinnicombe, Patricia 68, 221
violence 196
visibility 137, 141
vision quests 241, *241*

Vitlycke (Sweden) *178, 188*
vulvas 174–5, *174–5, 228*, 252

Wadi Mathendush (Libya) *123*
Wadi Tekniwen (Libya) *232*
Wadi Telisaghé (Libya) *43, 44*
Walbiri 180
Waller, Steven 202, 205
Walsh, Grahame *125*
wandjinas 33, *234, 242*
warfare 196
Wargata Mina (Tasmania, Australia) 161
water 132–3, 139

Weka Pass (New Zealand) 258
Westall, William *31*
West Tofts (United Kingdom) *86*
Wharton Hill (South Australia) 65, *162*
White, John 29
White Lady of the Brandberg (Namibia) 62–3, *63, 265*
Willcox, Alex 69
Willendorf (Austria) 75
Witsen, Nicolaas 9, 237
Woodhouse, Bert *125*
Worm, Ole 5–6
Worsaae, Jens *56*, 57
Wrangell (Alaska, USA) 262

Wright, Thomas 14
Writing-on-Stone (Canada) 196

Yam Camp (Queensland, Australia) 161
Yinshan Mountains (China) *1*

Zimbabwe 202, 230, 238, *266*
zoophilia 188–9
Zubialde Cave (Spain) 153, *153*